VOYAGE TO GREENLAND

VOYAGE

A Persona

TO GREENLAND

Initiation into Anthropology

FREDERICA DE LAGUNA

W · W · NORTON & COMPANY · INC · NEW YORK

Published simultaneously in Canada by George J. McLeod Limited,
Toronto. Printed in the United States of America.

Library of Congress Cataloging in Publication Data
De Laguna, Frederica, 1906–
Voyage to Greenland.
1. De Laguna, Frederica, 1906–   2. Eskimos—
Greenland.   3. Ethnology—Field work.   4. Greenland—
Antiquities.   5. Anthropologists—United States—
Biography.   I. Title.
E99.E7D385 1977   998'.2'00497   76–51808
ISBN 0–393–06413–1

This book was designed by Antonina Krass
Typefaces used are Electra and Delphian
Manufacturing was done by Vail-Ballou Press, Inc.

1 2 3 4 5 6 7 8 9 0

To Therkel Mathiassen
(5 September 1892–14 March 1967)

Inugsungme Tíkilip ikíngutâta tássa ukua atwagkiai Tíkili-mutdlo nagsiúpai aussarsioqatigîgdluarnermingnik ergá-issutigerkuvdlugit.

His comrade on Inugsuk has written this book and sends it to Tikile in memory of a happy summer.

Contents

	Preface	. 11
I	Plans	. 21
	Background [1975]	. 22
	Preparations for Greenland (1930).	. 24
II	The Voyage (June 1–13)	. 37
III	Within the Circle (June 13–21)	. 49
IV	Upernivik (June 21–26)	. 85
V	Inugsuk (June 27–July 12)	.101
VI	The Medieval Eskimo (July 12–August 14) . . .	.139
	Waiting for the Ship	.139
	Exchange of Letters [1975]	.156
	Digging Again	.165
VII	Farthest North (August 15–19)	.191
VIII	Home to Inugsuk (August 19–25)	.209
IX	The End of Summer (August 25–September 14) . .	.225
X	Farewell (September 14–November 2).	.255
	Upernivik Again	.255

Southward Bound. 265
The Last Greenland Towns 273
The Voyage to Denmark. 275

Epilogue 281
Acknowledgments 285

Illustrations

Our camp and the midden, Tunúngassoq, from Sangmissoq   *Title page*

Preceding page 21

    Map of Greenland
    Disko Bay to Ūmánaq
    Ūmánaq to Inugsuk
    Prøven to the Devil's Thumb

Following page 166

    The *Hans Egede* from above Qutdligssat, midnight, June 15–16
    Kayakers and *Hans Egede* at Ūmánaq
    Kayaker with auks, Ūmánaq
    Eskimo children, Ikerasak
    An Eskimo woman entering her turf house
    Eskimo women, Upernivik
    Upernivik church
    Our tents from the cliff, Tunúngassoq
    Washing in the sea: myself and Mathiassen
    Ane Møller dressing Peter while Malia watches
    Robert washing our dishes, Inugsuk
    Ole and the pups
    Removing turf from below House II
    It was a perfect sealskin mitten

Mathiassen painting the baleen mat
The Geodetic Survey visits us
Karl and I go kayaking
Eskimos, Kûk
House with old-style gutskin pane, Kûk
Old-style skin tent, Kraulshavn
A Greenlander with his young dog, Kraulshavn
Old woman with a pipe, sewing, Kraulshavn
Martin Nielsen and his family, Ikermiut
Man and daughter with new-style skin tent, Kraulshavn
Skin tents and sod houses, Ikermiut
The Devil's Thumb, Quvdlorssuaq
The *Natarnak* at the Devil's Thumb
Eskimos watching us dig, Holms Ø, the Devil's Thumb
Mathiassen asking the men of Quvdlorssuaq about ruins
Hobbled dogs, Ituvssâlik
Abel Danielsen carries his kayak past his umiak, Ituvssâlik
Caspar Petersen, two girls, and a youth stop at Inugsuk
Umiak and kayak from Tugssaq
Robert and Mathiassen opening a grave on Sangmissoq
The interior of the grave on Sangmissoq

Illustrations in text

Runic stone from Kingigtorssuaq 35
My sketch of deck tennis for the passengers' book
    of the *Hans Egede* 65
Map of Tunúngassoq Island in Inugsuk Harbor 105
Map of Inugsuk Island 113
Plan of the midden on Tunúngassoq 117
Specimens from the "new midden," Tunúngassoq 134
Objects of the Inugsuk culture from the
    "old midden," Tunúngassoq 151
Objects showing intercourse with Norsemen
    from the "old midden," Tunúngassoq 183
Paper dolls of West Greenland woman and girl 187
Specimens of the Inugsuk culture from the
    "old midden," Tunúngassoq 248

Preface

This book is about my voyage to Greenland and sojourn there through the summer of 1929.

The journey really began that spring when I went from London to Copenhagen for a few weeks to study the famous Danish Eskimo collections. Unexpectedly, the trip led on to a great voyage across the North Atlantic to Arctic Greenland (and ultimately to a Ph.D. in anthropology). But, more important, it was a journey into a new life, and for me a new way of looking at the world.

Here began my association with the Danish anthropologists Therkel Mathiassen and Kaj Birket-Smith, later both expedition comrades. It was their influence and example, almost more than my training at Columbia under Franz Boas, Ruth Benedict, and Gladys Reichard (or one term in 1929 at London under Malinowski), that made me an anthropologist. At least, my first week's contact with the Danish scholars in the National Museum of Denmark in Copenhagen convinced me that anthropology was what I wanted most in the world. Having once set foot in Greenland for a stay of almost half a year, I could not turn aside from that long journey or that vocation, even though I had to give up the man I loved.

The first field trip of an anthropologist is probably the most momentous occurrence in his or her professional life—more than the Ph.D., this marks the real initiation, and the true beginning of a professional career. The experience can be traumatic, exhausting, disgusting, frustrating, or terrifying, so much so that the budding anthropologist may be frightened away. Or this revulsion can occur even on a later field trip and doom him to a merely academic or museum profession. How fortunate I have been that my first field experience was so happy, and that it led to so many more. I knew, from the beginning, that this Greenland summer was to be glorious, no matter how strange, and because I was so sure of this, that made it so.

Anthropology is a way of life—not just another academic discipline in which one tries to pass on to students what one has learned. In the deepest sense this is perhaps impossible, for what one learns in living with and studying others in that alien world is not only those others but, ultimately, oneself. The first field trip is therefore truly an initiation, for it effects a transformation and, like all field experiences, by offering new opportunities for self-expression and living, demanding new adaptation to the queer and the uncomfortable and the alien, forces one to develop potentialities that might never have found fulfillment in ordinary life. In discovering and remaking oneself, of course, one discovers the world of man, where alien thoughts and feelings mask common humanity. Having become a citizen of that world, however humble or ignorant, one never returns as the same person to one's own native country.

This book was written in 1930 when I was fresh home from my first field trip, and a copy of the manuscript was sent to Dr. Mathiassen. Even then I had planned it as a book about these first field experiences, not only because I thought others might share my enjoyment, but because anthropology students in those days had very little to read about the experiences of other students in the field. What we learned as preparation came mostly by word of mouth. But I purposely delayed for years in offering this work for publication, because it was so personal a record, and as a still active teacher I was shy of my students. Now at the end of the long journey, unforeseen in 1930, during which I not only made many archeological and ethnological field trips to Alaska and founded the Department of Anthropology at Bryn Mawr College, I face retirement with enough confidence in myself and in my very young colleagues to make publication seem possible. For reading this manuscript and offering both wise advice and generous encouragement, I thank my old friend, the famous Arctic archeologist, Dr. Henry B. Collins of the Smithsonian Institution.

Perhaps my story may help or at least entertain the new young anthropologists. I have not dared to change it since it was first written, for that would have been to betray that younger self of 1929–30. The Greenland of those days now no longer exists, either. War and waste have destroyed the old simple ways and the innocence of old dreams. Yet it is my fondest hope to be able to return to Greenland, to Upernivik, and there to search out the old people who were young when I knew them in 1929. How much their own life stories could illuminate the changes in Greenland life!

The dedication to Mathiassen remains as written in 1930, for no one dies so long as someone remains to cherish his memory.

Bryn Mawr, Pennsylvania   FREDERICA DE LAGUNA
1975

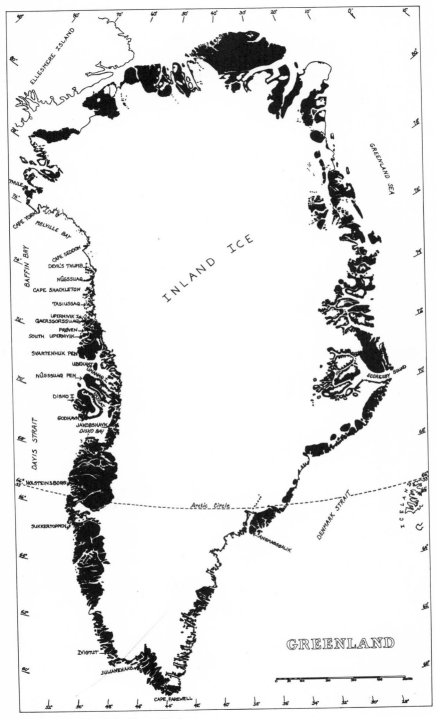

Map of Greenland, by Susan Kaplan

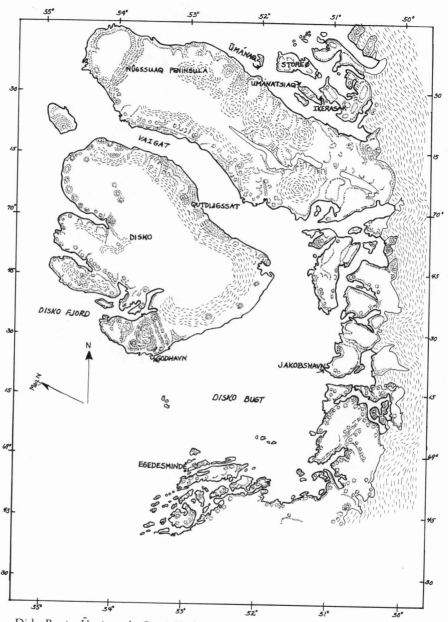

Disko Bay to Ūmánaq, by Susan Kaplan
Scale: One degree of latitude equals 60 nautical miles.

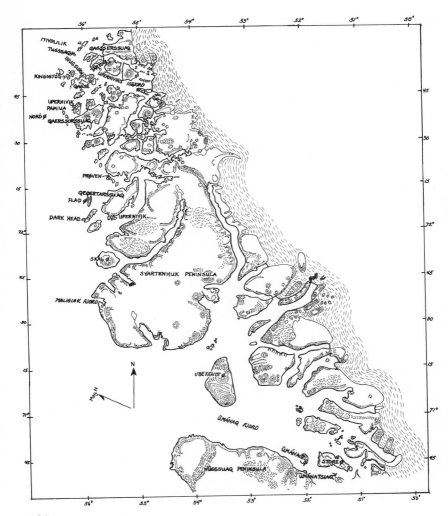

Ūmánaq to Inugsuk, by Susan Kaplan
Scale: One degree of latitude equals 60 nautical miles.

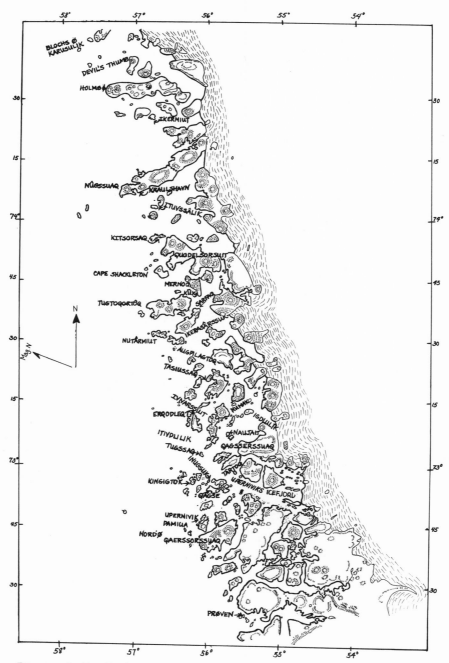

Prøven to the Devil's Thumb, by Susan Kaplan
Scale: One degree of latitude equals 60 nautical miles.

Voyage to Greenland

I

Plans

This is the story of my summer in Greenland, as told in the letters which I wrote home to my father and mother at Bryn Mawr College in Pennsylvania, where they taught, and to their summer cottage in Greensboro, Vermont. I have changed very little, except to cut a few passages, and to add explanations which I found were needed. [Major additions made in 1975 are in brackets.] Another account of this summer has been written by Dr. Therkel Mathiassen, called "Inugsuk, a Mediaeval Eskimo Settlement in Upernivik District, West Greenland," published by the Danish government in the *Meddelelser om Grønland* for 1930. This is a splendid scientific monograph, containing the fruits of our summer's labors, but since there is very little about ourselves and our adventures in uncovering the old Eskimo village, perhaps my own story can add something. I have not written it so much for others, though I hope they will enjoy it, but because this summer was the most wonderful of my life, and to relive it in this way brings great happiness, and also a touch of sadness.

Background [1975]

I had studied anthropology, then a relatively new discipline, for one year at Columbia under Professor Franz Boas. Knowing that I planned to spend the next year abroad, he suggested that I try to learn as much as I could about European prehistory and the new developments in Eskimo archeology, to see whether there was any evidence of connection between Eskimo and Paleolithic art, as had been claimed. This problem eventually became the subject of my doctoral dissertation, "A Comparison of Eskimo and Palaeolithic Art" (*American Journal of Archaeology*, vols. 36 [4] & 37 [1], 1932–33).

So I went abroad to spend the summer of 1928 with a group led by Dr. George Grant MacCurdy of Yale, visiting prehistoric sites in England, France, and Spain, and excavating a Mousterian rock shelter in the Dordogne. It was with this party that I saw the wonderful Magdalenian cave paintings at Altamira, encountered the famous Abbé Breuil sketching the remarkable frieze of horses under the "sorcerer" on the rock walls of the cavern called Trois Frères, and was led by one of the original discoverers for whom it had been named, sons of Count Bégouen, into the mysterious depths of the adjacent cave, Tuc d'Audoubert, where the bare footprints of prehistoric men and boys are still fresh in the mud. After an autumn studying in Paris, partly under the guidance of Drs. Paul Rivet and Marcelin Boule, attending lectures on Paleolithic art by the Abbé Breuil, and sketching designs on Paleolithic specimens in the Musée des Antiquités Nationales came a long awaited Christmas vacation in Switzerland, with a party of English skiers, not the least of whom was my fiancé.

For the spring before, when I was in my first year at Columbia, I had fallen madly in love with a young Englishman who was there studying mining engineering, but who, unfortunately for me, was planning a career in the coal mines of Wales, even though he had received an offer to teach engineering at an American university. Nevertheless, we were engaged. He had visited my family in Bryn Mawr, and I had visited his parents in England on first going abroad. D—— still had a year's apprenticeship to spend as a coal miner in Wales before he could receive his mine manager's certificate and earn enough to marry me, and I fully intended to get my Ph.D. in anthropology, which I expected to do in another year.

Although I hoped to persuade my future husband to settle in an American academic community, I realized that it was likely that we might live for some time anyway in England, so after Christmas I returned to London, to read at the British Museum, and matriculated at the London School of Economics (to be able to take my degree there, if necessary).

The course with Professor Malinowski was an unpleasant disappointment, for he regularly spent the first hour of the weekly two-hour seminar in attacking the United States and the nasty habits of Americans, represented in his class by another young woman and myself. I was his particular butt, since he had conceived a violent hatred of Dr. Boas and lost no opportunity to reveal my ignorance as an illustration of Boas' poor teaching. Eventually I discovered that the entire material for the seminar was contained in his article "Magic, Science, and Religion," which I committed to memory, and my being able to answer his questions in his own words spoiled his fun. I had wanted to see Sir Arthur Keith to ask his opinion of the alleged Eskimo affinities of a French prehistoric skull (Chancelade man). Although I had met this distinguished human paleontologist the previous summer with Dr. MacCurdy, Professor Malinowski (he was always "Professor," not mere "Doctor") insisted that only an introduction from himself would be proper, an introduction which he never gave. Instead, thinking to punish me, he sent me to study physical anthropology with his archenemy, the extreme diffusionist, W. J. (*Children of the Sun*) Perry. But the latter was kindness personified, interested himself in my Eskimo-Paleolithic problem, and gave me his copy of A. Irving Hallowell's now famous paper on "Bear Ceremonialism in the Northern Hemisphere," then recently published as his Ph.D. dissertation (*American Anthropologist*, vol. 28 [1],

1926). I also took a course on Africa with Professor Seligman, and another in philosophy, but since I remember nothing about them, it is obvious that there was little at the London School of Economics to stimulate an interest in anthropology for a student who had known Boas and Benedict. The intellectual atmosphere seemed alien and narrow, and I doubted if the School would ever be interested in helping me to a professional career in anthropology. (Yet this profitless personal encounter with Malinowski has never lessened my great admiration for his work as a descriptive ethnographer.)

So after the Lent term (February to Easter), I set out, as originally planned, to visit Scandinavian museums to study the Eskimo, Lapp, and Siberian collections which might be pertinent to my dissertation problem, but never dreaming that this relatively brief Scandinavian tour was to change my whole life.

Preparations for Greenland (1930)

Thus, I came to Copenhagen shortly after Easter, 1929, to see the Eskimo collections in the National Museum, and brought a letter of introduction to Dr. Therkel Mathiassen, an archeologist and Arctic explorer attached to the museum. The collections in which I was most interested were those which he had brought back from the Fifth Thule Expedition (1921–24), from Baffinland, Southampton Island, and Melville Peninsula in the Canadian Arctic. The finest specimens were on exhibit in the museum, but the bulk of the collections were stored in a ramshackle old building on Stormgade, since torn down to make room for the new wing of the museum. In this old house I spent many happy hours during my three weeks in Copenhagen, drawing pictures and taking notes, and listening to the stories of Lieutenant Thron, who had been a government official in Greenland for many years, and was now retired and employed at the museum. Dr. Mathiassen used to come in every day, and the three of us would bring sandwiches for a picnic lunch among the specimens. Mathiassen was busy with plans for his next expedition. He was being sent by the Danish government to make an archeological survey of Greenland, the first ever undertaken there. It was now over eight years since that wonderful day when Knud Rasmussen, the famous explorer, came to the little country school where Mathiassen was teaching and asked him to go on the Fifth Thule Expedition to Arctic America. I had read about that expedition in Rasmussen's book, published in English under the title *Across Arctic America*, and I had also studied some of the scientific reports, written by Mathiassen and Birket-Smith. Mathiassen has also written a popular account of his experiences, published in Danish and German, but unfortunately not in English. I could understand what going on such an expedition meant to the obscure young teacher, who wanted so much to find a place in the world of science, but for whom little Denmark could offer only a country school. His was the privilege of making the first extensive and systematic archeological excavations in the Arctic. He discovered an old Eskimo culture different from that of the modern Central Eskimo in the region about Hudson Bay. He was away for more than two years and had his share of hardship and glorious adventure. But that was years ago, and he had not returned to the Arctic since then. It was no wonder that he was happy now.

I had been in Copenhagen about a week, and was just beginning to get used to the (for me) very exciting experience of being alone in a foreign country whose language I could not understand. I was so delighted at the royal reception which Mathiassen and Birket-Smith had given me at the museum that at first I found it hard to eat or sleep. And then the most wonderful thing of all happened. That day, when Dr. Mathiassen was showing me the collections from West Greenland, he began to tell me about his plans for the summer—that he was going to Upernivik, the northernmost colony on the Danish West Coast of Greenland, a virgin field for the archeologist. He hoped to find what had been the culture of the first Eskimo inhabitants. He had been told of a promising village site on the island of Inugsuk. It was going to be a wonderful summer.

I could not help exclaiming, "How I wish I could go, too!"

"Well, why not come as my assistant? Would you like to?"

I thought, of course, that he was joking. The idea was extraordinary, sublime; nothing like this had ever happened to me.

But he was serious. He needed an assistant, but the government had not given him enough money for one. If I could pay my own expenses—and they would not be heavy—he would be glad to have me. It took some time for the full glory of the proposal to dawn upon me. All I could think of at first was that my fiancé and I had planned to be together during his holiday in August, and I did not know whether I had a right to cheat him out of the good times on which we had been counting. The rest of the summer I was supposed to be studying in Germany. It seemed quite impossible to fit Greenland into the schedule. But Mathiassen and I almost ran back through the halls to his office to look up sailings. Mathiassen was to leave Copenhagen on the *Hans Egede*, June 1, due to arrive in Upernivik some three weeks later. There was another ship, the *Gertrud Rask*, on which I might return to Copenhagen by the end of August. Mathiassen, of course, would stay on until the last boat in the fall. My trip was not an utter impossibility after all. What was a summer in Germany compared to one in Greenland? I still had some money of my own, my parents would certainly give me permission, and my vacation in England could be arranged somehow for later in the year.

We began to discuss equipment, at first very much in the conditional mood. If I should go, I would need a tent of my own, sleeping bags, etc., etc. I did not dare to think of it except as the most hypothetical of chances, for fear that I should be disappointed. In five minutes, however, we were already on the subject of sealskin boots and pants, and other necessary items of Eskimo clothing. Of course, we would have to wear proper clothes, like the natives. That was the only way to be comfortable. My outfit, passage, and share of the food would come to about $325. Mathiassen hoped I liked pancakes. He had been considered quite an expert in the pancake line on the Fifth Thule Expedition (as consumer, as well as cook, I thought to myself).

Then we rushed over to the office on Stormgade to tell Lieutenant Thron; at first he was speechless and could only point a finger at me and whistle. While he burst into an incomprehensible flood of Danish for Mathiassen's benefit, I headed for the nearest cable office.

One thing, I confess, troubled me, but only for a little while. Just what did Mathiassen really think about taking me? When I first met him, I had immediately sized him up as the ideal type of Arctic explorer—big, blond, hearty, easygoing, enthusiastic, and endowed with that essential supply of good humor which one demands in any companion or close associate. He really looks the part of an Arctic explorer, which is more than do most of those whom I have met. There was no doubt in my mind that he was the best possible person to initiate me into the Arctic, but I wondered—and this is a very subtle consideration—would he think it very unconventional of me to go alone with him, since aside from a few Eskimo workmen, who would hardly count, we should be quite alone together? If he were to feel that the situation were in any way peculiar, the atmosphere of shyness and constraint would be intolerable. As for myself, I was ready to feel as he should. Somehow, I did not worry about the attitude my family would take, for I knew that if it were really all right, they would see it so, and I knew that D—— would feel as I did. I did go to see a Danish friend, however, whom I had met through friends at International House in New York. I asked him if anyone in Denmark would think what I was planning to do was queer. He laughed. People in Denmark, he told me proudly, did not have stupid conventions. I felt ashamed of myself.

My family were really quite splendid about the whole thing, though at first they understood that I was going on a large expedition, and it must have been a shock to them to discover that it was only a man-and-a-half affair.

Later my father and mother told me of their consternation when they learned that their young daughter was going to Greenland with a strange man. They at once telephoned Dr. Boas in New York, and fortunately he was able to reassure them that

Dr. Mathiassen was a reputable archeologist and a fine person, and that the Greenland trip as his assistant would be a most valuable anthropological experience. So they cabled their consent and the necessary cash. D—— also telegraphed his approval.

I was amazed to see how everything was changed as soon as I knew that I was really going. Mathiassen became a new and even more wonderful person. I can hardly remember how he appeared that first day when his companion on the Fifth Thule Expedition, Dr. Birket-Smith, introduced us. I confess that they were both very romantic figures because of their connection with that expedition. I am afraid that I regarded them both with the small boy's feelings of hero worship. The great Knud Rasmussen came into the museum one day, and I was almost too shy to say anything.

Mathiassen and I went shopping for our equipment. He took me to the sporting-goods store on Gothersgade which makes a specialty of supplying Arctic expeditions. Mathiassen made me buy a really fine sweater with a high turtleneck collar, though I thought it pretty heavy for summer wear. We also ordered our tents. Mine was to be about eight by ten feet, and made of eight-ounce duck. It is the official Danish Boy Scout tent, supposed to hold seven boys, but how is the mystery. Mathiassen's tent was to be somewhat larger and of nine-ounce duck, for he expected to use it a good deal in the Arctic. We were each to have a blanket sleeping bag and an eiderdown bag, either considered adequate in an ordinary climate, and a spare blanket and waterproof undersheet besides. Mathiassen is at least six feet tall, so he ordered extra large sleeping bags. I insisted that mine be the same size, which made everyone in the store laugh, since I am only five foot three. I had my own way, however, and it was just as well. My bags are exactly the right length to pull up about my ears, while Mathiassen's come only to his shoulders.

From Copenhagen, I went on to visit museums in Stockholm, Helsingfors (Helsinki), and Oslo. The warm reception given in Scandinavia to the young student by established scholars and museum curators, with the chance to discuss anthropological problems with real and sympathetic anthropologists, all offered a sharp contrast to my experience at the London School of Economics. Even then I could clearly see the greater opportunities for active research in Arctic archeology if I could become connected with an American university or museum, and dreaded the intellectual isolation I would suffer in a Welsh mining town, or perhaps even in England.

As I wrote home:

Helsingfors
May 7, 1929

Dearest Mother:

I daresay you know all about my trip to Greenland now. Your last letter, written just after you heard from Boas that Mathiassen was O.K., pictures you in a state of curiosity. The best thing about it is that it may lead to all kinds of professional chances in the way of excavation in Alaska, for there are mighty few properly trained people in America, and the museums are wild to have stuff from Alaska. I've told this to D——, and suggested that I might be able to go and to take him with me, in the hopes that it may influence his decision about Wales vs. America. After this glimpse in Scandinavia of what real anthropology is like, I can't bear the idea of having to give up my work. And that I'd have to do if we live in England. It seems such a needless sacrifice. I want to be a first-class anthropologist. I'm not afraid of the drudgery, but I want my chance. . . . I get awfully upset worrying about our future. So afraid D—— will want to live in Wales.

Love,
Freddy

On my return to England, I joined my fiancé for a weekend visit to the headmaster of his old school, and we discussed our future. Although naturally disappointed about the postponement of our summer vacation, he generously helped me to prepare for my Greenland trip, even lending me his finest camera and advising me about films. But marriage plans remained uncertain. I realized that my chances of winning a Ph.D. soon (within a year, I foolishly hoped) would be more certain if I returned that fall to Columbia. Should we be married in England before I sailed, or would the separation then be worse than the delay of another year? And while I preferred to be married at home, could he afford to come to America for the wedding? Nothing could be settled.

After repacking in London, I returned to Copenhagen the last week in May, bringing with me a heavy canvas sheepskin-lined officer's coat which I had bought in Sweden.

Just two days before sailing, I wrote:

Copenhagen
May 29

DEAR FAMILY:

The site we are to excavate is on a small island twelve or thirteen miles north of the settlement of Upernivik. At Upernivik Mathiassen hopes to rent a motorboat to take us to the island. The Danish government has been encouraging the fishing industry among the Eskimo, especially in districts where the seals have been killed off. One of the Danish fishmasters near Upernivik, whose duty is to instruct the natives in modern methods of net fishing, has two motorboats, and we will try to get one of them.

We will take along an Eskimo family, and one or two young fellows besides. The men are to help with the heavy work and will supply us with fresh meat; the woman will keep our skin clothes in repair, and I offered to do my share of our cooking. Mathiassen will take a rifle and shotgun with him. The game will be birds, eggs if it is not too late in the season, seal, walrus, and perhaps white whale (beluga). Mathiassen is taking a supply of mustard and curry to flavor the seal meat, of which he is not really fond. He hopes that we can get bear meat and white whale skin. These are great delicacies. He does not know if there is any fresh water on the island. If not, we will have to capture a small iceberg and use it.

There will still be snow on the ground when we arrive. We

may have to clean it off the midden before we can begin to dig. Dr. Mathiassen has warned me that I may have to wear goggles for fear of snow blindness, but the snow will serve as a convenient refrigerator, which we may have to supplement with blocks of ice from an iceberg. Dr. Birket-Smith says that the blue ice is the best for drinking purposes.

I do not know how bad the mosquitoes will be. Greenland has a bad reputation, so we are taking enough netting to drape over our sleeping bags and to make into head nets. Mathiassen hopes that, since we are to be on a small island, there will not be much of a breeding place for the pests and that the sea breezes will blow them away.

We have two Primus stoves. One is all that we will really need for cooking purposes, according to Mathiassen, but since one is sure to go wrong, it's best to be prepared. We are taking very little canned food. It is very expensive in this country and the Danes do not eat much of it. Besides a good supply of canned meat, a reserve if the hunting fails, we have only four cans of asparagus and eight of peas. These will be for "feastly occasions," as Mathiassen puts it. We will also take potatoes, dried onions and soup herbs, rice, flour, coffee, tea, sugar, salt, a cheese, a ham, and a large sausage. This about exhausts the list of our provisions except for a little chocolate, some canned milk and canned butter. Mathiassen hopes that my "stomach is good."

Lieutenant Thron has been issuing grave warnings against constipation, so I am going armed with a full line of laxatives, though Mathiassen thinks the native prescription of blubber is good enough. I am also taking a box of castor-oil capsules, for I want to be able to sample all the kinds of native food without fear of ptomaine. [Lieutenant Thron also told me that if I went on a motorboat trip I should take a bucket of some kind, since there would be no facilities aboard for women to relieve themselves, and this later proved to be helpful advice.]

When I was outfitting in London, I did my best to find out about photography in the Arctic. Burroughs & Welcome, Ltd., gave me a table of exposures for taking pictures from four o'clock in the morning until eight o'clock at night, which sounds like the snapshotter's paradise. [Of course, this was long before the days of exposure meters, and one had to estimate the exposure from the condition of the light, aided by tables worked out for different latitudes, seasons, and time of day, as well as speed of film, the black and white being then even slower than our modern 1975 color film.]

There are many formalities about getting into Greenland. You see, it is a closed country, administered for the benefit of the natives. No white men are allowed to settle there, no tourists or traders are admitted. The only white people in Greenland are the government officials, who carry on the trade for the government and rule the country, the government doctors, nurses, teachers, and priests. For an outsider to get into Greenland, he must convince the government that he has a scientific purpose, leave a sufficient deposit in a Danish bank to pay for his passage back, and pass a medical examination two days before sailing so that he will not introduce any disease. [The Eskimo have little or no immunity to our ordinary diseases. I had to pass the tests, but was excused from those for venereal infections!] Only a Danish government expedition is permitted to take away archeological specimens. One is not allowed to buy furs from the Eskimos, because that is a government monopoly. Skin clothing to wear in Greenland is exempt from this prohibition, as are bird skins, sealskins, and dogskins, and Lieutenant Thron suggests that I invest in some of these. We'll see however.

A few days ago Lieutenant Thron took me to see the *Hans Egede,* named after the first Danish missionary to Greenland. She is a little three-masted ship. He knows the officers very well. They all speak English and seem a jolly lot. I am to share a cabin with two other women; one is the wife of the chief engineer, and the other is a nurse, Miss Østerby. There will be eleven passengers in all. The ship is supposed to have a limitless capacity; the captain claims they once carried sixty, but they must have stood all the way. I asked the captain what the tonnage of the ship was, but he did not know. My question was referred in turn to the first mate, the first engineer, and so down the line, without getting any answer, until the third engineer told me it was about five hundred tons. As ordinary ocean liners are measured by thousands of tons, you can get some idea of the size of our ship. She is technically termed a steam schooner. She carries a spare propeller in case the regular one is broken by the ice, and she ordinarily uses sails whenever the wind is favorable.

Mathiassen says he has a job for me on the voyage. He is writing an article for the *American Anthropologist* which he wants to translate into English. It is a criticism of Birket-Smith's theory of the origin of the Eskimo culture, as set forth in his new book, *The Caribou Eskimos*.

We are going to excavate our village site in the proper way. The height of the midden above sea level will be determined, since it is an important factor in estimating the age of the deposit. The Eskimo always live as close to the shore as possible, and the Greenland coast has been sinking. In Canada, Mathiassen found that the land had been rising, so that the oldest houses were farthest from the beach. Our midden will be divided into fields two meters square, and we will dig in layers twenty centimeters thick, keeping the finds from each section and layer separate. We are to use geological spades, with handles a meter long, notched into tenths, as measuring sticks. The ideal in excavating is to know exactly where every specimen came from, and how it was lying, so that, if necessary, one could put everything back into place again. The ground will be frozen, of course, but we expect it to thaw out at the rate of two inches a day. In Alaska, where there is plenty of wood, one can help the sun by lighting fires on the ground, but here there will be no wood. We do not know if there will even be enough driftwood to build a platform under our sleeping bags.

Our only difficulty is that Mathiassen has never seen our island and does not know where it is, for it is not marked on any map. Furthermore, the man who told him about the midden is no longer in Upernivik. He hopes, however, to find some Eskimo who knows of the place. He had originally planned to excavate a

very rich site in Holsteinsborg District, notorious for its mosquitoes, but he changed his mind as soon as he heard about Inugsuk,
for the sea is washing the ruins away.

The *Hans Egede* will touch at Holsteinsborg, Godhavn,
Ūmánaq (in the most glorious part of Greenland), and perhaps at
Prøven, a small post in the southern part of Upernivik District. At
Prøven, or Upernivik itself, we will leave the ship and continue
the trip to the site by motorboat. I hope we can take lots of motorboat trips, and that we will have a chance to do some mountain
climbing. I should like very much to get onto the Inland Ice. . . .

D—— thinks he can come over to America to marry me.
One trouble is a question of time, for he doesn't dare stay away
from his work too long. Would that mean a Bryn Mawr or a
Greensboro wedding?

Don't worry about me.

Much love,
FREDDY

But these were only plans, and the real Greenland proved much
finer than that for which my imagination had prepared me.

I think I ought to add a few words about the old village at
Inugsuk. The man who discovered it was Dr. Andersen, the
former doctor at Upernivik. He believed that the house ruins were
Norse, but the specimens he found and sent to Mathiassen are certainly Eskimo, and seem to be very old. In any case, Mathiassen
tells me that the Norsemen did not live in the northern part of
Greenland. They had to live in the south, where there was fodder
for their animals. In 1824, however, a runic stone was found in a
cairn on Kingigtorssuaq, a large island a few miles west of Inugsuk. The inscription says: "Erling Sigvattsön and Bjarne Tordssön
and Enride Oddssön erected this cairn on the Saturday before soc-
cage day and . . ." Professor Finnur Jónsson reports that the style
of writing is that of the latter half of the thirteenth century. So we
know that at least an exploring party of Norsemen came to the

Upernivik District in the month of April in the latter half of the thirteenth century. In *Danish Greenland* (London, 1877), Dr. Henry Rink also mentions this stone. The translation which he gives is: "Elling Sigvathson and Baanne Tortarson and Enrithi Osson on the Saturday before Gang-day raised these beacons and . . . (this clearing) 235" (or A.D. 1235). Gang-day is the same as St. Mark's Day, and is the twenty-fifth of April. In 1235 it fell on Wednesday, so the previous Saturday was April 21. Dr. Rink was puzzled that Norse ships could have reached a point so far north at such an early season. [Since Dr. Rink's day we have learned that the climate was much milder during most of the time the Norsemen lived in Greenland. This enabled them to journey so far north to hunt. Later the climate worsened, stunting livestock and men. Malnutrition, the cessation of trade with Scandinavia, and the attacks of the Eskimo led to the abandonment and destruction of the Norse colonies.]

The Eskimo tell this story about Inugsuk. I have copied it from Mathiassen's report, in which it appears in a somewhat abbreviated form. As the tale is also told about several other places in Greenland, it cannot have much historical value.

In olden times Norsemen lived on Inugsuk, and they have left a cairn and the ruin of a big house; at Qagsserssuaq lived Eskimos at the same time. Once the anqakoq (the shaman) flew from Qagsserssuaq over Inugsuk, and saw that the Norsemen were in their house. So

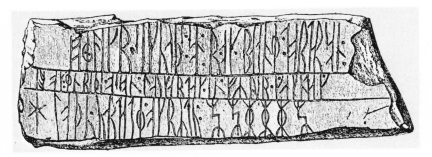

The runic stone from Kingigtorssuaq
(*Meddelelser om Grønland*, vol. 77 [4], 1930, fig. 2)

he returned home and said to his countrymen: "Tonight we will all go to Inugsuk, kill the Norsemen and take all the things they have." They immediately set off with their sledges and came to Inugsuk, where the people were just retiring to rest. They had taken off their clothes, as they used to sleep naked. Some were already entirely unclothed, while others still had their boots and dog-skin trousers on. Then the Eskimos forced their way into the house and killed them all with their bows, with the exception of three, who fled. One of them, who was quite naked, fled to a place not far from Augpilagtoq, but on the way the soles of his feet and his back were frostbitten. When he reached the Eskimo settlement and sought refuge in one of the houses, the skin of his back being frozen, went to pieces as it rubbed against the entrance passage. The angakoq there could not do anything to help him because he was a Norseman, and his cure could only help Eskimos; and so he died. The other two, a man and his wife, fled to a steep cliff some miles south of Upernivik, where they climbed up and turned into stone; the cliff is still called Qavdlunarssuit [the Norsemen]; but the figures have fallen down. When the Norsemen were killed the Eskimos were about to share the spoils. The angakoq took a big chest standing in an outhouse; but he was too tired and had no dogs; so he had to work all night dragging the chest to Qagsserssuaq. But when he got home and opened the lid, it only contained a recently dead Norseman in a white dress. Even in the memory of people living now the inhabitants of Kingigtoq and Qagsserssuaq feared the vengeance of the Danes.

[1975: Although there is now a standardized orthography for the Eskimo words used as Greenland place names, I have retained those we used in 1929. Thus "Upernivik" is now "Upernavik," and "Ūmánaq" is "Ūmának."]

II

The Voyage

On board the *Hans Egede*
June 5, 1929

DEAR FAMILY:

Well, this is June 5, such as it is, and we will all be glad to get out of this jeezly boat. She is rushing along at the incredible speed of ten knots, and is rolling through an angle of thirty or thirty-five degrees, at a conservative estimate. This may not sound like much to a mathematician, but just try it on a ship! I have to hold on to my chair with one hand, and hold the typewriter on the table with the other, which makes typing a little difficult. Birket-Smith warned me about this ship, but I did not believe she could be as bad as he reported. In fact, I can't really credit my senses now. By all the laws of gravitation we should have turned turtle long ago.

We sailed from the Greenland dock in Copenhagen about ten o'clock on the morning of June 1. Before I got up that morning, I had taken the precaution of consuming two tablets of Karmit, that infallible, money-back, gilt-edged seasick remedy, and it had given me a wonderful jag all through breakfast. [This was before the days of Dramamine.] I took another dose for good measure just as we sailed. Half of Copenhagen collected to bid us farewell. Dr. Thomsen, Curator-in-Chief of Ethnology at the museum, was there with a box of candy for me; Birket-Smith came too, and gloated with a veteran's callousness over how seasick we would be. He knows the *Hans Egede* of old. She is the unsteadiest tub on the high seas, and doesn't stop rolling until she has been tied up to a dock for three days. Lieutenant Thron and his wife came in from the country with a couple of jars of preserves for the expedition. Mrs. Thron kissed me many times and called me "*meine süsse Tochter.*" German was the only language we could use together. The Lieutenant dragged me around, introducing me to all sorts of curious people. All I could catch was my own name, and "*rejse til Grønland,*" which, pronounced in that inimitable Danish fashion, never fails to make my heart beat faster. Mrs. Mathiassen, the three little M. girls, and M.'s sister, and a sampling of grand-parents were there, too. Poor Mrs. Mathiassen looked pretty sad, and I felt sorry for her. Her eagerly awaited little boy had been born only ten days before. Even the other children looked un-happy, but they were not too depressed to consume the candy I gave them.

Ten o'clock arrived at last, and the friends and relatives were herded off onto the dock, all but a select company who were to go with us as far as Helsingør (Elsinore), where we were to pick up more cargo. We were a long time in pulling out from the dock, and getting into the channel. Our arms were tired from waving goodbye. Thron's was the most energetic handkerchief. The last figures we could distinguish were Mathiassen's little girl twins in white coats, standing well to the front.

Lunch was served at eleven o'clock with plenty of beer and *snaps.* When we came up on deck again, the liquor combined with the seasick cure had produced extraordinary effects. I re-member standing by the rail and talking fluent German to a lady guest and the members of Dr. Krüger's geological expedition to Ellesmereland [Ellesmere Island]. And my German could not have been so bad, either, for they were interested in what I had to say, and we conversed for some time. (This feat, I should add, I have not been able to repeat.)

The ship was already beginning to roll in a mild way when we reached Helsingør. There a tug came out to us, bringing a cargo of high explosives from a Swedish nitroglycerin factory at Helsingborg, across the straits, to be used at the Greenland coal mines at Disko. The tug took away the visitors.

Then we waited. We were to take on some provisions and explosives for the Hobbs meteorological expedition at Mount Evans, on the edge of the Inland Ice, halfway between Holsteinsborg and Sukkertoppen. The supplies were expected on a truck from Copenhagen, and we had to wait for them, said the captain, if it took us a month. There was nothing to do. Mathiassen was so impatient that he tore around the deck like a bear in a cage. I tried to take a nap but found it impossible to sleep. At last, with considerable relief, we saw the tug with the provisions. These were loaded aboard in record time, and we answered the cheery hails of *"god rejse"* with enthusiastic *"tak"*s.

The ship did not roll much that first afternoon, but what did upset me was the frequency with which meals appeared. Lunch at eleven, afternoon coffee at three, dinner at five, and evening tea at eight. There was no time to digest. The second day we steamed slowly up the Skagerrak. It was marvelously sunny during the morning, and I spent it lying on the after hatch, wrapped up in my Swedish soldier's sheepskin coat, watching the southernmost tip of Norway to starboard and talking with Bjare, the young Dane on Krüger's expedition.

Bjare tells me that he has lived for five years in Greenland. He is full of exciting stories, mostly about his wonderful dog team, but I suspect he is straining the truth a bit in order to impress me. He said that he had driven ninety miles in one day, but I don't see how that could be possible, even with smooth ice, good weather, an empty sledge, and a fresh team. His dogs loved to travel, and when his boss dog grew too old to go, he still used to come when Bjare was hitching up the team and whine to be taken. Bjare is to be Dr. Krüger's assistant on the expedition and have charge of the non-scientific side. The geologists are looking, I understand, for a particular rock formation which outcrops in Greenland and in Ellesmereland. This summer the four men will travel about Greenland waters in their motorboat, and then two of them will return to Germany, leaving Krüger and Bjare to go on to Ellesmereland alone. The country is quite uninhabited except for three Royal Northwest Policemen, who have a post there in order to claim the land for Canada—a rather silly business. It is in the High Arctic, and winter there, especially for two men, one of whom has never wintered in the Arctic, will be no joke.

While we were sitting out on deck, Mathiassen read to us some Eskimo stories from Rasmussen's new book, *The Intellectual Culture of the Iglulik Eskimos*. These were the Eskimo among whom the Fifth Thule Expedition lived. Being a scientific report, there had been no attempt to mutilate the stories to please European prudery. The first story was innocuous enough, but the second, "Women Become Dangerous When They Have No Husbands," which Mathiassen had struck at random, was—how shall I say?—typically Eskimo. I was curious to see what Mathiassen would do. He was a little embarrassed—so was I—and yet he felt that it would be too ridiculous to stop in the middle. I am glad to say that he read bravely through to the end; then looked up, laughing and a trifle flushed. "Well, I don't think that was a very suitable story to read to a young girl!"

He has been telling me something about his experiences on Southampton Island, north of Hudson Bay. He had gone there with his assistant, Jacob Olsen, a Greenlander, to do two weeks' digging in an ancient village site, but while they were there, the channel separating the island from the expedition's base on the coast of Melville Peninsula filled with floating ice, so that it was impossible to force a boat through. When their food gave out, they were dependent upon the natives. Then came a run of bad luck in hunting, and they almost starved to death. There was sickness, too; Mathiassen almost died from having to eat rotted meat, and the woman in whose house he lived was covered with syphilitic sores.

The shaman blamed it upon the strangers because they had robbed the graves of the old people. Mathiassen and Olsen feared for their lives. They had to spend the winter in that dreary place, until at last the channel froze over, and their comrades could send a dog team to fetch them. On the map of Southampton Island, which Mathiassen drew, there is a place called "Prison Gate," named, so he told me, because it was from there that they made their escape to the mainland. Mathiassen has wonderful things to tell, but it is not always easy to make him talk. Some of his experiences are ones he would like to forget. But for me this has been the jolliest day on board.

By June 3, I felt that the danger of seasickness was over, and succeeded in getting a game of deck tennis started. Since the game was unknown to the Danes, the first thing was to explain it and get some rope rings. One of the ship's officers spoke to the crew and the latter generously kept us well supplied. Soon the game became quite popular among the passengers.

It began to get rough the third night, but yesterday, June 4, it was really snorting. Almost everyone was sick, except the engineer's wife, Dr. Bertelsen, and the more hardy Germans. I can proudly boast that I have not missed a single meal, but when the ship pitches like this, we cannot sleep, for we are constantly flung about. It is hard work even to sit in a chair. I was the only one appearing for evening tea, and so it was handed to me unceremoniously from the galley.

June 13

We are now off the coast of Greenland and have seen our first iceberg!

I have been helping Mathiassen with his article. At first he translated the Danish to me, which I transposed into better English and typed. Then we read over the whole thing, correcting mistakes and trying to improve the idiom, and finally I typed it again, making a carbon for Birket-Smith, whose thesis is being criticized. Mathiassen dictates to me, and holds down the typewriter with one hand. The rolling of the ship has made the machine seasick. If it is set crosswise to the roll, every time the boat heaves over, the carriage flies up and shifts into capitals. If the machine is set parallel to the rolling, the carriage sometimes has to go up so steep a hill that it balks. So I have to wait until the ship is leaning over to starboard and then type furiously to make up for lost time, before she begins to swing over onto her other side. And with one hand I grab the typewriter and the edge of the table. It has been interesting work. Mathiassen's paper is well argued, and I don't see how Birket-Smith can answer him. The difference in opinion between them seems to be due to a difference in method. As both methods are good and both men scholars, what is a poor beginner like me to believe? I should like to have some theory to trust. I have worked very hard on the paper. It was often a puzzle to find just the correct expression for what Mathiassen wanted to say. He has been a good sport, and has not been angry at my criticisms. Mathiassen always knows exactly what he wants to say, and sometimes will come out with a phrase so excellent that it would do credit to an English writer.

I have learned quite a bit about Eskimo archeology already (or think I have). Mathiassen's theory is that the Eskimo culture originated about the Bering Sea, where there are plenty of whales to hunt and plenty of driftwood for houses, boats, etc. Eventually the Eskimo began to expand their domain, migrating from Alaska into Arctic Canada, until then (he believed) uninhabited, finally crossing into Greenland in the Middle Ages. These early Eskimo were great seamen; they hunted whales from big skin boats (umiaks), and they also had smaller, one-man, decked-over kayaks. Their houses were permanent structures built underground, with walls of stones and whales' skulls, and whales' ribs for rafters. Their weapons for harpooning sea mammals were skillfully contrived; and, like the modern Alaskan Eskimo, they were not without a certain artistic ability, especially in the decorating of bone and ivory objects. This was the culture which Mathiassen discovered in the oldest ruins in Arctic Canada, and which he called the Thule culture, after a great kitchen midden at Thule, Northwest Greenland, where Captain Comer found the first implements of that culture. This Thule culture of the first Eskimo is very different from that of the modern Central Eskimo in Canada, who do not build whaleboats, are very timid in kayaks when they use them at all, and who live in snow, not stone, houses in the winter. The culture of the present-day Greenlanders and Alaskan Eskimo is more like that of the Thule culture natives. In fact, Mathiassen has been able to guess a great many things about these Thule Eskimo—for example, how they harnessed their dogs, and how they cured skin, etc.—because similar practices in Greenland and Alaska suggest what used to be the customs in the Central Regions, though they are now different. In this way, he has filled in many "missing links."

The difference of opinion between Mathiassen and Birket-Smith is this: The former believes that the Thule culture is the original Eskimo culture, but Birket-Smith thinks that the first Eskimo were not coast dwellers like the Thule people, but inland, nomadic hunters, like the Athabaskan Indians of Canada. The Caribou Eskimo of the Barren Grounds represent, to the present day, he believes, the primitive culture of the first Eskimo. Mathiassen, however, calls the Caribou Eskimo degenerate Thule people who left the seacoast and wandered into the interior to hunt caribou, at last forgetting everything they knew about the sea. It is a tremendous problem, and makes a good argument. There is much to be said on both sides. Birket-Smith and Mathiassen are good friends and criticize each other in a sporting way. Up to now neither will give ground, and I am wondering if, and how, it will all be decided.

[Mathiassen's article, "The Question of the Origin of Eskimo Culture," and Birket-Smith's "The Question of the Origin of Eskimo Culture: A Rejoinder," were both published in the *American Anthropologist*, vol. 32 (4), 1930. But the summer that we were in Greenland, newspaper clippings mailed to me by my family indicated the recognition by Henry B. Collins of the Smithsonian Institution of the great antiquity of the Old Bering Sea culture, originally discovered in Alaska by Diamond Jenness in 1926. We did not then realize that it was in some respects ancestral to the Thule culture. Nor was Mathiassen then aware or ready to recognize that the Canadian Arctic and Greenland had been occupied by still more ancient Eskimo before the Thule Eskimo arrived from Alaska. This different culture had been identified by Diamond Jenness as early as 1925 from specimens sent to Ottawa from Cape Dorset, southern Baffin Island. Mathiassen had actually found some Dorset remains, too, but had failed to recognize them as distinct. Dorset and pre-Dorset, or Sarqaq, are now assumed to date back probably to 2000 B.C., while the oldest Thule remains are only about a thousand years old. The Canadian and Greenland Dorset Eskimo seem to have been absorbed by the Thule immigrants.]

Here one feels cut off from all the world. It is a wonderful feeling, and I can't describe it. I feel as if there were no use in trying to tell you what happens here, because I am in a different world, and the ordinary everyday words I have to use don't have the same meanings. Values are somehow changed. Food, for instance, has taken on a new significance, especially for me, since I can't tell whether or not the meal will prove a total loss. This Danish sweet fruit-juice soup, a kind of watery misplaced dessert, just about makes me cat. I don't see how Mathiassen can stow away a whole bowl of it, and he, of course, laughs at my inability to taste it.

I made a chessboard and set of men out of cardboard. The knights were pretty funny, I confess, and my efforts elicited many scornful wisecracks from the others, especially from Dr. Krüger, who discovered that there was a real set on board. With the boat heaving as she does, however, the real set is useless, and my non-skid chessmen can stand their ground except in the very worst weather.

Mrs. Bertelsen has recovered and Dr. Bertelsen has been giving me Danish lessons. Both he and his wife are charming people, and I am devoted to them. He is making a medical inspection of Greenland.

Dr. Drescher, the poor young German, has been sick all this time. He looks like a ghost, and we feel very sorry for him, also for old Dr. Nieland, who shares his cabin. They are the two who are not going to Ellesmereland. I don't like Dr. Krüger. He thinks too much of himself and is always putting other people in the wrong. His mouth is that of a spoiled child, and he seems to cherish a sense of injury. I am glad that I don't have to spend the winter alone with him, as Bjare has to do. Bjare is really very sensitive and touchy, in spite of his affectation of boldness and his teasing manner. One really can't joke with him. I am afraid that he and Krüger will not get along well together, especially since Krüger knows nothing about the Arctic winter. I should not be surprised if there were serious trouble, and I would not blame Bjare too much, either. I tried to find out what he thought of Krüger, but he was tight-lipped, and I was afraid to question him directly. One never sees them together, and there does not seem to be any spirit and enthusiasm in their expedition as there is in ours.

I took the bad weather as an excuse to abandon my skirt. It is wonderful to be in breeches again! I feel just like a small boy, and act like one, I guess. I have been wearing my ski boots, too, for they are warm and waterproof, and I want to soften them up a bit for walking.

On the tenth we came to Cape Farewell, the southern tip of Greenland, but could not see it. We passed a ship in the night, and her wireless told us that there was heavy ice along the southern and western shores, so we have kept well out to sea, much to the disappointment of the passengers. Yesterday we rounded the cape, and ran into a storm, with a "number ten" gale (the real thing). Luckily, the wind blew from behind us, for I think it would have swamped the ship if it had been from the side, and we could not have moved if we had faced it. Our poor ship reared and plunged, quivering, with the propeller frantically churning the air as often as the water. Mountains of water, with driving spray, rushed past us and over us. There was hail, too, that stung one's face like the devil, and in the afternoon it grew colder and snowed. We have been more or less shut below, for the ordinary decks have been swept by waves, and even on the forward deck under the bridge it is too cold and wet to be much fun. A wave broke the wooden support for the canvas cover of one of the lifeboats, and another smashed in the steward's porthole; the water went all over the ship. I was sitting in the smoking room reading when a wave came over the side, and a bit of it sloshed through the closed porthole and went down the back of my neck. We all went to bed between lunch and tea, for we are exhausted from lack of sleep. The day before yesterday I was flung out of my chair in the dining saloon, and almost landed in Bjare's lap, after caroming off the wall. Luckily, Mathiassen grabbed the cup of tea out of my hand and saved it for me. In the smoking room I have twice been thrown under the table. One has to sit there with one's knees braced against the edge of the table, and if one gets tired and relaxes, the first good lurch sends one flying. Of course, you can't walk anywhere without extraordinary precautions.

Meals are quite exciting. The table is covered with wooden slabs, and every dish, glass, and cup has to fit, like a jigsaw puzzle, into its proper slot. It is impossible to keep the spoons from rattling. Soup has to be served in the bottom of large bowls, glasses and cups can be filled only halfway up, and the men put the beer bottles in their pockets for safekeeping. They serve beer and *snaps* every day for lunch, with red and white wine for dinner, and sometimes liqueurs after that. Though I am very fond of the beer and the white wine, I can't drink it every day, especially when I have the feeling that I am so churned up inside that I can't digest anything properly. Curiously enough, I have a splendid appetite and feel quite fine as long as I am at the table.

It is wonderful to look into the galley. Everything is anchored in place. Lids are clamped tight to the pots, and they in turn are held fast to the stove by iron racks. There as not been a day that we have not had regular meals, and the food is excellent. The china is kept in the dining saloon, worse luck, and our cabins open off from it, with only curtains in the doorways for ventilation, since the portholes are screwed tight. At night the dishes rattle horribly in their racks, and the ship creaks as if she were coming to pieces. Our suitcases and shoes bang up and down across the floor; there is no way to keep them quiet. Mrs. Thron's jam had an accident, and some of it was spilled. The only place where I can keep jars safely is in one of the tin seasick receptacles, which the stewardess hangs on the edge of our bunks with ghoulish anticipation.

This storm is one of the most beautiful and terrible experiences that I have known. We roll less now than we did with the wind on our quarter, but the ship staggers along as if she were frightened, and we are glad that we are a safe distance from shore. Luckily, the wind went down a little this afternoon or we should not have dared to head for port. At first there was some talk of not attempting to call at Holsteinsborg at all, and keeping on before the wind to Godhavn, our next stop. I think I shall always remember this storm, and will be able to recognize Davis Strait without a chart. It has been a fitting greeting to the Arctic. Mathiassen and I hope that we will have nothing like this when we are camping. No tent could stand against it.

We have just sighted our first land, a misty, cloudlike bump, that is the famous sugar-loaf mountain which gave Sukkertoppen its name. We are just under the Arctic Circle, and will reach Holsteinsborg tonight.

III

Within the Circle

DEAR FAMILY:

We are really in Greenland now. We have climbed the "icy mountains" and tasted Greenland food. I have so much to tell.

Before I went to take a nap after dinner on June 13, we could already see quite a lot of the mountainous country north of Sukkertoppen—jagged peaks, white with snow, disgorging valley glaciers—just before the tail of the storm overtook us. Again the waves were lashed into a smother of foam, and the land was hidden by mist and falling snow. Luckily, the weather cleared almost at once, or we should not have dared to approach the rocky shores. I had a sound sleep until nine o'clock, when Mathiassen pounded on the wall and told me that we were almost in the harbor. I hurried up onto the forward deck. Already we were close to shore, running between skerries and small islands. There were several icebergs near us, and at the time it seemed as if there were a great many, but compared to those that we have seen since, they were very few and inferior specimens. What excitement there was when we caught sight of the first sign of life! It was only a cairn of roughly piled stones on a desert mountainside. The colony is hidden from the sea behind a point of land which forms the harbor, and one does not see the houses until one is upon them. From the water one sees nothing but a desolate and rocky coast. It seemed folly to take a ship into such a place. We could not believe that there was anything more ahead of us than snow-covered mountains and bare rocks. A church spire suddenly appeared above the point of land, and we let off an earsplitting toot from our whistle. Mathiassen had promised me that Eskimos in kayaks would paddle out to welcome us, but in none of the places where we have stopped have the kayakers come out in the proper way. The natives seem to prefer dories and skiffs. I was disappointed that we did not tie up to a dock, but we were forced to anchor some distance out in the little harbor and wait until we could be taken ashore in boats. The first of these soon tied up to the side of the ship.

We looked eagerly over the rail, and grinned down at the occupants, who smiled at us and began to scramble up the ladder. These were the first Eskimos I had ever seen! The men were dressed in dark blue jackets of cotton cloth, *anoraks*, with close-fitting hoods, which most of them wore thrown back, for although I had on my sheepskin coat and was glad of it, they evidently did not consider it very cold. They had on ordinary trousers for the most part, a few of them wore sealskin pants, but not many, for I am told that seals are not very plentiful here any more, since the Norwegians have been killing off the herds that used to drift around on the ice from the East Coast. All wore *kamiks*, or waterproof sealskin boots. These are the most cleverly made footgear that I have ever seen and I was much interested in them.

The boot is made of two pieces of skin, the sole and the upper, which are sewn together without any opening to lace up, and yet it fits the foot far better than our laceless riding boot. The sole is turned up around the edges, and is slightly puckered at the heel and toe to fit onto the upper. The women have a special implement like a bone knife with which to pucker the soles, and on a well-made boot the gathers lie in neat tucks all pointing forward. The upper is seamed up the front of the leg and ends at the bottom with a triangular flap in front which covers the instep. The patterns for men's and women's boots are much the same except that the women's boots come up over the knee, with an extra piece set in for the bend, and are of beautiful red leather. The men's shoes are of the naturally dark, dehaired skins, and come up only to the bulge of the calf. A poor man's boot may come only a few inches above the ankle. Inside is a stocking of sealskin, hair side inside, with a furry cuff at the top above the boot. While wearing white men's trousers, the men tuck their trousers inside their boots, but the sealskin pants end in a cuff which is tied about the boot. In this way they can wade into the water without getting their feet wet.

The women were wearing white women's coats over their native costume. It is very interesting. Their jacket is like the men's, except that at the neck there is only the beginning of the hood, which is cut off. They wear bright-colored woolen caps which they knit themselves. Their jackets are of the brightest colors, and end at the waist with a belt of wide ribbon. Their trousers are ridiculously short, and barely bridge the gap between their short jackets and their boot tops. They are made of dark sealskins with wide stripes up the front of the legs, composed of bands of red skin, clipped white dog fur, and a strip with a mosaic pattern of tiny squares of variously colored leather.

These Holsteinsborg natives were not pure-blooded Eskimo; many were obviously half or three-quarters white, but the general impression from the whole group was of a brown, strangely small race. Many of the men seemed barely bigger than myself, but the effect was certainly exaggerated, for I have become used to the six-foot Danes. The Eskimos' hands were bare and incredibly dirty. They clustered about the top of the ladder and stared at us and we at them. I was overcome with shyness. They were totally strange, and I was strange, too. I could not help sticking like a shadow to Mathiassen. I think I even got behind him, and peered round him at the Greenlanders. I have never been so shy in all my life. More boats kept arriving, bringing some women and boys. They were all so small, and so browned by the sun, that I could not tell whether they were young or old. They all seemed to be children who had aged without growing. Bjare and Mrs. Bertelsen went over to them and they began to talk Eskimo together. Soon the two race groups broke up and mingled, and the natives began to help the sailors unload the mail and freight into a large barge which a dory full of young girls had towed out to us. The white people, the governor of the colony, his wife and family, and his assistant, came aboard and shook hands with all of us. Mathiassen introduced himself, and me, as *"min assistent."* I felt proud, I can tell you! I still do when I hear him call me that. These white people all wore *kamiks*, and some of the men also wore the Eskimo *anoraks*. It is not always easy to tell the white man from the almost-white Greenlander, except that the former usually carries himself with more self-assurance, and is cleaner.

We were dreadfully impatient to go ashore, but we had to wait until all the mail had been loaded into the boats. Then we tumbled after it. Two small boys rowed our boat full of people. Mathiassen gave them each half a crown (the usual tip is twenty-five *øre*, or eight cents, per passenger), and I gave them each a cigarette. The village consists of church, schoolhouse, governor's house and outbuildings, warehouse, cannery, and blubber storehouse, and a miscellaneous collection of tiny wooden shacks, scattered on both sides of a smelly, refuse-choked brook.

Holsteinsborg is a typical Greenland colony in many ways. The first is the filth. I was especially struck by it, for not only was this the first place we visited, but the dirt was concentrated in the narrow gorge. There were bones everywhere, bits of broken china, tin cans, cast-off boots, etc., and pools and piles of filth. I could not tell whether the excrement was that of men or of dogs. The white men's houses seem to be the only ones with W.C.s, so the natives must just go outside, though I have never surprised one in the act.

There are dogs here. Holsteinsborg is just on the Arctic Circle, and is the place farthest south where people have sledge dogs.

I saw several dogskins hung up to dry. On account of the scarcity of caribou and polar bears, the Greenlanders have to use dogskins for their winter furs. The dogs have fine thick fur, but nothing to compare with that of bears and caribou. The colony governor had a fine team of dogs. I made friends with them at once. Eskimo dogs are very fond of licking one's hands. The leader—or, rather, the boss dog, for there is no leader in an Eskimo team—was evidently used to receiving the most attention, and kept shouldering the other dogs out of the way. There is quite a difference between the dogs of white men and Eskimos. The natives never make pets of their animals, so they don't come up to be fondled when you call them. They usually pay no attention to you, and if they do, they only bark suspiciously, or watch you with timid and distant, though not unfriendly, behavior. They will run if they think you are picking up a stone. I have never been growled at, though I have been quite close to dogs who were tied up because of their bad character. Not all the dogs are fine and big. There are always some thin, puny beasts, and some with mange, but on the whole they are splendid animals, and I like them tremendously.

As soon as Mathiassen and Miss Østerby and I stepped ashore at Holsteinsborg, we went up to climb the rocks back of the village. It was queer to be on solid land again; only the land wasn't steady, but swayed like the ship, and we staggered along. It was astonishing to see that there was really grass and heather and ground willow growing, not to mention a little white weed and a domed purply flower, which Mathiassen called by its Latin name, *erica* [heather]. There was, of course, plenty of moss and lichen on the rocks. It was good to throw ourselves down on the top of the hill, and pant, and look back at the village and the good old *Hans Egede* looking so very inadequate against the snowy, mist-wreathed mountains.

When we came down, Mathiassen and I went to call on an Eskimo woman who had been Lieutenant Thron's servant. She lived in a frame house, typical of the more civilized Eskimo establishments. It was not walled in with turf, as are the houses farther north. In fact, there was only one real turf house in Holsteinsborg. As usual, there was a separate entrance hall to this house, and the roof was so very low that Mathiassen had to duck under the rafters, and even I had to stoop to go through the door. The woman's husband came in with us. The woman was lying on the wooden bed platform on a pile of featherbeds. There was a child asleep at her feet. The woman was in her nightgown but did not seem to be embarrassed. Mathiassen spoke to her in Danish, and then tried some Iglulik Eskimo, which raised a laugh. He isn't very fluent, and there seems to be quite a difference, anyway, between the Iglulik and the Greenland dialects. The air in the house was pretty bad, and it was rather hot, so we did not stay more than a minute. The husband showed us with pride a toy two-car garage that stood on a table. There was a tin wind-up car in it. Mathiassen and I both laughed delightedly, and were much impressed, for we were seeing the only motorcar in Greenland. The people were pleased.

Then we went to the government agent's house (in Greenland one just walks in, through a series of outer entrance rooms and passages, with only a perfunctory knock at doors, until one locates the inmates). The governor was entertaining all the people from the ship with tea and coffee, not the colored water they serve on the ship, but real tea and real coffee. I was incredibly weary, and could hardly sit in my chair, for the whole house seemed to sway with the motion of the ship, and I was afraid of falling. I saw a radio set, and was tremendously excited when I learned that they could get stations all the way from London and Copenhagen to San Francisco. I begged them to tune in some American station, and soon was eagerly listening to the American voice of the announcer at KDKA, Pittsburgh. It was not a beautiful voice, but it sounded so honest and friendly and familiar. Then came the music—"Yankee Doodle," as it would be rendered in different countries, with even the old wisecrack at Prohibition: "And now we go to the country where they make the Scotch Coca-Cola." There was a chair in the room upholstered in the same dark blue shiny material that is on two of the chairs in our own living room at home. I felt very near to home, then, as I listened to the music and looked at the chair. I was homesick, after all these long months away from home, but yet so happy to be in Greenland that I would not have left it for anything.

The whistle tooted for us at midnight, so we hurried down to the ship. But what a night it was! As we steamed out of the harbor, we had to buck the waves left by the storm and, when we turned northward in the open sea, felt their full impact on our port side. I tried to wedge myself firmly in with blankets, but it was impossible to get them packed tightly enough to keep from being bumped about. With one awful lurch I was almost thrown out of the upper bunk. Some of the bedcovers fell onto the floor, and I cried out, so that the people in my own cabin really thought I had fallen out. We could not get to sleep until three. Then in the morning at seven-thirty, with the fatality of Judgment Day, that hard-boiled stewardess stuck in her head at the door and waked us as usual with raucous clamor. We journeyed that day surrounded by mist and snow and rain. I could not believe that there was land near us. Holsteinsborg seemed like a dream, coming to it, as we did, in the twilight night, when I was still drowsy from a sound sleep.

We made Godhavn on Disko Island sometime that evening. We were now inside the Arctic Circle. Godhavn is the seat of government for North Greenland, and in consequence has a great many white men's houses, and the Greenlanders here are very civilized, for most of them are in the pay of the government. Many of the boys have to wear rubber boots because there are so few sealskins. It can't be good for their feet. Quite a few people came on board to welcome us. This time I wasn't shy but grinned at the Greenlanders and waved to the people in the boats. It's not hard to make them smile back at you. Dr. Morten Porsild, who is an authority on every kind of science connected with the Arctic, invited us to visit him in the morning. His house is called the Arctic Station and is a kind of hotel for scientists, with a fine library and laboratory. That evening we called on an old friend of Mathiassen's who runs an earthquake and magnetic deviation observatory. There we had smokes and apples and whiskey. People in Greenland always get out their best when the ship comes to port. It was snowing most of the time, so we could not see the midnight sun, though it was fairly late when we went back on board.

The next day, June 15, was to be very long, though we did not realize it when we got up, bright and early, to go ashore. It was still snowing, though the weather gave promise of clearing soon. Everything was white, but by ten o'clock it had all melted, and the ground was a squidgy mire. Godhavn looks much better than Holsteinsborg. It has an excellent landlocked harbor, made by the building up of a big bar between a small island and Disko, and the village is spread out more, and there is less dirt. Mathiassen and I walked a quarter of a mile across the narrow neck of the peninsula, and along the coast to Dr. Porsild's house. We looked inside, but, as we heard no movement, judged that everyone must be asleep, so we went on across some swampy ground, bright with the purple *erica*, to the beach, where several icebergs were stranded.

Then we went back to Dr. Porsild's house, where I played with the dogs. Young Erling Porsild, the doctor's son, came out and began to feed them with *angmagsset*, a small, oily fish, like smelt. They are scooped out of the sea by the hundreds and spread on the rocks to dry; they make good dog feed. At Holsteinsborg we took on many bags of these dried *angmagsset* for Rasmussen, who wants them for his dog team at Cape York.

Inside the Arctic Station we were entertained with coffee, etc., and young Porsild showed us the magnificent photographs that he took on a botanical expedition in Alaska, and around Back River and Slave Lake, in Canada. He is going to the Mackenzie next year to take charge of a herd of tame reindeer which the Canadian government is buying from people in Alaska, to give to the natives. The animals are to be paid for, *when* delivered across the frontier, at $75 a head. Years ago the Canadians made an attempt to introduce reindeer breeding among the Eskimo, with reindeer imported from Lapland, to the tune of $500 apiece. It was a failure. It was originally Stefánsson's idea, but it miscarried because the captain of the ship bringing the reindeer was afraid of getting stuck in the ice, since the season was late, and put the Lapp herders and the deer ashore on the west coast of Hudson Bay in such a hurry that by the time the Lapps had got ashore safely, the herd had disappeared. "No doubt there was good caribou hunting that year," was Mathiassen's comment.

[Dr. Morten P. Porsild, born 1872, who ran the Arctic Station, was a distinguished botanist and an authority on all Arctic flora and fauna. His son, Alf Erling Porsild, born 1901, was to become a botanist even more famous than his father, an expert on Arctic, alpine, and subarctic flora, with many scientific publications to his credit, and a distinguished career at the National Museum in Ottawa.]

I told young Porsild that I would like to taste an *angmagsset*. He had been telling me how he and his brother, when they were children, used to go out to the storehouse and eat quantities of the dog feed. So he took me out and prepared one for me. They have to be deheaded, pulled open, and definned. Then one eats the whole thing, or if one is very particular, one can pull off the skin. The fish are about the size of a sardine, so you can imagine how much is left. They are very tough, and have quite a peculiar taste, which one does not notice so much at first, but which sticks in the mouth and grows ranker and ranker. My impression of the fish, of which I was able to master only three-quarters, was of very greasy, moldy, tough cardboard. I had to wash my hands and drink a glass of water, and smoke a cigarette right away, but the taste persisted until I could get back to the ship and brush my teeth. It made me feel a little sick. How the others laughed when they saw my struggles to eat the fish! Young Porsild told me that once he had had nothing to eat but dried fish—salmon, I think he said—and that all dried fish taste alike. (1930: This is not quite correct. Since writing this, I have tasted Alaska dried salmon, and it is much better than *angmagsset*, but since the salmon is smoked in the process of curing, that may partly account for the difference in taste.)

We had to go on board for lunch, and since the ship sailed at noon, there was no time to go on shore again. At Godhavn we took on board the inspector, or governor, of North Greenland, and his wife, and several families of Eskimos who are going to Upernivik. The Greenland government allows the natives to travel on the ships free of charge, except for their food, part of which, at least, they supply for themselves. A Greenlander who wants to travel has only to get permission from the governor of the colony where he lives, and convince him that he will not be a charge upon the people where he intends to go. Quite a few of the more adventurous young men have traveled all over the West Coast in this way, just to see the country.

Our next port of call was a tiny coal mine on the Vaigat, the fjord which separates Disko Island from the mainland. We sailed up Disko Bay from the southeast, rounded the end of the island, and went up the Vaigat to the northwest. The weather was fine; we saw the first sun we had seen for a week, and the only calm sea since we left Scandinavian waters. We basked in the sun and trained our glasses on mountaintop and iceberg. The island of Disko is made of carboniferous sedimentary rocks overlaid with basalt. The top is a more or less level plateau, about four thousand feet high, cut up into mesas by ravines, and covered with eternal ice. It looks as I should imagine one side of the Grand Canyon would look if it were dipped into the sea and covered with snow. The basalt lay in stepped-back cliffs, or palisades, with glaciers spilling over the edge, like thick white frosting on a chocolate layer cake. It fairly made one's mouth water. The sky was a dazzling blue, the sea was bright, and the icebergs floated on it like blocks of white marble, with cracks and lines filled with sapphire.

We reached the coal mine at Qutdligssat about ten o'clock that night. There were several mountains behind it, and Mathiassen and I were dying for a climb. We discovered that the boat would be in port only until ten the next morning. We were disappointed, for we had thought it would take a much longer time than that to coal. They can get it aboard at the rate of ten tons an hour, which is quite fast, considering that the coal has to be run by hand in little trucks up to a dump, from which it is spilled into a barge, and then taken out to the ship. Mathiassen and I had a mountain already picked out. Now we realized that we must either climb during the night, or give up the trip altogether. It did not take us long to decide. We had the steward put up some sandwiches for us, I dumped my camera and films into a knapsack, and we were ashore by eleven-thirty.

The mountain has no name. We met a native who claimed to have been up it, and he pointed out the way. The mountain is a collection of jagged peaks, rising sheer from the sea, and connected with some higher, dome-shaped, glacier-covered summits to the west and to the southeast. Our way was to be up a gorge to the foot of the lowest basalt cliffs, which seemed to be cut through by chimneys, and then onto the saddle behind the mountain. The sun was shining over our left shoulders as we climbed. I was afraid that we would find ourselves very poorly equipped, for we had no nails in our boots. I made Mathiassen look for some kind of staff or pole. He found a child's harpoon with a short iron foreshaft, and we bought it for a *krone* from the owner's astonished mother. Coming back that way in the morning, we left the harpoon near the house, so I hope the little boy found it.

The first part of the climb took us across a very swampy hillside, from which the snow had just melted, and we stepped gingerly from one tuft of heather to the next, working toward the gorge on our left. I noticed that a thin scum of ice was forming over the pools; soon it was fairly thick, and cracked into large cakes when we struck it with our pole. We had climbed two hundred feet, by my pocket barometer, when we were warm enough to take off our coats and sweaters. Mathiassen wanted to leave his raincoat behind, and spread it out on the grass so that we might find it again, but I protested so vehemently that he took it with him.

At midnight exactly I stopped to take a photograph of the *Hans Egede*, lying between enormous icebergs, and dwarfed to a toy. This halt delayed us, so we were anxious to get ahead. Mathiassen climbs very fast, too fast for me at first, but he likes to rest frequently, especially during the first hour.

A short time later we discovered a pile of stones, set on a large, flat rock. Mathiassen's first thought was that it was an Eskimo grave. I felt a sharp revulsion of horror when he went over as if he intended to open it, and I told him that it was too small, more because I did not want it to be a grave, I guess, than for any other reason. The place was so desolate, and the hour so eerie—I felt the midnight, even though the sun still lingered above the horizon—that I could not face the prospect of grave robbing with any enjoyment. As soon as we examined the pile of stones, however, we found it was a fox trap. There was an inside chamber and a ridiculously tiny passage leading to it. Across the middle of the entrance passage was a slab of rock, which, when the trap was set, could be suspended by a string, probably attached to a peg in the back wall of the inner chamber, though we could not see in as far as that. The bait would be put on this peg, so that when the fox snatched it, the peg would come out, let slip the string, and drop the slab to close off his retreat. The trap looked as if it had not been touched since the winter. The skins are worthless at this time of year.

We crossed the first patch of snow in the gorge and began the ascent of the steep, barren slope beyond it. This took a long time. When we reached the foot of the basalt cliffs, we were well above the snow line, though the hillside here was too steep for snow to stick to it. Luckily, the stones and gravel were frozen solid, so the climbing was not too difficult. The basalt is red, with clearly marked hexagonal columns, some of which are twisted out of the vertical in a fantastic way. We scrambled up through a cleft on a pile of talus, and came out on the more gentle slope behind the mountain. We were now in its shadow. We found plenty of snow here, which made walking easy, though occasionally Mathiassen would crash through the crust, and flounder in the drifts below. The snow finally ended in a narrow tongue that licked straight up the mountainside toward the summit, in a narrow slit between very sharp peaks. We had a choice of routes. The wide valley which we were following led on to a high pass, which seemed to offer an easy, though very long, way to the top of the mountain; the tongue of snow took the more direct path, but the going looked pretty difficult to me. I would have preferred the longer way, but Mathiassen seemed to think that the shorter would be the better, so up we went.

It got steeper and steeper, until the ground below, on the shoulder of the mountain over which we had panted, looked level, and it made one hold tight to the rocks. And still it got steeper. I don't see how we came as far as we did. For the last bit I was crawling on hands and knees. I had on only canvas ski mittens, with suede gloves inside, and they were soaked. At last we reached the first needle peaks. The talus slope narrowed between them to a few yards, and we could see where rocks and stones had fallen down. I was pretty tired by this time, and a bit scared, for we slipped a good deal, and there seemed to be nothing firm to hold. I dreaded the descent. Soon it became a matter of summoning all my strength for the next yard—for squirming up to the next stone which I could embrace, and where I could rest before the next spurt. Above us, almost bending over us, were rocky points, as sharp as needles. We could see the sun shining wanly against them, so we knew that the summit could not be far.

Mathiassen saw how tired I was and suggested resting at the next cliff, where there was a little shelf on which we could sit and eat our sandwiches. To our right and a little below us was the monolith which we had seen from the lower slopes and thought to be the summit. I thought Mathiassen wanted us to go to it, for from it one could see the fjord and the mountains on the other side. I started to climb out to it, but Mathiassen called me back. It really would have been dangerous. As soon as he called me, and I realized that I had misunderstood his first directions, I saw how truly awful the few yards of traversing would have been. I was so tired, however, that I had hardly noticed the precipice below, but was obeying him like an automaton. When we sat down with our backs pressed against the cliff above, and our feet dangling over the drop below, I felt suddenly sick with fear and fatigue. I could hardly answer Mathiassen when he spoke to me, and I remember turning away my face so that he might not see my expression. He picked up a stone and shoved it over the edge. There was a rattle of gravel and a purr of sliding snow, then thud—a pause—thud—silence—and, miles below us, a thud which we could barely hear. I told Mathiassen not to throw stones down, but in a few minutes he did it again. Afterwards, I asked him if he had heard me when I begged him not to do it. He said yes, and admitted that he knew that it got on my nerves, but I could not make him tell me why he had, nevertheless, continued to throw stones. As a matter of fact, it was good, because one soon got used, in a way, to the idea of the drop below. We got out our sandwiches. I was famished. That was one reason why I was so exhausted. Mathiassen could hardly eat one sandwich, but I wolfed two.

I took several pictures. Mist was rising and the view back toward the inland peaks was not as fine as the seaward view would have been. My barometer registered an altitude of 3,500 feet. This was the highest that Mathiassen had ever reached in Greenland. It was bitterly cold, and I shivered so that I could barely hold the camera. The thermometer was down to 25 degrees Fahrenheit, but I do not know if the mercury had time to sink as far as it should. I had taken off my gloves and mittens, and when I came to put them on they were frozen solid. Mathiassen put the gloves in his pocket to thaw, but I had to push my hands into the mittens, and when they melted, they felt still colder.

It took us almost fifteen minutes to go down the first few yards. Mathiassen went first with the pole, and I waited until he had braced himself to receive my weight if I should slip. I was delighted to find the descent was not half as bad as I had anticipated, and at once began to feel ashamed of my timidity. As soon as we reached the first narrow slit, about twenty or fifty feet below our resting place, I no longer needed moral support. I took a picture of Mathiassen below me, his cap perched over the hood of his *anorak,* and his raincoat frozen stiff and standing out like a ballet dancer's skirt. Then I climbed down to him, and he took a picture of me. I had poised myself on a rock below him and was all ready for the picture, when he called that the camera was jammed, so I had to climb back, take off my mittens, and try to repair it. I am afraid the film got soaked with snow. Finally I discovered the cause of the trouble, and twisted the shutter back into its proper place. This was very hard work for the fingers, and Mathiassen was afraid that mine would freeze, but when I inspected them they were still red, and all too painful.

It was with great relief that we got off the talus onto the snow. It was packed hard and the slope was steep enough for us to slide, which we did, standing upright as though on skis, Mathiassen stick-riding to balance himself over the soft parts. My friends in Switzerland would have approved of my style, for my feet left but a single track. We rested by the first boulder at the bottom, where I devoured another sandwich. Here the snow was already soft, and Mathiassen fell through the crust at almost every step. He was taken by surprise each time. Finally we both crashed through together, and wallowed in the snow, helpless with laughter.

The last part of the descent seemed very long. My knees were now lame and tired, and I stumbled over everything. By the time we reached the village, we were both walking with feet wide apart, and with legs as stiff as wood. How surprised our shipmates looked when we arrived, in the middle of breakfast, wet and dirty! Even Mathiassen was pale with fatigue, and the captain told me I looked drunk. We fell into bed immediately, crawled out for lunch, and slept again till dinner.

It was a wonderful trip, and although 3,500 feet does not sound like much of a climb, it was one of the hardest mountains I have ever tried. Curiously enough, we did not feel the usual first half hour's exhaustion before the second wind. Mathiassen thinks that was due to the cold. I felt rather badly when he admitted afterwards that if he had not been afraid that he would have a hard time getting me down, he would have tried to reach the top. Just as we were leaving our resting place, I had asked, probably in a not too enthusiastic voice, if we were not going higher. I was relieved when he said no, but I had thought he spoke as much for himself as for my sake. I keep wondering now if we, or if he alone, could have reached the summit. The slope seemed to end in a cliff above us. Perhaps no one could have gone on. Mathiassen seemed to be rather impressed that I was not more tired. This trip has certainly improved the spirit of our expedition. We have done something together, and the fact that it was the highest point in Greenland which Mathiassen has ever reached makes up for his disappointment in not getting to the top, and I admire him for not being impatient with me. He's a good sport.

At dinnertime we were already well on our way out of the Vaigat, and were rounding the end of Nûgssuaq Peninsula, which separates the Vaigat from Ūmánaq Fjord. Near Ūmánaq there is a splendid mountain, Qilertinguit ("the women's topknots," suggested by the columnar basalt), which we had been talking of climbing. It is about 6,000 feet high, and one would have to be taken to the foot by motorboat. Mathiassen got halfway up once, but was turned back by bad weather. We had been talking about this climb for a long time but at the last minute abandoned the idea because Dr. Bertelsen invited us to go on a motorboat trip.

Years ago, when he was a young man, Dr. Bertelsen was the doctor at Ūmánaq. At that time his territory also included Upernivik District to the north, a stretch of three hundred miles of coastline. Mrs. Bertelsen's father was the government agent at Ūmánaq, and that was where he met her. The father, old "Onkel Jens," is quite a character, and I had heard many stories about him. He has many other children, all married to Greenlanders. It seems hard to believe that gentle and refined Mrs. Bertelsen came from such a primitive community. Her husband is far more than an ordinary physician. He is a real man of science. He has banded hundreds of birds at Ūmánaq, and traced their migrations to all parts of the world. He is also an artist with a camera. "Onkel Jens" now lives at a little trading post up the fjord about three and a half hours by motorboat, and Dr. and Mrs. Bertelsen were going to visit him while the ship was at the colony. There were supposed to be old Eskimo ruins at the village, so they invited us to come with them.

Now arose the problem of sleep, which has been a distressing question ever since. The weather was fine again, we were approaching the most beautiful part of Greenland, so why go to bed? On the other hand, we did not know when this motorboat trip would take place. Mathiassen solved the question by going to bed and getting eight hours' sleep; he had a bad cough. But I had just slept all day, so I stayed up all night with Miss Østerby and Bjare.

I was asked to draw in the ship's memory book, for on each voyage someone makes an appropriate picture to head the page of the passengers' signatures. Mathiassen suggested a sketch of deck tennis, a popular innovation. So I tried to show Bjare in his *anorak* and plus fours, Miss Østerby with hair flying, myself heaving the ring overboard, and Mathiassen falling over a stanchion in his effort to catch it.

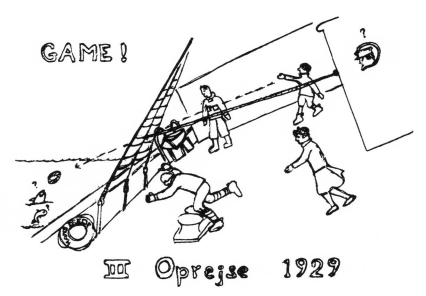

My sketch of deck tennis for the passengers' book of the *Hans Egede*

Everyone has talked a lot about the midnight sun. I had come to regard it as a kind of advertising slogan, and wondered how the sun at midnight could be so very different from the sun at any other time. It has a quality of its own, however. It is more beautiful than any sunset, or midday sun, and more mysteriously lovely than any moonlight. The night hours between 6 P.M. and 6 A.M. are by far the best in the twenty-four. The sun at night, though it hardly warms at all, yet seems to have the power of drawing out and enhancing all the hidden colors in rock and snow and sea. The calm waters of the fjord become opalescent, the cracks in the monster bergs and the water in their shadow glow with an incredible blue-green brilliance, the sky is violet and deep, and the shadows across the mountains reveal the true relief which has been hidden under the glaring sunshine of the day. Over everything is cast a rosy glow which seems to come more from an inner light than from the sun. I have never seen anything so beautiful as Ūmánaq Fjord at midnight. Greenland is the most lovely country in the world.

It was devilishly cold. We played a little deck tennis, rushed inside for a smoke and to warm our fingers, and came out again. Dr. Drescher, who is now recovered from his seasickness, whistled while Bjare and I danced. A dance at midnight, in the Arctic— romance can offer no more! There were multitudes of icebergs all around us, more than I had ever seen before. We were not far from the Inland Ice; once, in fact, we caught a glimpse of that high horizon line of ice in a gap between the mountains on the east. One really does notice a decided drop in temperature when passing close to a big berg. I had left a can of oil on deck after oiling my boots, and when I went to get it at two o'clock in the morning it was frozen solid. The icebergs were so thick about us that I did not see how we could find a way between them. They were enormous, and of fantastic shapes. It was all the more impressive when one remembered that nine-tenths of their bulk is hidden under the water. Most of them showed gouges across their sides, marks of former waterlines. Icebergs often break in two, or drop pieces, and then have to turn over to gain a new equilibrium. We could hear them cracking. Even the dropping of a small lump booms like thunder.

Greenland, strangely enough, has had a very warm winter. (This was the winter of 1928–29, when the terrible frost cracked every water pipe in England, froze in ships in Scandinavian waters, and even bridged the straits between Denmark and Sweden so that my Danish friend, Struck, had actually walked on skis over to Sweden, a perilous and almost unheard-of feat.) In Greenland, however, the sea ice did not form until February, instead of December. This meant poor hunting. In return, they have had a very late spring. Three weeks ago there was fine weather, according to young Porsild, but now there is fresh snow on the mountains, and it is so cold that I live in my sheepskin coat. The winter ice is already gone from Ūmánaq Fjord, but we could see masses of berg fragments which had become cemented together during the winter. I think the cold we are feeling now must be unusual for this time of year. Mathiassen says that it is much colder than when he was here before, the first week in July.

Ūmánaq means the "heart-shaped thing." The mountain rises straight from the sea, with a low pedestal of rock at its foot, on which the colony of Ūmánaq is built. The mountain has been a great temptation for mountaineers, but expedition after expedition, even those equipped with Swiss guides, have failed. I think it will never be climbed. There are several clefts running to the top, the largest of which, on the south side, bisects the mountain, at the top becomes a precipice, and is too wide to serve as a chimney. Except for the talus slopes at the bottoms of the cracks, the sides of the mountain are walls of gneiss so sheer that no snow can cling to them.

The icebergs were massed thickly about Ūmánaq Island, so that we had to go very cautiously. As soon as we could see the flagpole on top of the hill, we let off a couple of re-echoing toots, and the rocks swarmed black with people. Under the flagpole we saw the hospital which Miss Østerby will run. How the people shouted when we rounded the point below them! The harbor was packed almost solid with icebergs. A boat got out to us, and took our cable ashore. We dropped an anchor, and then began a very skillful play of hauling first on the cable and then on the anchor, to worm us into the harbor. There was a schooner in there, the *Hvidfisk* ("White Whale"), which belongs to the colony, but she was imprisoned in the ice. It was three o'clock when we finally reached our proper place. Fresh ice was forming on the water, like a thin scum. Sea water freezes at about 25 degrees Fahrenheit. It did not seem to be as cold here as up on the mountain, where the thermometer said only 25 degrees, so I think that up there it probably did not have time to register correctly when I looked at it.

When we were finally at anchor, we all went below for some bread and butter and tea. We were more or less intoxicated with sleepiness and were very noisy, though we knew that Mathiassen and some of the Germans were trying to sleep. I remember that we played "smile tennis" with great enjoyment, which is one of the most inane occupations imaginable. Then we tumbled into bed, and slept through breakfast.

Mathiassen had already gone ashore when I got up. We were completely surrounded by ice, and the barges and boats that were plying between the ship and the land had to fight their way through. I made the stewardess open my porthole while I took some pictures. Then I went on shore, and wandered about looking for Mathiassen. The village is much more primitive than Holsteinsborg or Godhavn. Practically all the Greenlanders' houses are turfed, though they are planked inside and have glass windows. I went up to the hospital, and Miss Østerby showed me around. It is not yet finished. A native carpenter built it. Some Eskimo women were painting it, and having a good time. It has capacity for twenty children; they will probably all be tubercular patients. The hospital has by far the best location in the village. It is on top of the hill in the sun, and from it you can look across the fjord to the mountains on the other side.

When I went back to the shore, I climbed some rocks to watch a party of kayakers who were hauling their little skin boats out of the water. Mathiassen called me, and in my hurry I slipped and skinned my arm rather badly, so that my clothes were all dirtied with blood by the time I got back to the ship. Every time I go ashore I seem to have some minor accident. On the mountain it was the seat of my breeches, which will never be the same again. It is all due to my excessive *joie de vivre*.

In the afternoon, though I would have preferred to sleep in the sun, I went with Mathiassen to a little island about two yards from the mainland, forming the south side of the harbor. It is called Turf Island, a *lucus a non lucendo*, for there never was such a barren rock, and sometimes it is called Oil Island, for there is a small storehouse on it for gasoline. There is said to be an old site on this island where implements of siliceous slate have been found. Mathiassen was anxious to find some himself, for they have never been properly excavated. Implements of this kind have been found at a sea-washed cliff at Sermermiut ("the people dwelling near the Inland Ice"), in Jakobshavn District, and at Qeqertaq ("the island"), in Ritenbenk District, at the southern end of the sledge route across Nûgssuaq Peninsula from Ūmánaq Fjord to the Vaigat. Dr. Solberg at Oslo thinks these stone implements belong to a very ancient stage of Greenland culture, which he has called the "Greenland Stone Age" to distinguish it from the more modern "Bone Age." Mathiassen thinks that the stone implements are not very old, and that the only reason they appear to form a special non-bone culture is that they have been picked up on the beach, while the bone implements that belonged with them have been lost or washed away. [They have since been proved to be pre-Dorset.]

We had brought a spade, and Mathiassen set to work with it in the most stone-infested bit of earth I have ever laid eyes on. The gasoline storehouse had, of course, been built on the only decent part. The earth was soaked with oil, probably seal blubber. Our hands got gloriously dirty, and my poor nails, which were broken in deck tennis, were just about ruined. We found very little: one broken slate blade for an arrow, a long flake, and the broken point of a drill. While we were working, two little Eskimo boys came over and watched us, and Mathiassen asked them the names of the things which we had found. It was hot in the sun, so we stopped very soon, washed our hands, and fished out a lump of iceberg to suck. We went back for tea, and after that I slept until dinner. We were to go on our motorboat trip at six o'clock.

The *Umarissoq* was a wonderful little boat, with a very noisy engine which blew off perfect smoke rings from its exhaust pipe. There was the engine room aft, a tiny hold amidships where cooking was done, and a little cabin forward, with two bunks, a table, and a stove. The man who runs the boat is Master Sørensen, of the Royal Geodetic Survey. He is a submarine officer in the navy. He and three others are mapping Ūmánaq District, and there are more men at work near Holsteinsborg. Sørensen is one of the few people I have liked very much at first sight. He does not look like a Dane; he seemed to me to be an American, and of the finest outdoor type. I kept feeling that I had met him before. He speaks English quite well. He wore *kamiks* and a bright blue *anorak* with the insignia of the Geodetic Survey Corps sewn to the pocket. He made these common Eskimo clothes seem a uniform. Besides him, there was an Eskimo to help with the engine. We had a little trouble with it, for there was water in the gas, but that did not stop us. The Eskimo had white patches on his head, and Sørensen explained them by saying that he was a half-breed! He looked as if he had been caught in an explosion, and that they were the scars from burns, or perhaps from freezes (if there is such a word). Besides Mathiassen and myself, there were Dr. and Mrs. Bertelsen and her sister, who lives in Ūmánaq, in a typical Greenlander's house. She was dressed in regular Eskimo clothes, with a European coat over them, for it was chilly, and the effect was rather incongruous.

Ikerasak, the outpost, is at the eastern, or farther, end of a long island in Ūmánaq Fjord. There is a mountain on the island, called Ūmánatsiaq ("the one like Ūmánaq"). Mrs. Bertelsen's father [Jens Fleisher, 1847–1930] is now about eighty-two years old. He used to be a post manager at Ikerasak, but is retired now, and there is another manager there. When "Onkel Jens" was manager, his brother was the post manager at Qeqertaq, at the other end of the sledge route across Nûgssuaq. Once, when some liquor was being sent to "Onkel Jens," the brother took out half the bottles, and sent the rest on with the note, "Brother, I *skaal* you!"

It was a beautiful night, windless, and not too cold. The fjord was filled with icebergs. It was cold enough to make me want to go to the toilet, so I asked Sørensen for an old pail. He could not understand, so called Mathiassen, and I had to explain it all again. The pail was produced finally. Lieutenant Thron had warned me never to go on a sledge or boat trip without having such a pail. He told me of one poor woman who was caught without one, and who was in a bad fix until an Eskimo loaned her his drinking cup!

When we reached Ikerasak, the present post manager came down to meet us, followed by the usual joyous rout of Eskimos and dogs. Mathiassen asked him if I could sleep at his house. The Bertelsens were to stay with "Onkel Jens," Mathiassen and Sørensen and the Eskimo were to sleep on the boat. That was where I wanted to sleep, but knew that there was no use in asking as long as there was a respectable bed ashore. We all went up to call on old Jens Fleisher.

There were any number of Greenland women and girls in the house, probably his own children or the families of his two sons who have just died. The house is like a native's house, with low ceiling, very low doorway, and dark—Mathiassen gave his head a hell of a bump, which swelled up like an auk's egg—turf wall outside, and boards inside. It has several rooms, however. The place was as hot as an oven, and smelled like a chicken house. There was a curious collection of furniture, including the wooden platform on which the old man lay, and a grand piano. The walls were hung with the usual assortment of religious pictures, chromos vaguely suggestive of the great masters, and sloppy prints of children and guardian angels. There were also some Danish country scenes. The old man sat up when we came in. He looked very old and feeble. There was a thong hanging from the ceiling above his head with which he hoisted himself up. I think he had consumption, but it may have been only old age. We sat and talked to him. He could speak some English, but mumbled the words so that I could not understand, which made me feel very stupid. We were all invited to tea, which we accepted, of course, though we did not really want any. The heat and the close air were making me feel very sleepy. Mathiassen got as red as a beet, and his face seemed to swell up until I thought he would burst. While they were making tea, we rushed outside for a breath of fresh air and to inspect the bed I was to have. Then we came back, took a long breath, and ducked down into the house. The old man had managed to pull on his boots and hobble into the dining room. Mrs. Bertelsen acted as hostess. I managed to drink a cup of very black tea, but could not eat anything. Then I was escorted back to bed. I was to come down to the boat for breakfast at eight. As it was now only eleven, I should have time for a good night's sleep.

There was a *dyne* (featherbed) on the bed. Enough said! Dear family, do you remember about my struggles with the *dyne* in Copenhagen, and how I finally was beaten and had to have it taken away? Do you remember how, night after night, I went hopefully to bed, only to find that this wretched oversized pillow, which was the only top covering I had, could not be made to cover my shoulders and my toes at the same time, though I am sure that it was not an unreasonable hope? How do the six-foot Danes keep warm? That is the question which should have worried Hamlet. Supposing, for the sake of argument, that you are more or less covered by the *dyne*, but that you want to roll over, what then? By no effort or strategy was I ever able to prevent the *dyne* from slipping off onto the floor. It is never the right temperature. It is always too hot, while your toes and shoulders, and the exposed portions of your anatomy along the edges, are too cold. I had thought that I was free of the *dyne*, but here it was again.

In my excitement over the boat trip I had forgotten to pack my pajamas. In my knapsack I could find nothing but an assortment of photographic appliances; there was not even a toothbrush. I was afraid that it would be cold, so I left on all my clothes but my breeches and my footgear, though I opened the window wide. I woke two hours later, stripped to my undershirt, heaved off the *dyne* with an oath, and took to my soldier's coat, which was at least disciplined enough to stay in place. The arm which I had skinned was stiff and ached. From time to time the dogs outside would begin to howl, the silliest, puppiest kind of shrieking that cut through the stillness like a fire siren. The sun shone in at the window and it was very bright. I wanted terribly to sleep, but I lay awake for three mortal hours, and finally dozed off only after wrapping a sock around my eyes. A mosquito or two, the first we have encountered so far, got in a few good bites between the sock and my coat, but I had the satisfaction of a bloody revenge in the morning. I overslept, of course, and was cruelly roused by Mathiassen's shouts under the window.

Going to the W.C. was an experience. It was the usual type of wooden outhouse. As soon as the dogs saw me headed in that direction, they sprinted up. They could not get to the back of the privy, for it opened into a wired-in yard. In this yard was a dog, however, and as soon as I lifted the wooden cover off the seat, he poked his head in at the back and looked up expectantly. I nearly died laughing, and for some minutes could not function, for thinking of the dog below. He gobbled up everything that came down to him. For toilet paper, there were some numbers of a Greenland magazine. I snitched a few pages. It was printed in Eskimo, and contained a poem, news from the East Coast, two historical articles, one about Nero and Agrippina (how funny it was to see these Roman names with Eskimo prefixes and suffixes), and one about the Indians of Pennsylvania. Mathiassen had a good laugh when I produced it. Next time I went to the W.C., I took along a stone, which I heaved down at the cur. He only looked up at me reproachfully, and stuck to his post. I must say he kept the place clean. All Eskimo dogs have this curious appetite, according to Mathiassen, who has told me the funniest stories. Apparently the dogs have to eat human excrement to satisfy some fundamental deficiency in their diets, a deficiency from which dogs in other parts of the world apparently do not suffer. [I never heard of this peculiarity among Eskimo or Indian sled dogs in Alaska, but the latter are usually kept tied up all the time, so hardly have a chance to exhibit it. But all dogs do have rather nasty tastes at times.]

My notebook for the day has the following entry:

"One has to have a whip when communing with nature to keep them off. Mathiassen tells of a man who had diarrhea and in his hurry had forgotten to provide himself with a whip. When the dogs saw him let down his pants, they collected in hundreds, and the poor man was helpless, for he couldn't hold in long enough to get a whip. He jumped and kicked, but it was no use.

"The sanitary arrangements in an igloo provide a urine pail. The Aivilik look down on the Netsilik [both Central Canadian Eskimo tribes] because, as the former claim, the latter use the same vessel as urine pail and cooking pot. (See also Rasmussen's last book, in which one woman is said to report that they just relieve themselves all over the place, even on the platform.) For larger calls of nature the Aivilik build a low stone-walled enclosure, or if they are very swanky, a snow hut. This is to keep the dogs away. When the place gets too full, they make an opening in the side, and in a minute it is cleaned out."

After breakfast Mathiassen and I went to look at an Eskimo grave. We had talked of taking a skull back in my pack, and I was all keyed up for the job. There was only one grave, however, and it had been demolished, and since the top of the skull had been kicked off, we did not take it. We followed the shore around to the right, and found some house ruins. These were just overgrown outlines of stones, with a litter of old animal bones scattered about. We poked into some of the ruins, but they promised little of archeological interest, for we found bits of crockery and glass. Some dogs from a nearby house had followed us and sat down on the top of a ridge to watch us. I drove them nearly frantic by barking and miaowing at them. The mosquitoes were out in force. It was hot, so I took off my sweater, and that let the beasts get at my arms and back, for I was wearing only a thin flannel shirt. Mathiassen put up the hood of his *anorak*, and I tied a bandanna around my head. The mosquitoes seemed to prefer Mathiassen to me. While we were digging, a kayaker landed, and the dogs rushed down to him. We welcomed the excuse to stop and watch the dogs gobble up the great hunks of flounder which the man threw out to them. Then some people gathered and inspected what we had found, and even poked about in the dirt a little for themselves. One small boy tagged after us all the way back to the village.

We had lunch with the post manager. We had meatballs of auk meat, and auk's eggs. These were fried and tasted like hen's eggs, except that the egg taste was more pronounced. The white is more transparent, as if the egg had not been cooked long enough. It will never become opaque. The shells are blue with brown splotches, and are enormous. They are very pointed at one end; this is to make them roll in a circle and so prevent them from rolling off the ledges on which the auks breed. The auk meat was very good, too.

After lunch I wandered out with my camera and tried to get acquainted with the Eskimos. One man and his wife were very cordial. They showed me their dogs, and warned me about two who were tied. The man showed me his kayak, set up on top of a rack out of the reach of the dogs, and took down his harpoon and lance. He told me the names of the different things, and when I repeated them, they both roared with laughter, and so did I. They must have been rather well off, for they had an umiak, and the man had started to build the frame for a new kayak. There was another man also building a kayak, and I watched him. He was very white for a Greenlander. He worked very cleverly, for many pieces of wood had to be spliced. The slats were made of ridiculously thin pieces. One wondered how it could possibly be strong enough for a seagoing craft.

Soon Mathiassen appeared again with the spade, and "Onkel Jens" came too, followed by all his womenfolk armed with knives and other digging implements. He said that he knew of other old ruins on the other side of the village. I took a picture of him, and he insisted that someone take another of both of us. He posed with his arm around my neck—the old sugar daddy! (1930: He died that winter. I had a postcard from Sørensen the next summer telling me that old "Onkel Jens" was dead. I am sorry, for in spite of his uncouthness, he was a grand old man.)

The ruins proved to be mythical; we did not find even a soup bone in the ground. There were only some modern turf houses at the place. On top of one was a scooter with rubber tires! Where did the little boy scoot, I wondered. I played with some pups while Mathiassen and the others looked around.

It was all very boring, and above us the summit of Úmánatsiaq was inviting. Sørensen told us that he and his colleagues had built a cairn on top as part of their geodetic work, and he had pointed out the way up. Since there was no real archeological work to do, I suggested to Mathiassen that we climb the mountain. It was now only half past two, the Bertelsens did not want to leave until eight, so we would have plenty of time. So we went back to the village, collected our junk, had a cup of coffee, and went down to the boat, where we roused poor Sørensen and his Eskimo out of a well-earned sleep. They took us in the boat around to the foot of the mountain, half an hour from the village, and set us ashore. They said they would call for us at half past eight, on their way back to Ūmánaq. Sørensen loaned Mathiassen his pack rack, for Mathiassen wanted to take his camera with him, and it is very bulky. I took my pack with both my cameras and our raincoats.

The way up was not difficult. There was no swamp to cross, and no loose stones to slide, only smooth rock and large piled-up blocks. We had to work around to the left (west), cross the ridge through a cleft, and ascend to the summit proper from the far (south) side. We could see the tracks left by the other party in the wet moss and snow, so it was not hard to find the way. Mist was coming up the fjord. We reached the summit about seven o'clock, after three hours' climb. The clouds had now already covered the top of Qilertinguit and Ūmánaq. Fortunately, I had taken a picture of Ūmánaq just in time. The beacon on top of the mountain was an impressive affair, four meters high, and was swathed about the middle with a piece of white cloth. My barometer gave the height as 2,700 feet, but Sørensen had found it to be only 2,500 feet. From the top we could see the Inland Ice at the head of Ūmánaq Fjord, like a vast white sea, fringed by mountainous rocky "islands" called nunataks. The fjord all around our island was filled with monster bergs. The shoulder of the mountain hid the village.

We stayed at the summit only ten minutes, just time enough for a few pictures, and then started down, with the mist fast overtaking us and snow falling. We had only one hour in which to catch the motorboat, and though we knew that we could not reach the appointed spot in so short a time, we hurried as fast as we could. Except for the steepest places, where we had to use our hands, we literally ran down the mountain. The snow which had hindered us going up was our friend on the way down. While we were still some distance above the place of rendezvous, we heard the boat's whistle, but thought it was only the goodbye signal to Ikerasak. After a few minutes, however, we saw the boat. She had already left the place where she was to pick us up and was heading for Ūmánaq. We shouted and waved frantically. Then we ran harder, heading for the shore near the boat. This took us away from the best route, and as we did not know the country, we came to cliffs several times, and were delayed until we could find a way around them. Finally, the Eskimo on the boat saw us and waved. He had caught sight of Mathiassen's white *anorak*. They told us afterwards that they had decided to go to Ūmánaq without us, and let us find our way back to Ikerasak, where the post manager could have loaned us his boat. It was raining now, and we were soaked with sweat on the inside, too. Ever since I sprained my ankle last winter in Switzerland, I have hated to run downhill over rough ground, or to jump onto unfamiliar places. I was sure that I was going to fall, we were running so fast. Soon Mathiassen got ahead of me, and in my hurry to keep up with his seven-league strides I fell head over heels down a rock, in full view of the boat, and skinned myself again. I was a damp mass of dirt, sweat, and gore by the time we reached the shore. Sørensen himself came out in the rowboat to take us aboard. I was so stiff that I had to be heaved over the rail.

We took off our wet things. I had nothing dry but my soldier's coat, so I sent the men out of the cabin, while I stripped and put it on. My shoes were wet through and so were Mathiassen's. But Sørensen had some dry *kamiks* which he generously loaned me, and Mathiassen gave me a pair of socks. These *kamiks* were wonderful things, with the beautiful silvery seal fur on the outside, and they came up to my knees so that I could hardly walk. They had dogskin socks inside, and were the warmest and most comfortable things I have ever put on.

Sørensen poked his wet head into the cabin and wanted to know if I could "smile" (*spejle* or "fry") eggs, so I went down into the hold and did my best with four auk eggs and a Primus stove. It was my first experience with either, and being tired and in a hurry, I broke all the yolks. They tasted pretty good, just the same. Mathiassen seemed tired, too. It was raining very hard outside, so we stayed in the cabin. The stove made it warm and cozy, and I drowsed off, tucked behind Mathiassen and Dr. Bertelsen on the bunk.

By and by Sørensen came in and put on his blue flannel *anorak*, lined with dogskin, so I knew that it must be pretty cold. I wanted to go out, too, so I did, with socks on my hands for mittens, and my raincoat draped over my head. Sørensen was quite surprised when I joined him where he was steering in the lee of the engine-room hatch. We had a good talk, standing in the stern, while he steered with one foot on the tiller, keeping a sharp lookout for bergs in the mist. He looked like the real thing in Arctic explorers with the soft dogskin about his face and his black pipe drooping out of the corner of his mouth. He promised that I could take his picture next day in this costume, so that I could show my friends that it is cold in the Arctic, but it happened that this was impossible. He is talking of coming up to Upernivik later in the summer, and if he does so, he will visit us. I can't think of anything nicer. We tried to lure him with promises of *pâté de fois gras* and other delicacies which we had brought for special occasions. He and Mathiassen are about the nicest men in Greenland. He seems to have taken quite a fancy to me, and that makes me tremendously proud.

We were back at the *Hans Egede* by midnight, and it took me no time at all to climb stiffly into my berth and fall asleep. When I woke in the morning, I was still lying on my back in the same uncomfortable attitude which I had assumed when I first lay down, which shows how soundly I slept. While my boots were drying, I proudly wore Sørensen's. Everyone called them *dejlig*, and Mathiassen took a picture of me in them to send home.

It was a gray day, and Mathiassen and I wrote letters during the morning. While I was at late breakfast, Bjare rushed in, looking for his boss, Dr. Krüger. Their motorboat had been unloaded here from the *Hans Egede*. While they were testing it, the screw had fallen off and now lay on the bottom of the harbor under fourteen feet of icy water. It seems the accident was due to a defect in the mechanism. The engine had reversed and just shot the propeller off. Bjare looked tired and dirty and almost ready to cry. He has had to take charge of the unloading of all the expedition's equipment. Coal dust from the hold and sweat were caked into his skin, and he looked haggard. I could hardly bear to look at him; no man should look like that. I guess Krüger has just about given him hell these last few days, and it did not help things that Bjare and not Krüger had been on hand when the accident occurred.

Sørensen was called on board. He had served on a submarine during the war and has had some experience in diving. There is a complete diving outfit on our ship to be used in case the screw is broken in the ice. The first officer is a diver, and it was arranged that the two men should take turns in going down and hunting for the motorboat's propeller.

The mate went down first. It was horrible to see him being screwed into his heavy rubber suit, to see the leaden-soled shoes strapped on his feet, and the lead breastplates hung on, and finally to see his tense, set face shut inside that monstrous and inhuman helmet. He went down a few feet at first to test the suit, then came up, and went down a second time. When he came up, he reported mud on the bottom, which did not sound good. He wore only ordinary woolen gloves on his hands, and the water must have been devilishly cold. Sørensen, meanwhile, was at the air pump supervising everything in a very efficient way, which inspired confidence. Then the mate was undressed and went to his cabin, and Sørensen prepared to go down. While Sørensen had been managing the air pipe and the ropes, he had slipped and fallen against the ladder. The upright of the ladder caught him under the arm and almost broke a rib. But though it must have hurt, he said nothing.

We watched while he submerged for the first time. He went down so quickly and in so resolute a way that I wondered if the mate had not been rather timid. When he came up, he reported that there were strong currents and that he could not orient himself. He wanted the ladder on the side of the barge extended to the bottom. While he was down, there was only the second mate to take charge above, and one could not help wishing that there were someone as efficient as Sørensen in the barge. Krüger had been hovering around the barge, trying to help, but no one would let him touch anything. Bjare, however, seemed to be pretty useful.

Thinking that nothing much was going to happen, Mathiassen and I went ashore and called on the post manager and had some coffee. When we came out, we were told that Sørensen had located the screw on his next trip down, that he had walked to it, but finding himself unable to lift it in his hands, was struggling to put a rope around it when he fainted. Fortunately, he was able to give the danger signal, three jerks on the hand line, in time, and was hauled up. Bjare's theory is that he was out of practice and submerged too quickly. We called on Sørensen in his boat later, and found him in his shirt sleeves, lying down, and looking pretty weary. He seemed pleased to see us, but we did not stay longer than to say goodbye and beg him to come to Inugsuk to visit us. I wanted very much to have his picture, but I didn't have the heart to ask for it then. He told Mathiassen that his side was paining him a good deal.

Mathiassen and I wandered up to see Miss Østerby in her new establishment. She entertained us with Benedictine. She had three deck-tennis rings hanging in her room, a present from the second mate. It would be funny if that game which I introduced on board should become a popular sport in Greenland! Before going back to the ship, Mathiassen and I climbed the rocks to the flagstaff and looked out over the cloud-shrouded fjord. I was sorry to have missed the view. Two little snow buntings were trying to get a drink from a pool of water. They hopped all around it, sampling it from every side, but found it hard to discover a convenient place where they would not wet their feet. They are the jolliest of little birds, a flutter of black and white and a trilling song reminiscent of the skylark and the American song sparrow. We could hear them even on the desolate mountains. On our walk Mathiassen told me many amusing things, that such and such a post manager has eight children every year. Here, no one is shocked by an affair between a white man and a native woman, they only laugh at him a little. Almost every explorer in the Arctic has left behind him an Eskimo child as memorial to his sojourn. Although he, of course, said nothing about it to me, I imagine that Mathiassen and some of his friends are the sole exceptions to this rule. He also told me many amusing stories about animals. He was rather shy at first, but now that he has found that these things do not shock me, he is able to give me many curious and interesting bits of information. One of the nicest things he ever said to me was to apologize and say that he could not always remember that I was not a boy.

Some of Mathiassen's stories I wrote down in my notebook and repeat them here:

"The West Greenland dogs have team spirit. Do they also have a village spirit? Mathiassen doesn't think so. They seem to breed much as they choose. A female is usually chosen as the leader dog. The Polar Eskimo, however, are great dog breeders, and keep their dogs tied up. There is only one female in the team, and she, of course, belongs to the strongest male. The others are dreadfully punished if they so much as look at her. When on a sledge trip and the pups can't be cared for, the dogs eat them as soon as they are born. The Central Eskimo don't have big teams. They are too hard to feed. There is no team spirit, and one man may borrow another's dogs to supplement his own.

"The [West Greenland] dogs never leave the camp during the winter, though in summer, when they are more or less neglected, they will go hunting along the shore for fish. In the winter they are afraid of the wolves. Sometimes foolish young dogs who perhaps can't tell a wolf from a dog wander too far from the others and are carried off. Mathiassen doesn't take much stock in stories of dogs mating with wolves. The dog that tried would be eaten up."

When we got back to the ship for dinner, we found that the screw had been salvaged by the second mate, who had gone down after it twice. It was found badly broken, and the engineer was at work on it all night.

The day was again gray and it snowed. I went to visit Miss Østerby for the last time. I was dreadfully sorry to say goodbye to her. She cannot speak much English, but I am beginning to understand a little Danish, so we talk to each other in our native tongues and trust to luck. I think it shows wonderful courage for such a young woman to come here and assume alone the responsibility of such a hospital. I complained that my hair was too long, so she undertook to cut it for me. There is now quite a white line across the back of my neck that will need re-sunburning, and it feels very bare when a good wind catches me. How we laughed over the operation! We kept thinking that we heard Mathiassen's step on the stair, but he didn't come, and when he did see me next, like a man, he noticed nothing strange in my appearance.

Once while I was ashore, I went to admire some pups playing in the passageway of a turf house, and was bitten by the mother. She gave no warning, and slunk off at once with her tail between her legs as if she expected to be flayed alive. It was not a hard bite, and I was not sure how intentional it had been, so I didn't retaliate. I think she showed real spunk, for the Eskimos beat their dogs cruelly when they misbehave. This ought to be a lesson to me not to play with pups without first asking their mother's permission.

We sailed at two o'clock after what seemed an interminable delay. By this time the Germans had fixed up their boat, and they followed us out into the fjord for a little way. We were glad, for Bjare's sake at least, that it had ended happily. The screw is not really mended, for it cannot reverse. Still, they can go forward.

Mathiassen bought some cotton cloth in Úmánaq and had an Eskimo woman on the ship sew it up. She made him three dark blue *anoraks* and one for me. She also made me a canvas hood for my soldier's coat. I am to have some more *anoraks* as soon as the goods from the *Hans Egede* are unloaded at Upernivik.

Not much happened on the last part of our trip from Úmánaq up here. We passed by Dark Head, a little island on which the *Bele* was wrecked in 1921. She was the ship carrying the Fifth Thule Expedition and some other scientists. It was very foggy weather, and the captain was not sure where they were. While they were all on the bridge arguing about whether the nearest land was Dark Head or Skal Ø, the big island next it, the ship struck a reef. Everyone got ashore safely, and they salvaged enough stuff to make themselves comfortable, but most of the expedition's supplies were lost. The *Bele* was a Swedish ship, chartered by the Royal Greenland Trade, and was the first ship in Greenland to carry a radio. They were able to send a message to the warship which was carrying the king of Denmark on a tour of Greenland, and he came to their rescue. Through the king, Rasmussen was able to get more supplies sent in time for them to carry on with their plans. I was naturally very eager to see Dark Head, as there was a chance that one could still see the old wreck, so I asked one of the officers to wake me when we passed. It was a foggy night, however, and they did not call me. I could not have seen any more than Mathiassen did on his trip.

Yesterday (June 21) we had a fine view, however, of the famous bird cliffs of Qaerssorssuaq, where auks nest by the thousands. There are convenient ledges halfway up the cliff where the eggs and young are safe from marauding foxes. The rocks are stained white with excrement and are visible from a great distance. With the glasses we could see the birds flying about or sitting in solemn rows, wing to wing, like black balls in a bowling alley.

Shortly afterwards, in the early afternoon, we reached Upernivik.

IV

Upernivik

DEAR FAMILY:

We dropped anchor in Upernivik harbor on June 21, about two o'clock in the afternoon. The harbor is on the northern side of a rocky point, and the village (or colony) is on the other side, a quarter of a mile away. When we approached, we gave a couple of toots, and soon the governor, Mr. Otto, and his assistant (the post manager, a pleasant chap with reddish curly hair, whose name I have forgotten) came out to meet us. They came in a long dory, manned by Eskimos, fine strapping fellows, who rowed standing up and facing the bow. (Most Eskimo men seem to row that way, or else scull from the stern. One seldom sees them rowing in the orthodox manner; that's for Eskimo women.) These men were all dressed in sealskin pants, which showed that there was no lack of good hunting in this country.

The harbor was filled with icebergs, and we had to creep in cautiously. There were even some remains of the old winter ice, which, they told us, had broken up only on June 8, instead of going out by the middle of May. The season is three weeks late. The icebergs here seem much bluer than those farther south. Some of them are like blue glass all over, and no one can explain the reason.

The island of Upernivik is quite small. It is perhaps three miles long and a mile or half a mile wide. It is very rocky, with an abrupt shore, and there are only two possible sites for a village: one is where the colony is now; the other is on the southern side of the island, across from the "Old Ships' Harbor," at a place called Qaitarmiut ("where the old people lived"), where there are ruins of a former settlement.

Where we landed, there are only a few storehouses at the dock, which is only a small pier for barges, so the big ships have to anchor out in the harbor. There is a flagstaff halfway up the path to the colony, with three funny little cannon around it, relics of the "wars" with the Dutch whalers. Blubber barrels were piled all around and in back of the storehouses, and men and girls worked hard all day, unloading the ship, and then rolling the barrels down and loading her up with them. The last was a filthy job, for the barrels lay half submerged in a blubber-flavored mud. Some of the dirtiest dogs that I have ever seen wandered about the barrels, licking up the blubber wherever they could find a leak. They seemed to live there, for every time I passed, I noticed the same ones, hungrily investigating the filth.

The village is not very attractive, no more than any of the other colonies, though it will be the great city for us this summer. There is the district governor with his wife and daughter, Ruth, the doctor and his dentist wife, the post manager, the priest, and the schoolteacher, and the usual assortment of natives and dogs. The governor's house is well placed on a rocky knoll. His assistant's house is not far off, and in front of it the Greenlanders collect every evening. Farther along is the doctor's house, and a couple of hospital shacks. There is also the store, the old church now used as the meetinghouse for the native district assembly, a turfed house which is used as a jail on rare occasions, and the new church, which is the highest building on the hill, and is pretty fine for a simple wooden structure. The graveyard is extremely grim. There is no earth in which to bury the coffins, so they are laid on the surface of the ground and covered with a little turf and a few stones. Many of the graves have come apart and the bones are sticking out.

When we first came to Upernivik, I was a little disappointed, for it was dull weather and the land seemed to be broken up into smaller and less majestic pieces than at Úmánaq. There was nothing to see but low islands, rocks, brown moss, and snow, not even glaciers. The land is so much lower here than in Úmánaq District that the scenery lacks that grandeur and spectacular beauty which prevents one from noticing how very desolate it really is.

The wind is blowing from the north and forcing icebergs into the harbor. We would laugh if the ship got stuck here. There are still big patches of snow on the northern slopes, and there is not much green showing yet. Only the bright purple *saxifraga* is blooming. Mathiassen is terribly afraid that we will not be able to get a spade in, but the snow is melting and the first good sunny day will clear the ground. I'm glad I saw it like this, for now it seems really the Arctic. Last night was not very cold. It may have been freezing, though it did not feel so cold. Our tents will not be too comfortable if the weather of the past ten days stays with us.

We won't be able to have a motorboat for the whole summer. The inspector, who came up with us from Godhavn, is expecting his motorboat to join him here, and he will take us out to our island. We shall be marooned there. It is uninhabited, but is not too small. There is a cairn on top, which has given the island its name; *Inugsuk* means "cairn" (literally, "the thing like a man," from *inuk*, "a man").

Yesterday we walked up to the top of Upernivik Island, where Governor Otto has built a summer house. We could see far out across Baffin Bay and up the fjords to the north, and probably saw Inugsuk also, although we did not know which island it was. To the south was Qaerssorssuaq, where the auk cliffs are, a great snowy mountain which dominates the whole Upernivik District.

To the east stretched the Inland Ice. (We hope there will be a hill on our island with a view of the Inland Ice, and a good gravel beach for pitching our tents.) The fjord back (east) of Upernivik is called the Dark Hole because of the color of the steep cliffs which form its sides. The waters of the fjord are incredibly blue. Far to the north the sun was shining and the clouds were unwinding from the mountaintops. We realized then that even this frost-bitten place is beautiful, too. How happy I am!

This letter with all my love to you sails today (June 23) aboard the *Hans Egede* while we wait at the Ottos' until we can go to Inugsuk.

June 26, 1929

As soon as we had landed at Upernivik (June 21), we visited Governor Otto and his family. There were the usual coffee and cigars. I had to try a lady's cigar, for there were no cigarettes, and I did not find it very satisfying. Then there was nothing to do but sit in the hot room—they had a stove going, and we were dressed in sweaters and *anoraks*—and listen while people talked in Danish. This is always very boring for me. Occasionally, when I listen very hard, I can discover what the conversation is about, but I seldom understand what is being said. The effort of attention is too great to be kept up for very long, so usually I am reduced to fidgeting, to looking out of the window, and finally I am driven out of the house to look at the Eskimos and play with the governor's dogs. There has been a lot of coffee drinking and a great deal too much Danish, at least for me, during our stay in Upernivik.

That first night we had the traditional Captain's Dinner on board to celebrate the arrival of the first ship of the year. (There are only two!)

I sat between the chief engineer, who is an amusing chap, especially when well primed, and Dr. Bertelsen, who is a dear at any time, and whom I call "Onkel." We did a lot of hefty *skaal*-ing. In Denmark one is not supposed to drink at table unless one is drinking to and with someone present. When you are thirsty, you must fix your victim with a glittering eye—it is not necessary to say anything—raise the glass while he follows your movements, then down with as much as you can manage without choking or making a face! Then hold out your glass again, give your opponent a glare, as if to say, "See all I managed to drink? How much did you get down?"—and the awe-inspiring ceremony is over. On no account is one allowed to smile or look as if one were enjoying the drink. Our informal way of drinking or toasting is regarded as childish. These Danes take life seriously. Between dinner proper and after-dinner coffee and liqueurs we were allowed to go on deck to recuperate. The women from the colony had on thin summer dresses, and I was shivering in a sweater! In the warehouse the Eskimos were dancing. After another intermission we had fruit and whiskey and soda. Most of the women got very red in the face and the party was rather merry, though perfectly dignified, of course. I had a full glass of each of the seven kinds of drink offered, except the red wine, which I don't care for, and the whiskey and soda, but of these I took just enough to be able to *skaal* properly. I was surprised that I did not feel the effects; it was rather disappointing.

The next day more coffee and Danish, and a mad scramble with the mail. In the afternoon Mathiassen and I walked over the top of the island to see the ruins at Qaitarmiut. It is on the western side of the island between a chain of little lakes and a small bay. The island is very low at this place, and the island opposite Qaitarmiut, Pamiua ("the tail"), has a similar valley. Both valleys are on a line with a glacier which is on land still to the west of Pamiua, and I think that this glacier must have scooped through both islands in former times. The Eskimo call such a corridor an *itivdleq*, because it is "easy to walk across." We had a little difficulty in locating Qaitarmiut at first, for we came out on the beach too far south and had to scramble along the top of a cliff which fell straight into the sea. We could not resist the temptation to throw stones down. There were also many patches of snow to cross.

The first thing that we saw of the old village was some graves. They are just piles of stones, more or less oval in outline, on the bare rocks. The first one we came to was rather round, so we did not recognize it as a grave at first, and we looked at it for some time, trying to find a crack to look inside. At last I found a bone sticking out, which Mathiassen said was human, so the matter was settled. There were eleven graves altogether, some of which had been opened and their contents scattered, while others still preserved their growth of lichens undisturbed.

This village consisted of six house ruins and several meat caches. The latter are piles of stones, smaller and less carefully made than the graves. The houses were of stone, either square, or long and rectangular with three rooms to accommodate several families. The modern houses are also square, but are built of turf. The older houses were necessarily of stone or bone because there was no imported lumber in those days to timber a turf house. One of the houses at Qaitarmiut seemed to have been built upon the ruins of a still older and larger structure. The walls were fairly well preserved. The roofs, of course, had long ago fallen in, and all that was left of the houses was the tumbled-down outline of their walls. We scratched in the ground around the houses, but found the soil frozen under the sod. All we have ever found at this place has been a few pieces of china, not very interesting to an archeologist. Nearby was a modern stand with a kayak on it, but the owner had not visited it since the last snowfall. There was still much snow on the ground, and quite a bad swamp, for the surface of the snow had melted in places, and the water was dammed up by the frozen earth below. Along the beach was the ice foot of the winter sea ice. Mathiassen was pleased with the look of the place. He thought that if we had time to dig down deep in front of the house doors we might come to some old stuff. He was especially keen about the graves, for though plenty of Greenland graves have been robbed, none has been properly excavated.

On Monday (June 23) we got a small boat, a shovel, and a wooden box, and took our lunch around to Qaitarmiut. We rowed around to the nearer end of the corridor, just beyond the harbor, and walked across to the old village. It was hard going through the deep, soft snow and the mud. We had a native with us to help row the boat and carry our stuff, but as soon as we arrived at the ruins,

Mathiassen sent him back on foot to Upernivik, because he does not like to have natives around when he is grave robbing. A bitter cold wind was blowing. The first thing we set about was to measure the houses and draw a sketch map of the place. I tried to draw the map, but it was so poor that in the end Mathiassen had to do it. He is very clever about such things. We also took photographs of the village and of the best houses and graves. Then we had lunch, sheltering ourselves as much as possible from the wind in a hollow in the rocks. The dampness from the moss soaked up to us so that we were glad to hurry through the meal and get back to work.

We attacked grave number six, first with the camera, then with our hands, heaving the boulders off the pile and rolling them down the hill. The crushed lichens gave off a musty smell. When the loose boulders had been taken off, we could see the inner chamber, a rough coffin or box made of large stones. This had to be photographed before we could lift off the top slabs and look inside. There were two complete skeletons, frozen in a solid lump of ice. We did not try to touch the bones, but hacked away at the ice with our geological spades. Finally we had to abandon the attempt to cut the bones out, and leave the grave open to thaw. I made a sketch of the grave and its contents for Mathiassen. There was something extremely pathetic in the attitude of the skulls. One was sunk forward on the breast, the other turned away from its companion. There was earth and moss in the eye sockets, and shreds of decayed vegetable matter dripped away from the teeth. Mathiassen had to retire for a moment, and I felt a little uncomfortable, left alone with these grim companions. We looked carefully between the stones about the coffin for the things which should have been buried with the bodies, but were disappointed. There was a fissure in the ledge of rock just above the grave. I peered into it and found another skull. A small stone had been pushed into the crack to close it. I pulled out the skull and gathered up the fallen teeth but found nothing else. The crack was too small to hold any more bones. Mathiassen believes that the grave goods were originally put in the fissure, and that when they were taken out the skull was put in their place. It may have been taken from another grave by robbers, or pulled out by foxes.

We examined two more graves. The ones that were still intact were filled with ice, and the others did not seem to be worth the trouble of tearing down. We returned home finally with only one skull and a handful of teeth to show for our day's work.

We came back to the ship just in time for dinner. The *Hans Egede* was to sail that evening at eight o'clock. As we were rowing back, we noticed that the icebergs had drifted away from the mouth of the harbor, and thought that the ship would have no difficulty in getting out. We had talked all along of how we should laugh if she were stuck in the ice. For dinner there was sweet soup, which I abominate. I felt very ill used, for the cold and the digging had made me very hungry. I was, however, able to make up on the meat course. After dinner I went into the smoking room but fell asleep there.

When I woke, it was time for the ship to leave. The night was beautiful, with bright, mellow sunshine, but the bergs had drifted back again with the rising tide and now filled the harbor. All the white people from the colony came on board, and we solemnly drank the captain's health and wished him a good journey. May I sail with him again to Greenland! Then we all climbed into the governor's boat and rowed out a little way to watch the *Hans Egede* back and twist and push to clear a passage. It was a chilly, tiresome wait. At last she was clear. They fired off the three cannon and dipped the flag to her, and she replied with mighty blasts from her whistle. Then we rowed around the point to the village. From time to time we could catch glimpses of the ship slowly moving between the icebergs out toward open water. Three more shots were fired. She was gone. I was glad, for now we had really arrived.

The night was so lovely that I hated to sleep under a roof. We turned in about one o'clock, but not to an unbroken rest. I am not yet trained to feel sleepy when the sun is shining. It is now the dogs' mating season and they are hard at it. There is something decidedly unattractive about dogs' love affairs. They do not have nice manners. The big ones are mean to the little ones and to the females. The small boys and men also tease the smaller animals. These Eskimo dogs are either bullies or cowards. All night long we could hear the males fighting and the bitches yelping. As soon as the dogs hear one scream they all begin to howl, until the whole colony is in an uproar. I thought I would go crazy. It seemed to me that the governor's team deliberately chose the path below my window for their orgies. I am very sick of it all, and will be glad to get away to our island.

The next day we fiddled about the village. We went in to see the family which Mathiassen is going to hire. They live in a turf house near the point. The doorway was ridiculously low and the room inside incredibly dirty. The man's name is Karl Møller, and he told us that it was his forty-fifth birthday. His wife, Ane, is much younger than he, and quite pretty. She has charming, gentle manners. There is Niels, a small, undersized boy of fourteen, who seems to help his father quite a bit, a girl of ten, Malia, then another boy, Ole, and at last Peter, the baby, who is still learning to talk and walk. Karl has several dogs, which he will leave behind, but he wants to take two half-grown pups, because they are not old enough to take care of themselves. He owns a kayak and a big wooden dory, which he has to paint before we go.

Ane was commissioned to make each of us a pair of sealskin pants. She undertook to make them without taking any measurements. The theory is that Eskimo women are such wonderful seamstresses that they don't need to measure, but can cut clothes to fit after one glance at the prospective occupant. These trousers were beautiful to look at. The skins were fine and soft, and prettily marked with a silky sheen of silver. They were sewn up in the traditional way, with the light underpart of the skins down the middle of the front, over the seat, and between the legs, with the dark spotted skin from the seal's back down the outside of the legs. This is how the color is on the seal, according to Karl. My trousers were finished with red leather at the top and bottom, and Mathiassen's with dark blue bands. They have two pockets, and open with a flap down the front, like old-fashioned pants. I was very proud of mine. We were disappointed, however, when we put them on. Mathiassen's were so small around the waist that he could not get into them, and mine were so large that they could accommodate someone else at the same time. Even after Ane had cut them over, mine were not very comfortable. I had to have them slit farther up between the legs. The bottoms of the legs are tied down around the middle of the calf. The skins are not really as soft as they look, and they chafe my legs. It is hard to get in and out of them, for they are very stiff. The first days I could hardly sit down or bend over. I understand now why the Greenlanders, especially the women with their long boots, do not sit down with bent legs, as we do.

Another woman undertook to make our *kamiks*. She measured our feet, but the boots came back miles too big, and had to be made smaller. Ane did such a good job of it that they will not come up over the tops of my pants. They were always sliding down, exposing a convenient patch of bare leg, down which dirt went sliding. Now I have tied a tape to the tops of the stockings, and with this lashed about my legs am managing to keep pants and boots in conjunction, until Ane can make me a proper pair. How she laughs at me! We were supposed to have dogskin socks, but there was only one skin in Upernivik; the rest of the winter's killing had all been used. So we have had to content ourselves with dogskin soles in sealskin stockings, which is not so warm. Hay is packed between the sole of the boot and the stocking. They say that white people usually go lame when they put on the thin-soled *kamiks*, but I have escaped that; what with the trouble with my pants and my boots, I have been broken in gradually. The *kamiks* are certainly fine for climbing over smooth rocks, but they are poor between loose stones which pinch the feet. The sealskin trousers are very warm.

We have also seen another man, Robert, whom we are taking with us. He is twenty-five, and quite a large man. He is the happy-go-luckiest, most shiftless fellow in the world, and, as Mathiassen says, he is not the great brains of Upernivik. He owns nothing but the rags he has on. He has no gun, no house, no kayak, no dog team, no wife, and not a care in the world. He lives by visiting his friends and doing a few odd jobs for the white people. He came originally from Prøven. The carpenter and smith at Upernivik, a Greenlander, wanted to adopt a young fellow, and was taken with Robert's looks, but he was too lazy. He sat around the house and did nothing. When sent out to hunt, he had no success. They say he was once away for a day and a half and came back with only one *teist* (a little black and white water bird like an auk, but much smaller; it is called "rock duck" in Alaska). Finally, the smith passed him on, and he lived with various people until they got tired of him. For quite a while he lived with an old woman who had no husband, but at last she threw him out, so he was glad to come with us. His first job was to grind the coffee beans which Mrs. Otto's Eskimo maids roasted for us. He is quite strong, so he may not be a total loss, after all.

One afternoon we saw a procession of kayakers paddling toward the colony. They were towing the carcass of a white whale (beluga), which they had found, several days defunct. They beached it on a tiny island a few hundred feet from the colony and began to cut it up. At first they tried to haul it up on the land, putting a line through slits in the hide and taking it around a big rock to make a sort of pulley. The beast was too heavy and the hide tore, so they set to work to flense it in the water. I was anxious to watch them, so the governor's assistant rowed me out to the island. The stench from the animal was awful. It bled bucketfuls until the water in the little cove was red. The men climbed out on the half-submerged carcass; their *kamiks* and the bottoms of their pants were drenched in blood. Their hands were red above the wrists. There were yards of intestines like a hose, and the stomach was big and black like a coal sack. The smell was so bad that even the Eskimos were talking about it, the assistant told me. The flesh about the stomach was black, and I wondered if they would dare to eat any of the meat. The dogs on the mainland had all come running down to the beach, where they ran up and down, not daring to enter the water, wild with the smell, and dribbling at the mouth with anticipation. By the time most of the vital organs had been cut out, I was so nauseated by the stink that I had to go away.

The assistant has a kayak, and when he learned that I was

wild to try one, he brought his down for me. I was still wearing my ski boots, which were too big to fit into the narrow space in the bow, so he loaned me a pair of *kamiks*. All the boys in town collected to watch me embark. It is quite a job to get into a kayak. You hold the boat steady by laying the paddle down across the deck with one end resting on shore, grasping it firmly to the kayak with one hand. Then you step carefully into the manhole, sit down just behind it, and gradually insinuate yourself into the bowels of the infernal contrivance. Once in, you are in for good. There was just room for my feet between the top deck and the bottom. The manhole was slightly too large around the waist for me, and there was no "half-jacket" of waterproof sealskin to fasten around the manhole at the bottom and around my body under the arms to keep the water out. The kayak is so long and narrow that you have to sit with your legs straight in front of you. One can be quite comfortable with a good piece of sealskin folded for a cushion. Ruth Otto, the governor's daughter, and the assistant followed me in a rowboat to rescue me if I should capsize. I wore no gloves, so every stroke of the double paddle dripped icy water down the blade and up my arm. The well-dressed kayaker wears long sealskin mittens, tied high above the wrist, with woolen mitts inside, so his hands stay dry and warm. In stormy weather he wears a complete sealskin jacket that ties tight about his face and wrists.

I pushed off from land somewhat timidly at first, but soon gained confidence. The kayak is the easiest craft in the world to paddle. The least motion with the sharp-bladed paddle sends you shooting forward, and you can turn on a dime. I outdistanced the rowboat in half a dozen strokes. It was great fun poking about between the icebergs. One is so close to the surface of the water, the experienced kayaker must feel himself part of his craft in a very intimate way. I paddled out to the island, where the men at work greeted me with shouts and laughter, and then circumnavigated it. It began to rain, and by the time I came back to land I was pretty wet, for not only had water spilled down the manhole from the paddle, but the boat had not been in the water for some days, so the seams were open and leaked.

It is beautiful to see the natives go out in their kayaks. They are dressed in white *anoraks*, with white caps on their heads, and the kayaks themselves are painted white. At first I thought it was horrid to use European paint on the sealskin, but Mathiassen tells me that it is camouflage. When the man and boat are all white, the seals, who have very poor eyesight, think he is only an iceberg. To help the disguise, the hunter also hangs a little screen of white cloth from the prow of his kayak. But they say this camouflage is effective only when the water is filled with ice. When there is no floating ice, the seal knows it's a fake.

Several additional ingenious inventions and improvements have been added to the kayak since the coming of the whites. One is the waterproof sealskin bag that lies on the forward deck to hold the rifle or shotgun. When the natives first got guns, they had no way of keeping them dry except down inside the boat with them, and many men were killed when the trigger caught while they were pulling the gun out. Another recent invention is the false keel. The kayak is quite flat on the bottom, and since it is so long and slender and draws so few inches of water, it is very easily capsized. Now the Eskimo have added a little centerboard or false keel, which is lashed on near the stern and which can be slipped off when going into shallow water, or when they carry the kayak up. That has made it much steadier. Everything has its place on the kayak deck. Just in front of the man, on the forward deck, is a round raised tray, or rack, on which the harpoon line is coiled above the wash of the waves. The harpoon with its throwing board attached is just at the hunter's right hand. The line runs up to the coil on the rack, and the end is brought back to the afterdeck, where the sealing bladder sits. Sometimes a man may have a lance and other weapons, and they are also fixed in their proper places. In the old days, before they had guns, the barbed three-pronged bird dart was in the middle, where the rifle bag is now. The deck of the kayak is crossed by several thongs, under which things can be tucked or thrust. It is wonderful to see a hunter come back, loaded with birds, all piled carelessly on the narrow deck behind the hunter, who paddles along without spilling a single bird.

Mathiassen was not particularly pleased at my kayaking. He keeps warning me how dangerous it is, especially for a white man who wasn't, so to speak, born in a kayak. A white man at the colony was drowned this spring. South of Holsteinsborg, where there is open water all year, there are many more native women than men, simply because there is such an opportunity for the men to drown themselves in kayaks. The governor's assistant is loaning his kayak to Robert this summer, so I am planning to go out in it again, though of course I won't venture out without someone at hand in a boat to rescue me if I turn turtle.

On the twenty-sixth, today, we were up late, but decided to go back to Qaitarmiut to finish excavating the grave. We started off after lunch in the little boat, Mathiassen and I each taking an oar, and pulling first to one side and then to another, like tipsy sailors. We were armed with our digging sticks, two thermos bottles of tea which Mrs. Otto had given us, a big wooden box for the bones, and our full equipment of cameras, tripods, etc.—a very imposing expedition. We rowed around to Qaitarmiut, passing below the high cliffs on which Governor Otto has built his summerhouse. Mathiassen has amused himself on several occasions by heaving stones down them. We hoped that no one would imitate him while we were underneath. We found the grave pretty well thawed out and were able to take out the bones. There seemed to me to be enough legs in the collection to outfit several individuals. Part of one skeleton we were able to get out still embedded in the soil. This we wrapped up carefully by itself. The box was filled with bones when we left, but hunt as hard as we could, we failed to spot a single grave gift. This was quite a disappointment.

We rowed across the fjord to the harbor opposite Qaitarmiut. There were supposed to be ruins here, but we found only a meat cache. We had our tea, and mighty good it was, too. We caught sight of a kayaker passing, and hailed him. We gave him the remains of our biscuits and sugar, and he told Mathiassen that there were ruins, *igloqut,* just beyond, and he pointed up the cove. We accordingly re-embarked and rowed to the head of the cove. There was nothing to be seen here, however, but a valley filled with snow (the corridor across the island, matching that across Upernivik Island at Qaitarmiut), and the beach covered with the remains of the winter's ice. We landed and tied up our boat and, at my insistence, set off across the land following the little valley. The bottom was very swampy, so we scrambled along the sides, and suddenly came over the edge of a hill to confront one of the most beautiful views of all Greenland, the Dark Hole. Below us was a small harbor, fringed with ice; across the fjord snow-clad mountains disgorged a glacier. The high sides of our corridor shut in the view so that the fjord seemed a lake. The Eskimo would call such a place *tasiussaq*, "like a lake," from *taseq*, "lake."

On the heathery slopes above and about the harbor were many house ruins, very much decayed and overgrown with moss, so that they showed only the dimpled outline of their walls. This is the village of Umiarsuarârfik ("the old ships' harbor"), which we had been seeking. We took photographs, though it was already late and the sun was hidden under the habitual Upernivik clouds. Mathiassen made a sketch map, also. Then we examined the houses. These were mostly community houses, divided into three chambers, with the door passages facing the sea. They measured about eight by three meters, though some of them were so poorly preserved that it was impossible to see the exact limits. They were built of big stones and pieces of whale bone. Mathiassen was glad when he saw this. One of the buildings seemed to have several little storehouses built around it. We went about poking into the turf with our digging sticks, but the ground was frozen solid under the moss. In one of the storerooms of the largest house I found a stone that could be pried loose. Mathiassen heaved it up and found under it a human skull and several fragments of a soapstone cooking pot.

Now he was very much excited and announced that he was going back after his tripod and big spade, but that I did not have to go with him. Coward that I am, I could not relish the idea of being left alone in that dreary place, with only the slimy green bones of a very defunct Eskimo for company. The wind moaning among the boulders brought the faint noise of an animal's howl. It might have been a dog, or only my imagination, but I looked to see a wolf coming over the hill. I would never have thought of a wolf, of course, if I had not heard Porsild arguing that the wolves in Greenland were not really extinct, as was commonly supposed. I had to tell Mathiassen that I was nervous—it would have been too childish to have invented an excuse—and we both laughed at me as we went back to the boat. Still, I was some use after all, for I helped him to haul the boat above the tide, and brought along my pack, in which the skull journeyed to Upernivik. I did feel foolish, I admit, and I hope that when the summer is over I will have outgrown this unscientific horror of bones. When we were opening the grave, I made a point of jumping in and picking up as many bones as I could. At first I hated to touch the slimy things, but now that feeling is gone.

When we got back to the ruins, Mathiassen set to work with his spade while I took some photographs for him with his big camera. By the time I was finished, he had cleared away everything that was movable, but had found only a few more bones and a few potsherds. There seem to have been two bodies in the house, but most of the bones were still frozen fast in the ground, and the collapsed roof had crushed the other skull. Mathiassen thought the place would make rich diggings, for the presence of the unburied bodies in the house showed that it had been abandoned in a hurry, so probably many things were left behind. The great age of the ruins was evident from the style of their construction. We were quite disappointed that we could not do more. It was a beautiful spot, but very grim, especially in the overcast night. We should like to come back here and camp; perhaps we shall, when we have finished at Inugsuk.

V

Inugsuk

Inugsuk
June 27–July 12

DEAR FAMILY:

We are at Inugsuk, camped on a desert island. It is wonderful to be shut away from the world, alone, and to feel self-reliant and self-sufficient, and the hub and center of our own microcosmos. I take such pride and joy in my tent. I can't tell you what it means to be in my own house again, after so many months of knocking about in hotels, among strangers. You know how I have always longed for the Arctic; it was always to me the Promised Land, and it has not betrayed me. Everything is full of wonder and surprise, and yet I feel at home and part of it. I can be myself. Don't you sometimes want to be able to roll on the ground like any free animal? I can here. I feel as if I had never been really alive before. Every morning I wake, happy, and look around my little tent, and think again: I am in Greenland, I am in the Arctic, and it's really myself here! I want to feel the hard, cold ground, and know again, with all my power of being sure, that all this is real. But when I think that this is only temporary, that someday I must go back, that I will see the sun begin to set again and the nights lengthen, as the ship sails south, until at last I am back in the ordinary world, and all this is as past and done as if I had never lived it—this makes my life here seem a dream, and somehow less real. But then I can feel the cold wind, and look around, and see and smell and touch these friendly Greenland things, and know that this is the true reality, the real life—so real and so much a part of my existence that when it ends I think I must have something of it with me, not a ghostly memory, but something stronger and more abiding.

I am very happy.

June 27 was a great day for us, for the inspector's motorboat arrived from Godhavn, in which he and his wife are to continue their tour of the northern posts. They had promised to take us with them to Inugsuk. At the last moment Governor Otto and his wife decided to come, too. Our Eskimos assembled their worldly goods and ours and piled them in their big dory, until it was loaded down almost to the gunwales. The motorboat came around from the harbor to the colony wharf, and we proceeded to get aboard. In the midst of the confusion Niels, the oldest Møller boy, appeared dragging the pups. They were terrified, and yelped and struggled until one of them slipped his string and shot off across the rocks. I held the other while Niels chased him. After a short conflict, he was secured. Karl and the boy tumbled the poor dogs into the boat very unceremoniously by picking them up by the loose skin of their backs. They yelped piteously and lay on the bottom where they had fallen, without daring to move for some time. They were shoved out of the way under a seat, and disappeared from view for the rest of the voyage. The kayaks were piled on top of them. Then followed Ane, Malia and the baby, and Ole. Some seal meat was thrown in, too, which the pups soon discovered. I saw Karl pick up his paddle and give a couple of jabs between cracks in the baggage, which were well directed, for more yelps followed. The governor's rowboat ferried us out to the motorboat.

We were off! The motor chugged until the boat seemed to be

shaking to pieces, and our ark full of Eskimos bobbed along behind. The governor's dory hitched onto us, too, for a little way.
We went very slowly, about six miles an hour, so it took us a good
two hours to reach the island. I was sleepy, so I curled up in the
sun, to be awakened at intervals to be fed chocolate, or be shown
points of interest. It was a beautiful, clear, sunny day, the first in a
week. The water was blue, and the icebergs sparkled like sugar. At
last we caught sight of Inugsuk. It did not look very imposing, in
spite of the stone beacon on top. It was like any of the other
islands to be seen on all sides—nothing but gray rocks, a few
patches of snow, a jumble of low hills, cut through by wandering
valleys, a rocky shoreline, almost without a patch of beach, which
ran out into points and skerries about which the calm fjord lapped
gently. We were still some distance from land when we recognized
the midden, a black bank, topped with withered turf, that ran
along the bottom of a cliff, just above a gravel beach.

The motor stopped a little distance from the nearest point of
rock. We tumbled into Karl's boat. The dogs and children were
asleep but woke when we came aboard. We rowed to the nearest
place where we could step ashore, a shelving rock which broke the
cliff on the southeast side of the island. Mathiassen and I did not
wait to see what was done with our stuff. We ran up across the
rocks and the soft turf, and tumbled down over the low cliff onto
the midden. The sea had cut the edge of the midden into a bank,
from which bones, bits of wood, and great masses of baleen
("whalebone") hung down like fringes. Bones were scattered on
the beach. We poked about between the flat beach boulders and
soon had collected a handful of specimens which the sea had
washed from the bank. Mathiassen had a piece of a cooking pot,
and a sledge shoe of antler, but I claimed the first Thule culture
type, a knife handle of whale bone with a blade slit at one end and
a hole for a thong at the other. We knew we had come to the right
place.

We went back to the landing place and said goodbye to the
others. The inspector was anxious to be gone, and we did not want
to detain them. Mrs. Otto had thoughtfully provided us with sand-

wiches for our first meal, and we waited only long enough to wave politely from the rock before sitting down to work on them. We climbed down to a mossy ledge, halfway down the cliff overlooking the midden, and discussed our plans happily while we ate. The Eskimos were meanwhile transferring our possessions from the rocks where they had first dumped them to the north end of the little triangle of midden, where Mathiassen had decided that we should camp. It was not until then, I believe, that we discovered that we were not on Inugsuk at all, but on a tiny island in a bay of Inugsuk. The cairn was on a high hill to the north of us. Mathiassen thinks our island is about two acres big, but I don't see how it can be measured, for it is all up and down. All along the west side of the island is a cliff, running due north and south. Below its northern half is the midden. Almost directly opposite the middle of the midden is another small island, about as big as ours, which at first we thought was a point of Inugsuk. This island is connected with ours at the very lowest low tide by a spit of slimy stones. We were rather disappointed to find that we were to live on such a small island, for there is nowhere on it that we can go for a walk. (1930: Mathiassen has found from old records in the Upernivik church that our little island is called Tunúngassoq, the other little island Sangmissoq, so I will call them by their proper names, though we did not learn them until our visit to the colony in July.)

As soon as we had eaten our lunch, we went down and set up the tents. On the spot which Mathiassen had chosen there was just room for them to stand side by side. The ground is very uneven, and they tilt forward at a precarious angle. The midden is thin here, only a foot or so thick, and our front doorsteps are just on the edge of the bank. There are plenty of heavy stones on the beach, and these we used in setting up the tents. The pegs are hardly any use in the frozen ground, though I put in a few around the bottom flaps as an extra precaution. Mathiassen has now commandeered them to mark the corners of the fields on the midden. The Eskimos do not seem to know much about our sort of tent, so we had to do most of the work ourselves. The guy ropes had to be fastened to big boulders, and stones had to be laid along the sod cloth

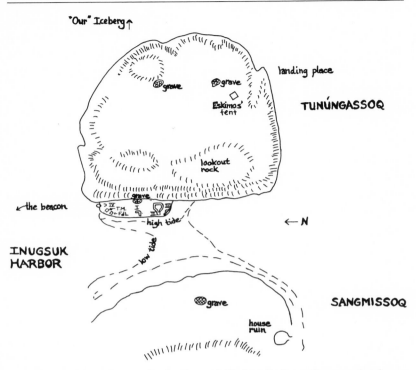

"Our" Iceberg

landing place

grave

grave

Eskimos' tent

TUNÚNGASSOQ

lookout rock

the beacon

grave

← N

INUGSUK HARBOR

low tide

high tide

grave

SANGMISSOQ

house ruin

Map of Tunúngassoq Island in Inugsuk Harbor. Redrawn from my sketch by Susan Kaplan

at the bottom, which we turned inside. Mathiassen's tent has three poles, mine has only two.

As soon as the tents were up, the Eskimos got into the boat and went on farther around the island. I was rather relieved that they were not to camp on the midden beside us. They chose a place on top of the island on the north side, but had to shift their tent a few days later to a spot almost above the rocks where we first landed, in order to be more sheltered from the icy north wind. Mathiassen commented rather unfavorably on their disappearing before our camp was really established. He said that the Hudson Bay natives would have stayed and helped us to fix up everything before going off to see to their own things. But since we did not offer to help them, I don't see that they should be blamed.

All the cooking things and most of the canned goods came into my tent, while the biggest boxes for packing specimens and the digging outfit went into Mathiassen's. The largest boxes we had to unpack on the flat rock by the water to make them light enough so that we could carry them up. We had an accident, which luckily was not serious. Mathiassen fished a bottle of alcohol out of one of the boxes and passed it to me, saying it was for the Primus stoves. Like a fool, I let it slip out of its straw wrapper, and the next instant it lay in fragments on the rock while the precious contents trickled away. I snatched up a spoon and tried to save some, but it was hopeless. I thought that it was the only fuel we had, and was puzzling to find out how we should get along without our stoves, when Mathiassen produced another bottle and pointed to the two cans of kerosene, which he had set between the tents. But, even before I realized that the disaster was not fatal, I could not feel discouraged. We were both too happy to be on our island to let anything worry us. I cried out that now we would have to use a real Eskimo blubber lamp, and Mathiassen laughed at me until the tears began to run, and I was laughing too. Later, when I dropped a tin of biscuits and scattered the contents all over the landscape, we acted as if it were the best joke we had ever known. Mathiassen is a splendid sport. He has never cursed me out yet, though he has had good cause.

We built a little kitchen place between the two tents and cooked our supper there. We had fried auk's eggs, hardtack, and coffee that first night, and thought we had a feast. Though we were rotten cooks, and still are, we are fast learning through sad experience. We ate our supper out of doors, but since then it has been too cold and windy, and we have moved the Primus stoves into my tent. Mathiassen made the coffee Danish fashion that first night, but I was suspicious of it. Next morning I made it in the American way, but I did not know how to regulate the Primus, and it boiled over, so now it seems safer to boil the water separately and pour it through the coffee in the bag, which is how the Danes make coffee. I think we can justly be proud of our coffee. It is always good and strong, and we drink lots of it. We had apple

cake that first night. It was one of the "feastly dishes" on the Fifth
Thule Expedition, and you should have seen Mathiassen grin
when he opened the can and reassured himself that it was the
same good stuff. What fun that supper was! There was no wind,
and the tardy sun shone straight across the harbor into our faces.
Mathiassen filled the Primuses and showed me how to prime them
with alcohol and how to judge the critical moment when one
shuts the air screw and pumps the real flame into being. After eating, we sat for a time, looking at the view and smoking, and then
Mathiassen produced his digging stick and we went around to the
other end of the midden, where it is thickest. We found a lump
that had fallen down on the beach and was thawed. We cut it up
and got out many good specimens. It was midnight when we finally turned in.

I felt that it was a pity to sleep with the tent shut up, so I left
the flaps wide open. It is the last time I ever do so, for a breeze
sprang up during the night and it became damnably cold. The
moss on which we had spread our bags was not far from the frozen
ground, as we were soon to discover when we began to dig, and
the heat of our bodies thawed it, until pools of water collected
under us. The surface of the ground was very rough, besides, and I
had to curl in and out between lumps of grass and stones. Altogether, it was not a very comfortable night. Our sleeping bags
are too narrow. The theory is that there should be no extra air
space inside them to warm. This means that once in, one is well
in, and it takes an enormous amount of squirming to turn over.
The legs of one's pajamas hitch up as one gets into the bag, and it
is almost impossible to push them down. One can't curl up inside
the bag, the bag has to curl, too, and when one rolls over it is
some job to untangle one's arms. All this we discovered during the
night. Mathiassen arose in the morning complaining bitterly about
the "damned swamp," which he pronounced to rhyme with
"damp."

He got breakfast. It took me ages to get into my sealskin
pants, stiff and new as they were, and besides, I still clung to the
old notion that one should wash before breakfast. I ran out of the

tent, without my sweater, with shirt sleeves rolled up, and washed my face—even my neck! I think, though, that I omitted brushing my teeth. By that time my hands were numb. It reminded me of old days in Vermont when I used to run down to the lake, wash my face and hands, and then plunge heroically into the water before breakfast. There is so much of my life here that reminds me of America. That is one reason why it is so happy. I feel that I am near home, and have left the conventionalities of England far behind me. Before-breakfast washing lasted exactly one day more. Now it is omitted. We wash our hands when returning from work for lunch, for afternoon coffee, and for supper, and we find twice a week sufficient to care for the less contaminated portions of our anatomy, that is, our faces and teeth. Mathiassen shaves twice a week, and Spartan work it must be, too, in ice water.

In Upernivik we had bought a hundred auk eggs and about sixteen birds. These we buried in holes laboriously cut in the large patch of old winter ice, just north of Mathiassen's tent. The eggs were in a box and we contented ourselves with piling snow over them. The snow and ice have melted, however, and at such a rate that every day we have to pile more on the eggs, while the auks have gradually emerged from the ice, looking very dead and squashed under the weight of the big stone we had put on them.

The sea ice furnished us with part of our drinking water. We set a washbasin under the edge to catch the drip, and found it quite fresh, except when bits of seaweed were washed up by the tide and fell into the basin. The first afternoon we discovered a wonderful little berg on the beach. It was clear as glass, not opaque and frosty as most icebergs are, and it was composed of small cubes which fell apart at a blow. I have never seen another like it. Mathiassen thinks it came from a crack in a glacier that filled with water and froze; it was evidently not made of the ordinary refrozen snow of the glacier. There is, of course, no running water on our island, so we have to rely on the bergs which the wind sends us and on the now almost vanished winter sea ice. It was very convenient to set out our water pail and washtub under the ice to catch the drip, until the very high tides began to come.

Mathiassen woke one night to hear a plaintive tin bumping, and ran out just in time to rescue the tub. Incidentally, we don't wash in it, it merely serves to hold water. For washing purposes, which are not many, I confess, we use the pools left by the sea on the big rock in front of Mathiassen's tent, or else ice water from the bucket. We have three washbasins and set out with the intention of devoting one of them solely to ablutionary uses, but they have become hopelessly mixed by this time. We use them as extra cooking pots, and one of them usually holds the sanguinary portions of an eider duck or auk, which Robert has cut up for our supper. Usually Mathiassen and I wash out of the same basin, and it's some water when we finish! The blubber-soaked mud of the midden certainly makes a mess, and one can't get it off. At best one scrapes off portions of the skin, and washing isn't very pleasant in such cold water. It's astonishing how soon the thin veneer of civilization wears off and is replaced by the happy dirt of primitive life. Some of the hardest excavating of the day is done when we poke under our fingernails. Mine look like my brother's when he was mending the car!

Our real digging did not begin the first day. There were many things to be done about the camp. Mathiassen called Robert and Karl and had them take the turf from the floor of our tents, and pave it with big, flat stones from the beach. They got two strips of slatting from the bottom of Karl's boat and put them down as platforms for our beds. I took some excelsior which came in the packing cases and spread it down for a mattress. It was fine and warm, but rather a nuisance, for it was forever shifting and wadding itself into lumps. Mathiassen objected because the pieces got strewn all over the tent and eventually found their way into the food, so I threw it out, and passed two miserable, cold nights before I discovered what was the matter and substituted my army coat for an under blanket. The slatting from the boat has been a great success. We live on the platform in my tent just like Eskimos. I push back my bedding during the day and spread my raincoat over it to keep off the dirt. We have our two Primuses on the ground in front of us, and cook there in the tent. I can really appreciate the platform now, as I could not when it was only an ethnographical element. I can't imagine tenting without one. One can't sit on the ground for long, and even our feet are apt to get cold if we leave them on the stones of the floor. Our platforms run the whole length of our tents, so there is plenty of room on them, and I have, besides, widened mine with some boards from one of the packing cases.

I have to laugh now when I think of my early notions about a tidy camp. That first day when we were unpacking, I went around and picked up the bits of paper and excelsior, and I strongly objected, much to Mathiassen's amusement, when he threw the eggshells down on the beach in front of the tents. When Ane came to clean an auk for us, I made her put the entrails in a basin and told her to give them to the pups, but she, not understanding the reason for the basin, promptly dumped the contents on a rock, and set about washing it. The bloody vitals she carried by hand back to her tent. Feathers were scattered all over the beach, and the bloodstains on the rock would not come off even when I poured water over it. But how my notions have changed! At first I did not want to have the cooking done in my tent because I knew that things would be spilled and it would soon become messy. I was right in my surmise, but it doesn't worry me. The high tides have cleaned away the rubbish from the beach, and although we are rapidly forming a "new midden" again, and archeological excavation would reveal remains of all the meals we have eaten on and between the floor stones of my tent, it does not seem to matter. The trouble with a messy camp in ordinary latitudes is that it attracts flies. Here we have seen them for one day only, then the cold weather and wind drove them away. As for mosquitoes—not a sign. It is much too cold for them, though to make sure, Mathiassen put a little kerosene on the pool of water in the middle of the midden. When we are a little more advanced in our excavations, we intend to drain the swamp, but the digging will be very slow, for it takes a long time for the ground to thaw.

It took us some time to get the regular camp life started, and for that reason the first days seemed very long and were full of surprises, so it is hard for me to remember exactly what did happen. Our second day on the island I was quite pleased that at low tide our island was joined to the other little island (Sangmissoq), though at that time we supposed it was a point of Inugsuk. I took my camera and tripod and slithered across over green, slimy stones to the other shore. Even going this short distance from camp made me feel like an explorer in an unknown land. It was then that I discovered that I was on an island in the harbor, and not on Inugsuk itself. On the shore opposite our island I found a grave—a big one, and apparently undisturbed, though one end had an opening through which I could look. I put my eye to the crack and saw a regular charnel house. There were eight skulls which I could count, and a confused mass of bones, half covered with horrible rotted filth. A snow bunting has her nest somewhere inside, so we are not going to open it until the little birds are flown. I also found one skull lying on the open ground, but when I returned a few days later it had disappeared. I think our Eskimos moved it, probably just kicked it aside, though they may have stuck it into a grave. Mathiassen soon joined me, when I called to announce the discovery of the grave, and found several house ruins and some more graves. Not knowing the name of the island, we called it "Grave Island," and were much disappointed that it was not Inugsuk itself.

One evening we went over to "Grave Island" (Sangmissoq) and dug for a little near the big grave. There is a midden there, which appears to be a continuation of the one on our own island, though it is much thinner, only twenty centimeters deep, as compared to two and a half meters, the maximum depth here. The land in this part of the world is sinking, which explains why so much of the midden has been washed away. In former days our island and the other must have been one island, and the middens on them were probably continuous. Mathiassen thinks that this island would have made the bay a wonderful harbor for umiaks. We found the same sort of things in the midden on the other island that we find on our own island. There, as here, there are remains of two periods of habitation, a modern village and an ancient one. In the midden on "Grave Island" we find a new deposit on top, characterized by bits of china, iron, and well-preserved bones, and underneath is an older layer with rotted bones, bits of baleen, and Thule culture types—but more about that later.

(1930: The church records at Upernivik, Mathiassen found, speak of a village at or near Inugsuk called Qeqertaq ["the island"]. It was inhabited between 1845 and 1857 and must be Sangmissoq and Tunúngassoq while they were one island.)

Our times for visiting the nearby islands are limited to evenings after work and Sundays. The government chart is on much too small a scale to show anything. Inugsuk is not even marked on it, though we are able to pick out a little black dot which we think is the island. We tried to make a map of the island, which did not turn out very successfully, so we used one drawn for us by Karl, to which we added a few corrections. Inugsuk is a jumble of rounded hills of gneiss, cut through by small valleys and ravines, in the bottom of which are streams and little lakes. The rocky sides slope down abruptly into the sea, and there are very few beaches. One gets the impression that the island is not a real unity; there is no sense to the pattern of valleys and hills; it is really a lot of separate islets thrown together. There is a deep bite taken out of the southwest corner, and in the mouth of the bay thus formed are Sangmissoq and Tunúngassoq.

South of Inugsuk is another island, which we could see from the top of our little Tunúngassoq, and south of it again are more islands. In the distance we could see the white pyramid of Qaerssorssuaq, and knew that Upernivik was in that direction also, though we could not see the island. From the southwest, where the open water is, all the storms come, and we could tell what the weather would do by observing whether Qaerssorssuaq was hidden in clouds or standing free. Often it was raining and snowing at Upernivik by the open sea when it was clear weather up the fjord where we were camped. On the west side of Inugsuk were other islands which also cut off the storms from Baffin Bay. These were Kingigtoq and Kingigtorssuaq, where the runic stone was found.

East of us was a big island, Târtoq, of which we saw only the western end. Just north of Târtoq and Inugsuk is the Upernivik

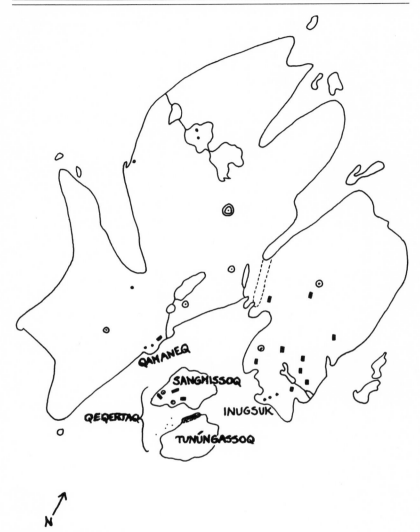

Map of Inugsuk Island,
from the original sketch by Karl Møller,
corrected in the field; redrawn by Susan Kaplan
Rectangles are house ruins; circles and dots are cairns or graves.

Icefjord, which brings down hundreds of icebergs from the Inland
Ice. In fair weather, when the north wind was blowing, the water
all around Inugsuk was filled with icebergs, and they even crowded

into the bay and drifted up on our shores. The biggest bergs went aground in a shallow place in the fjord between us and Târtoq, where they stayed until high tides and a southeast or southwest storm washed them back up to the Icefjord again. Across the Icefjord we could see other low islands to the north and east, and beyond them snow-covered mountains. The biggest of these was the high, square mountain called Qagsserssuaq ("the big dancing house"), and the village of that name, mentioned in the Inugsuk legend, lies at its foot. From our camp on the midden we could see very little but the bay and the hills of Inugsuk. From the top of our island we could look up and down the fjord, in every direction, in fact, but west, where the round hills of Inugsuk shut off the view toward Baffin Bay. Târtoq, of course, hid the Inland Ice from us.

There was quite a good deal of snow when we first came to Inugsuk. It lay on the north slopes and in the bottoms of the ravines. The snow lingered on well into July, but it all melted during the course of the summer. There were patches of winter ice at both ends of the midden, but they melted also. Our own island was unusually barren. Very little grew on it except various kinds of moss and lichen, coarse, stiff grass, a few weeds with yellow and white flowers, and ground willow, which is such a stunted plant that it seems to bear no possible relation to the tree. There was not even heather on the island, so Ane and Malia and the boys had to take Karl's boat over to Inugsuk to fetch fuel for their fire. In summer the Eskimo cook most of their meals on heather fires out of doors. We used to see our Eskimos going out almost every other day, wandering over the hillside across the harbor, and returning laden with sacks of heather. They seemed to enjoy the trip. Heather does not burn well, because it is so wet, and Ane had to sit beside her fire, lifting up the twigs with a wire to make a draft, and blowing hard if there was no wind to help her. It took a long time to make the pot boil. I used to enjoy visting the Eskimo camp on the other side of our island. They had a tattered old tent which Governor Otto had loaned them. The two pups were tied to a rock near the door. They were never allowed to run free, because it would have been impossible to keep all the eatables from them. One of the dogs was bigger than the other and made his life miserable. They were sullen, shy dogs and, whenever I tried to pet them, ran as far from me as their ropes would let them. The Eskimos threw out all their rubbish on the rock in front of the tent, where a great pile of junk soon collected. The children would pick up all our tin cans from the beach and keep them in a playhouse under an overhanging rock.

The inside of the Eskimos' tent was as dirty as the outside. They skinned the birds Karl shot, and all the birdskins, turned inside out, were thrown into a corner. I believe Ane saved the down from the eider ducks to stuff a *dyne*, but the other skins just lay around and rotted. Across the back of the tent there was a wooden platform on which the whole party slept and where Ane sat to do her sewing. The tent was khaki, and was very dirty besides, so the light inside was terrible, and we wondered how Ane's eyes could stand the strain. There were a few wooden boxes, which seemed to hold clothes, scraps of skin, etc., and these were also used to sit on. There was a tiny back room to the tent, hidden by a flap behind the platform, and this was where Robert slept. There was no platform there, and though I never peeked into his sanctum, I am practically certain that he had nothing in the way of a blanket. He apparently would lie down on the bare ground, in the clothes he had on, and sleep as soundly as the rest—more soundly, in fact, for he was usually the last one to work. Mathiassen was paying Robert two *kroner* a day, a little over fifty cents, Karl and his family three *kroner*, and one *krone* more for the boat, a little over a dollar. Just what arrangements Robert made for his board we did not find out. The assistant at Upernivik had loaned him his kayak, and Mathiassen let him have his shotgun and some shells, but he was certainly not self-supporting. He was forever shooting off his gun at the flocks and flocks of birds that flew past the island, but he rarely hit anything. I don't think that Karl had much use for him. Ane never mended his boots for him, which were usually in a sad state.

The second evening that we were here, while Mathiassen and

I were poking about in a bit of the tumbled-down lump of mid-den, we looked up to see two kayakers paddling toward us. They told us they were Mathias Petersen and Nikolai Eriksen, from Augpilagtoq, a village on Târtoq. They were real, full-blooded Eskimos, and grinned all over with pleasure at meeting us, and we responded with the same smiles. Mathiassen showed them what we had found, and they exclaimed and laughed over everything. The older man wore wooden goggles which he had made himself. The rim was carved out of a single piece of wood, with a slot at the top into which a piece of ordinary window glass was inserted. They had auks and eider ducks behind them on their kayaks and offered us some. Mathiassen and I suddenly decided that we were hungry, so he asked them to cut up a duck and invited them to share it with us. They prepared the bird but would not eat anything except some candy and a cup of coffee. Mathiassen did not pay them for the bird, because he thought the entertainment was a fair exchange. When they were leaving, the younger man picked up my cake of soap and asked if he might take it, which I let him do. The men came to visit us again, some time later, but they did not seem to be as jolly as the first time. They went up to see our Eskimos instead of us, and sat around gravely talking. Karl and Robert are certainly less jolly and irrepressibly good-humored than these two. Mathiassen says the others are more happy because they are more primitive. Our natives may have had a sobering effect on them, or they may have been displeased because Mathiassen did not pay them for the duck. One thing which had delighted them before was having their picture taken by "autoknips," my auto-matic camera shutter release. It has proved a great success, and tickles everyone, even Mathiassen.

The next day, June 29, we began the serious work of the summer. Before we could dig, we had to mark off the midden into fields, measure the heights, and map it. First of all, Mathias-sen ran a base line along the midden, just under the cliff, which is almost straight. We marked out the base line by four "ducks," or little cairns of stones. Our base line was just forty-three meters long. Then Robert and I were set to making smaller "ducks" every

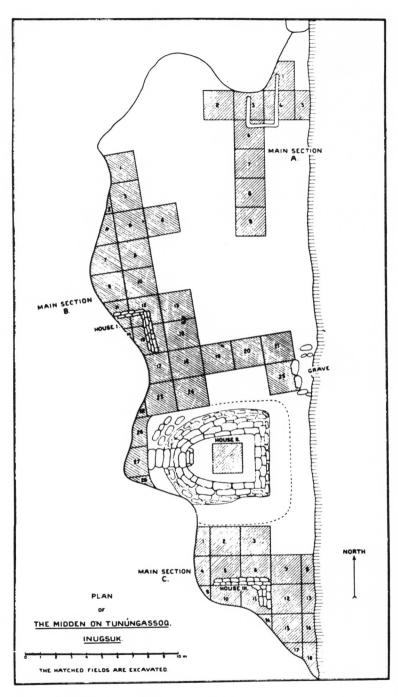

Plan of the midden on Tunúngassoq, Inugsuk
(*Meddelelser om Grønland*, vol. 77 [4], 1930, fig. 8)

two meters along the base line, to mark the sides of the squares. When we were through, Mathiassen took his little instrument for sighting right angles—I forget what it is called; it is a very simple arrangement of mirrors—and with it we soon ran lines out to the edge of the midden, at right angles to the base line, from every two-meter duck. These lines we measured with a steel tape, so that a map of the midden was very easily drawn to scale. The midden is only thirteen meters wide at the widest part, so you can see what a small place we live on. On our map we divided off the midden into squares, grouping the squares, for convenience, into three larger areas, A to C, and numbering the squares thus: A1, A2, A3, etc., then B1, B2, etc.

Our next job was to measure the height above sea level of various points on the midden. We had some argument as to what sea level really was, because the tidal range was so great, and during storms the waves washed high up to the edge of the midden. I forget what we finally agreed on. Mathiassen operated the hand level, and I carried the pole for him. With these we measured the height of all our points along the base line, and the ends of the cross lines along the edge of the midden. The midden is thickest at the southwest corner, where it totals two and a half meters in height, or well above Mathiassen's head. It was quite a job for me to climb up and down the bank there, until gradually our excavations lowered the top.

The top of the midden was overgrown with grass, which grew more luxuriantly there than in any other spot on the island. The soil was evidently very fertile. There were also the remains of four houses and a grave. Houses I and III were already mostly destroyed by the sea, which has been tearing away the midden. House II stands a little farther back, and was built on top of a big rock, which protected it somewhat. Although the roof had fallen in and the walls were crumbling, it was fairly well preserved; only the end of the long entrance passage had been washed away. The roof was still on the part of the entrance that remained, and Mathiassen decided to preserve the ruin, while excavating inside it and around it. The walls of the other two houses had to be torn down. House

IV was nothing but a very small structure built of turf, probably a storehouse, of which only the outlines of the walls remained in low relief. The grave was against the cliff at the edge of the swamp. The top stones were out of place, and we could see the skulls and other bones inside.

We began to work at the extreme southern end of the midden, because the lower layers there were fringed with baleen and gave promise of good digging. The men peeled off the turf, pulled up the rocks which were scattered through it, and began to dig down through the first layer. The ground was thawed to a depth of thirty centimeters. For the rough work of clearing the ground the men used spades and a pickaxe, but as soon as the real excavation began, Mathiassen produced the geological spades with little blades, which were better for the more delicate work. Robert invented a fine technique for taking off the turf; he skins it with a digging knife, just as if it were the hide of an animal. Later we worked very efficiently together, he cutting with the shovel while I pulled back the strip of turf. I think we underestimated his ability. He is a faithful worker, never complains or slacks, and does all the dirty work. He cleans our birds, and washes our dishes, and heaves down the biggest stones. Mathiassen says he is just like a big, willing dog.

That first afternoon Mathiassen gave me the digging journal and told me to mark the position of each specimen on a map of the square in which it was found. This was what he had done at Naujan, in Canada. However, he soon decided that it was time wasted, as the position within the square was not very important as long as the numbers of the field and of the layer were noted, so we gave it up. I was very glad when he suggested that I did not have to keep notes any longer, and I was free to squat in the dirt and dig.

Mathiassen sits down when he digs, swinging the handle of his digging stick across his knees to thrust the blade through the tough ground. At first I used to dig like the Eskimos, standing and bending over at the hips. It seemed easier to work this way, for my sealskins were still too stiff to bend comfortably at the knees, and it required considerable effort to cut the earth with the stubby spade.

In time, however, as my arms grew stronger, I learned to sit down and dig like Mathiassen, though my strokes are always longer and more energetic than his. He has enough strength to dig very gently, with small, delicate movements, but I don't think he is really any more careful than I or more lucky in his finds. I love the actual digging, the rhythmical swing of the arms and the bending and pushing with the whole body. The sun shines warmly over my back, the rich, sweet smell of rotted blubber rises from the saturated earth. The work is pleasantly interrupted by the discovery of some artifact: perhaps it is only a whittled wooden peg, which I know I can't persuade Mathiassen to keep; perhaps it is an elaborately carved piece of bone, which must have been used for something, though I can't guess what; or, best of all, it is a real specimen—the handle of a knife, a grotesque wooden doll, the wooden shank of a gull hook, or some other treasure. If I have found something very fine, I must call the others to admire, and they, too, shout, *"Taku! taku!"* ("Look! look !"), to announce their discoveries. The midden is so rich that we never dig through a section without finding something, though of course some squares and some layers are more productive than others, and scarcely a day passes that we don't bring back something very fine to gloat over.

When we go out to work, each one of us chooses a field to dig over. When it is finished—that is, when we have dug off the thin layer that has melted since the day before—the specimens found are entered in the digging book and then set aside to be packed in the evening. Robert is the one usually called to shovel off the tailings. I often do it myself, though Mathiasssen thinks the work too strenuous for me. I do not care much for it, though it is not very heavy, for while shoveling one does not find anything, unless it is something that was overlooked in the digging. It seems to be impossible to find everything. Mathiassen is usually the one to write in the digging book, which he does in Danish, but sometimes he sends me around with it to the fields where the others are digging. As each layer is dug, he makes a note of its character in his book, describing the soil and the various objects found which are not good enough to take as specimens. Thus, in the remains of Houses I and III we found "blubber-soaked earth, stones from the walls, heather (probably for covering the platform), chips and shavings, many bones, feathers, etc."

The real task of correlating the different layers will come when Mathiassen is back in the museum and can spread out all his specimens. Of course, the midden has such varying depths that "layer three," for example, does not always mean the same age in all the different sections. The surface layers, and in spots even the third, and the insides of the three houses are filled with quantities of junk—broken china, steel knives, nails, scraps of hoop iron, whittled wood, and even scraps of cloth in the frozen parts. Mathiassen saves samples of everything so that he can date these upper layers. The layers below contain much older things, but how old they are, and whether there is a gradual change from the older to the younger culture, or a sharp break in the midden, we do not know yet.

We do not work at the midden on Sundays, but go about to other places, looking for more ruins or other interesting things. June 30, our first Sunday, we had the Eskimos row us across the narrow strait to the north side of Inugsuk harbor. On the point at the mouth of the harbor which sticks out toward our island, there are three house ruins, very like House II on our midden. The one nearest the water is the largest. It is square, and is built of stone. We will excavate it someday. We took our digging sticks with us and dug a little on the slope in front of the houses. We found only knives, broken china, and other articles of European manufacture, such as we have been finding in the new midden on our island. While Mathiassen was making a sketch of the houses, he sent me up to the top of a high rock to take a photograph of the site. His camera is very bulky and heavy, so he had Niels, Karl's oldest boy, go with me to carry the camera.

When Mathiassen had tired of poking about the houses, we climbed up to the top of the hill just north of the harbor, where the beacon stands which gave Inugsuk its name. The hills are bare rock, rounded off and polished smooth by the mighty glaciers which once covered all of Greenland. Perched about in curious places are boulders of all sizes and shapes which the ice brought here and which were left behind when it melted. They are scattered in such a haphazard way that they seem out of place, and there is something about them which gives them an air of being alive when one sees them out of the corner of one's eye. Although the country is completely open, because there are no trees or bushes behind which anything could hide, these boulders look as if they might be sheltering something. This was the very vivid impression which they made on me at first; now I am used to the character of the landscape, and all the rocks seem to belong to it.

The cairn is a pile of smaller rocks on top of an enormous boulder, set on end. They are quite overgrown with lichens, and must have been put here a long time ago. We climbed up to the cairn and hunted for a record, but found nothing. It was not made by Eskimos. They sometimes make cairns to mark sledge routes across the country, but these are very small. In the Central Regions the Thule Eskimo built long lines of cairns, to form a lane down which caribou were driven to a lake or a river, or to some other place where they could easily be killed. To the frightened caribou the cairns looked like men, so they did not try to break through the lines. Mathiassen thinks our cairn was built by whalers. In the old days they must have come to this fine harbor.

From the beacon, or cairn, there is a magnificent view to the north across the Icefjord toward Qagsserssuaq. We walked across the top of the hill for a short distance beyond the beacon, but turned back at the edge of a steep ravine that crossed our path. By the edge of it was a fox trap of the same kind as the one we saw at the coal mine. Coming back to the boat, we passed several Eskimo graves scattered on the hillside. We found half a dozen or more in a gully just behind them. One of these was made of turf, not stones, and looked very recent. The grass had not yet grown up over the spot where the turf had been cut for it. Mathiassen says that we must open some of these graves, but we will wait until we are ready to leave before we touch them for fear that our Eskimos may not like it. Our trip was marred only by the dull sky. The first few days of glorious weather were already over.

Usually when I go to bed, I lie awake for a little while, listening to the noise of the ice, bumping against the rocks, knocking against each other, and sometimes letting off a boom of thunder when a big berg drops a piece and wallows in the sea until it regains equilibrium. During the day I do not notice the noise very much, but at night I am astonished to hear how loud it is. It does not seem to be a strange noise, for when I am half asleep I seem to hear the familiar noises of home: a train shunting, traffic going down the road, the subway roaring past. Sometimes two icebergs will knock together a few times, and then I am wide awake and sitting up to listen to what I am sure is the chugging of a motorboat. Again, an iceberg may knock against the shore with a hollow, wooden sound, and I am sure that someone is landing from a rowboat.

Mathiassen is fooled, too.

This night, however, we really did hear a boat. We were fast asleep but were awakened at one-thirty in the morning by the inspector and the Ottos coming back from the north. We jumped out of bed, dressed sketchily, and ran to the landing rock to welcome them. They came ashore and were much impressed by the few specimens we had set aside in the "Visitors' Box" to show them. Mathiassen got out a bottle of Madeira from the locked box which Mrs. Otto gave us to keep our wine in, and we all had a sip. The Ottos talked of visiting us at our island for a while, but a painter came to Upernivik, and they felt they had to stay at home to entertain him, so they have never had time to come back to Inugsuk. It was interesting to have visitors, but we had a happy feeling when they went away, and were glad that we were not going back to Upernivik. The next morning we slept till noon.

It was not until July 2 that we settled down to the routine of digging. Mathiassen is the first one up, and without waiting for me to wake, he gets dressed and comes to my tent. The first sound I hear is the noise of the Primus being pumped up and the hot flame roaring out. Then when I am almost asleep again, Mathiassen hands me a cup of hot tea and a piece of bread and cheese. That is all we have for breakfast. I thought I should miss coffee, but we have so much later in the day that tea for breakfast seems quite all right. I am usually too sleepy to eat very fast, and Ma-thiassen has finished his breakfast and is out in the field before I am done. Then I get up, and by that time the men come down over the hill, Karl first, and Robert tagging along some minutes later, with straw still sticking in the white knitted cap with a tassel which he always wears.

We each take a square and begin to dig over what has thawed since the day before. Robert soon has to shovel to keep up with us. Malia usually appears with the baby, which she carries every-where, though he is a very heavy load for such a little girl. She sits down on the ledge halfway up the cliff where Mathiassen and I ate our sandwiches that first day, and watches us. Occasionally the children come down on the beach and hunt about for specimens. Mathiassen gives them twenty-five øre for what they bring him. We work until the middle of the morning, which is psychological, not chronological, time, and then Robert is sent to wash the dishes from last night. He does a very thorough job, first licking them and then polishing them off with excelsior. He makes little use of water.

The first day or so Mathiassen and I did the cooking together, and I enjoyed this, especially since I did not want to be the only one to do the less interesting woman's work, but finally Mathias-sen suggested that we take turns with the meals, since there was not really work enough for two at a time, so I offered to get lunch and dinner, except dinner on Saturdays, which is pancake night. This has worked very pleasantly, especially since I am usually tired enough by mealtime to enjoy more quiet work than digging. For lunch we have fried auk's eggs, and a slice of some kind of tinned meat on bread and butter, followed with coffee and buttered bis-cuits. We take just time enough for a smoke while Mathiassen rests his back in the place of honor against my pack, and then we go back and work again.

We work until sometime in the late afternoon, when we have dug over all the fields, and then Karl, who is always puffing and panting as if about to die, is sent down to my tent to make coffee. Mathiassen always announces this with "*Kaffeliorpugut*" ("Now we are going to drink coffee"). Ane and the children are always on hand, and we all manage to crowd somehow into my tent. I sit at the upper end of the platform, Mathiassen next, then Karl and Robert, and lastly the others. We have only four cups, so the white people and the men drink first, and the woman and the kids, Eskimo-fashion, have to wait till later. With the coffee we have hardtack with margarine; the baby always gets a sweet biscuit. Mathiassen finds the hardtack too tough for his teeth, so he has a biscuit also. Then we all smoke and sit comfortably for a while, and Mathiassen talks to the others, while I listen enviously.

After coffee the men go hunting, and Mathiassen and I pack up the day's specimens. He reads off the numbers from the notebook and writes out a number on a slip of paper for each specimen, which I put with it, and wrap it up in newspaper and pack in a big box. The baleen objects have all to be painted with a mixture of glycerin and carbolic acid to keep them from decaying or from drying out and cracking. The more fragile bone things are also painted with it, and have to be wrapped in toilet paper. When this is done, it is time for dinner. My favorite meal is auk's or eider duck's breasts fried in margarine with mashed potatoes. I can eat more than Mathiassen.

After dinner we go out and dig again by ourselves. Mathiassen loves his little fields along the south edge of the midden so much that he works them twice a day, and never comes home without some treasure. We also cut down the bank along the edge of the midden, though Mathiassen does not really approve of this way of digging. One is more apt to confuse the depth of anything found, and it is impossible to get out the long objects which are frozen into the bank. One is tempted to give a heave on the free end, and that is very bad. The baleen things crack when they dry, so when we find something we can't take out, we wrap it in moss and leave it until it thaws. We would not "rob" the edges of the midden this way if it were not frozen and we did not feel pressed for time. Sometimes we go for walks on the hills of Inugsuk after dinner, and we hardly ever go to bed without climbing to the top of the island for a last look at the two big mountains. We also like to see if the big iceberg near the entrance to the harbor is still there. It is an old friend and we call it "our" iceberg. Before going to bed, we often make a cup of tea. Then Mathiassen crawls into his sleeping bag, where he sits with a small cigar in his mouth, his Icelandic sweater pulled on over his *anorak*, and his journal in his lap. It doesn't take me long to climb into my bag. We call good night to each other and are soon asleep.

On July 3 we tore down the walls of Houses I and III after photographing them, and hard work it was, too. It was still harder clearing out the debris from inside House II, for Mathiassen wants to save the walls, and all the stones inside have to be heaved over them. While someone is clearing it out, it isn't safe to walk along the beach below it without calling out to the men inside, for the stones fly out like cannonballs. This day *Hvalen* ("Whale"), the Upernivik schooner, stopped for a moment at our island on her way to the northern outposts. We are just on the main passage to Tasiussaq and, with the boats stopping here, are beginning to lose our delightful sense of isolation. The schooner, however, brought us our laundry and some red and blue cloth for my new *anoraks*, so she was not unwelcome. Mathiassen got a letter from Governor Otto with the latest radio news. This schooner is certainly not much of a boat. She has a half-breed captain and an Eskimo crew, though the captain looks as native as the others in his *anorak*, sealskin pants, and dirt. The former captain was drowned in a kayak this spring, and the present captain is only temporary; they are expecting another real seaman later. The ship was crowded with women and girls on their way north. They looked very fine in their woolen caps, bright jackets, beaded collars, and red boots. Some of the girls wore white boots, elaborately embroidered in colored skin mosaic like the bands on their trousers. These boots came only to the knee, so the upper part of their long sealskin stockings was covered by linen cuffs, embroidered and trimmed with lace.

On the Fourth of July we celebrated not only the birth of my native land but our first five hundred specimens. We worked as usual, but I prepared an elaborate dinner of auks, rice, canned beans, with coffee afterwards, and "sidecar" cocktails and *pâté* sandwiches to begin. The cocktail recipe is, as you ought to know, one half brandy, one quarter Cointreau, and one quarter lemon juice and ice. I had brought the ingredients with me in my trunk, for just this occasion, not realizing that I was breaking a regulation which requires all people coming into Greenland to register the liquor they bring in—in order to prevent liquor being sold or given to the natives. I had rather forgotten what a powerful mixture this cocktail was, so I made us each a teacupful. Mathiassen has the reputation of being impervious to the effects of alcohol, but he exclaimed when he tasted the stuff. He maintains that I had too much, that my hand shook when I poured the coffee, but I claim that he showed the effects of his drink when he went out to fill the water pail, and that he staggered so he almost spilled it. The dinner was a great success, however.

Apropos of the liquor regulation, he told me that in former days the post manager at Ūmánaq used to give all the natives a little to drink on Sundays. Finding that a little went a long way, he cut down the rations to a mouthful per man. What was his surprise to find that every Sunday there was always some one man who got drunk. On investigation he discovered that the natives were in the habit of drawing lots each week to determine who should get all the liquor. The entire male population would file past the man serving the drinks, fill their mouths, and then run outside to spit the contents into the mouth of the lucky man!

It was a beautiful night. After dinner we got into the little boat which the schooner had brought us as a loan from Governor Otto and rowed around "our" iceberg. We went across to Târtoq and landed near the northwest point of the island. From the hillside we had a magnificent view across the Upernivik Icefjord. I brought home a few of the purple *Saxifraga oppositafolia* to plant on our island, for it does not grow here. Later I collected a few more plants for a little garden behind my tent. I have a plant with yellow flowers, two with tiny white blossoms, the light green reindeer moss which explorers have cooked and eaten in time of starvation, and other lichens.

The next day Karl found our first example of a Thule type harpoon head. It was thin and slender, with an open socket to receive the point of the foreshaft. It looks very different from the broad, flat type with closed socket now used by the Greenland natives. It was a very much decayed specimen and came from the second layer among the modern stuff. Mathiassen says that originally it must have been lower down. Karl's own theory is that it was in the turf cut by the more modern inhabitants to use on a house, and he is probably not far wrong.

That night the wind changed from the north to the southwest, and "our" iceberg, to which we had grown quite attached, sailed away to the north in the gale. The next day it rained so hard that we were forced to quit work at noon. I spent most of the afternoon in the Eskimos' tent, while Mathiassen had Karl down in mine, talking about old ruins. He gave him tobacco, and they sat and smoked while Karl told him about all the old village sites in the district. He seems to be well informed. We all had coffee together and Mathiassen showed us pictures of the different Thule types which he hoped that we would find here, and offered a prize of twenty-five øre to the one who found the first example of each. The Eskimos were very much interested, especially in the things such as bolas for catching birds which are no longer used in Greenland.

Ane was softening skin for my stockings, and I tried to help her. She had already dried and scraped the skin, but it was still very stiff. The method of softening it is to take a fold down the length of the piece, with the hairy side in, and then rub the fold hard against itself. The Eskimo women hold the fold with the left hand palm down and the right hand palm up, but I found it easier to hold it with both hands palm down, and they laughed at me. It was a cold, damp day, so one's hands got sore more quickly than the skin was softened. When one had rubbed as hard as one could, there was nothing to see but tiny cracks of softened skin along the fold. One is supposed to keep at it until the skin has been folded all over, in every direction. Robert was in the tent filling shotgun shells. Mathiassen had bought the empty shells, the caps, and the powder and shot separately, and Robert had to put them together. He had a very ingenious homemade pair of nippers to press the cap into the end of the brass butt of the shell. Mathiassen also has ten empty shells for his rifle, but so far Robert has not found time to fill them.

[1975: I find the following entries in my notebook. Aside from these there are almost no other records of temperatures at Inugsuk:

"July 5–6, midnight. 39°F; 44° inside tent.

"July 6, 10 A.M. In tent, 43°; with Primus 47°; outside 43°."]

That night (July 6) there was a most amazing high tide that came up to within a foot or so of the midden, and tore away all the dirt which we had shoveled down onto the beach. It took out most of the old sea ice, washed away our water pail, which Mathiassen rescued only just in time, and made us haul our boat up still higher. The water broke into the little igloo of snow and ice which we had built for the auks. We discovered one of them floating merrily off to sea, and fished it out with an oar. Robert's first job next morning was to build a new storehouse for the remaining birds. The spot he chose was part way up the cliff directly above my private W.C., and the moment when he began to work was just when I was responding to one of nature's calls. He could not have failed to notice what I was doing, for he was only a yard or so above me, but he went on placidly collecting turf for the storehouse, and I was the one who fled. I thought I ought to tell Mathiassen, since I wasn't sure what sort of fellow Robert was, but Mathiassen only laughed at my misadventure, and reassured me that Robert was "all right," but that he had merely a more "primitive" sense of modesty than my own. I was relieved and began to think that Robert was right.

We were working Sunday morning, to make up for the time lost due to the storm, when Dr. Falkenberg from Upernivik came in his motorboat. At first I had thought it was Sørensen, and was disappointed, but not for long, for the doctor stepped ashore with a

portable victrola and a box of records. We showed him our diggings. He was especially interested in the graves. We entertained
him for lunch, while the natives with him went up to our Eskimos' camp. After lunch we sat on the beach outside our tents and
listened to the music. The best records were a collection of old
Danish songs, including the Danish version of "Oh, Susannah,"
and an American record with the "Song of the Prune" on one side
and "Down in the Canebrakes" on the other. We enjoyed them
thoroughly, and so did the Eskimos. Some days later I heard
Malia humming "Down in the Canebrakes" very prettily, and
when she had finished the tune she repeated it with variations. I
took an "autoknips" picture of everyone listening to the music,
which pleased them all very much.

We seem to have no end of visitors, for only the next day,
July 8, *Hvalen* came back from Kraulshavn in the north on her
way to Upernivik, and we received a short visit from Søren Nielsen, the "Old Man" or "King of Tasiussaq" or "King of Northern
Upernivik." He was a fat old fellow, very red in the face, and
dressed in the most beautiful soft sealskins I have ever seen. We
had great difficulty in helping him out of the rowboat and up the
rough beach to Mathiassen's tent, for he seemed very wobbly on
his legs. Mathiassen served a little brandy and showed him the
Visitors' Box. Then he wrote a note for him to take to Governor
Otto, while I showed Nielsen around the diggings. What impressed him most was the quantity of whale bones and caribou
bones, for there are no whales and caribou left in this part of
Greenland. Nielsen is a great man; for forty years he has been the
only white man in Northern Upernivik, and has ruled it like a
king. He made a trip back to Denmark and was returning to
Greenland on the *Bele*, on the same trip with the Fifth Thule Expedition, when she was wrecked. Mathiassen said that he looked
just like a typical Danish peasant on the boat, and one could not
imagine him as anything else, yet when they came to Úmánaq,
there was a Greenland girl in high red boots and skintight shorts,
swaying from the hips to rock the baby in her back pouch, with
her red hair—the only sign that she was not a pure-blooded Es-

kimo—twisted high on her head in an old-fashioned topknot. This was his daughter, by his native wife, and herself married to a Greenlander.

From this time on to the end of the month the fine days have become rarer and rarer. We were glad whenever it was not actually raining, for the bad weather is pretty bad.

July 10 was one of our hardest days. We demolished what was left of House I, and then shoveled away the tailings from the bottom of the midden below it, to find that the midden was two and a half meters thick there. It is built on an ancient moraine. Throwing down the stones from the house wall was heavy work; Karl and I took the smaller stones, Mathiassen and Robert the larger ones. We were all so tired at coffeetime that Mathiassen gave us all a little brandy. It was wonderful to see how we all cheered up. The men began to play cat's cradle with a piece of string. Robert was better at it than Karl, but they were not as dexterous as I had imagined Eskimos to be.

That night when we went up to their camp, as we usually do before turning in, both men were out in their kayaks. Robert is using Mathiassen's shotgun, and we hear him banging away at all hours of the night, but he is a rotten shot, so rarely gets anything. Mathiassen groans when he thinks of all his good cartridges being wasted. This time we did see Robert get an auk. Karl came back with several auks, a gull, and two eider ducks. We bought one of the ducks. It was interesting to watch them hunting. When a kayaker is about to shoot, he sticks one blade of his kayak paddle under the deck thongs in front of him, so that the paddle lies out horizontally on the water and acts as an outrigger. Then he pulls the gun from its waterproof bag on the front deck, and can shoot in any direction without fear of capsizing. They told us that one night Robert turned turtle and Karl had to rescue him. It is only the experts who know how to turn over in the water and come up again. That is a useful trick to know in case of an accident. The man fits so tightly into the kayak, especially with the half-jacket fitted about the manhole, that he could not possibly free himself from the capsized kayak. There must be another man to turn him right side up again, or he will drown. They say one drowns quickly in this cold water. None of the Eskimo know how to swim; the water is too cold for it.

There are hundreds of birds near our island. Flock after flock fly up or down the fjord, and the air is almost never without the sound of their wings. The little black and white auks seem very heavy in the body, with short, stubby wings, and they fly very low with noisy, laborious strokes. The eider ducks fly more gracefully, but do not glide as well as the gulls. We also see a raven or two on the land. The little snow bunting is still fluttering in and out of the old grave. We have not seen any ptarmigan, though on Inugsuk we have come upon their droppings. The auks are wonderful birds in the water. They usually dive when frightened, and will stay down for minutes, and when you think they must surely have drowned, they will pop up again far away, in some unexpected direction. I did not know until I came here that there were so many auks and ducks in the world. The auks nest on high cliffs, like the famous bird rocks at Qaerssorssuaq, but the eider ducks make nests on the ground. They are so easily found that the government has had to forbid the taking of the eggs; otherwise there is danger that the natives would kill off the birds. There was an eider duck nest on our island, but I am afraid we chased away the mother bird. There was only one egg, a large colorless, unappetizing thing, in the nest made of soft down. The female eider duck is brown with speckles, but the male, or king duck, is black and white with a low green crest. They do not look as if they belonged to the same species. We were glad to get one of the birds that Karl killed, for there was only one very dead-looking bird left in our cache.

We thought it would surely clear up, for the wind was from the north again, but this only brought us a fresh batch of icebergs. The wind soon shifted to the south and we had rain again. We were trying to drain the swamp in the middle of the midden. Mathiassen was planning to run a cross trench through the midden to the grave at the back. It is a long job, however, with all the rain, for the frozen soil will not let us dig a deep trench, and water collects in the swamp as fast as we drain it out. We also worked in

House II, and almost got through the floor. I cleaned out the passageway, and can crawl through it, though it is not in a very good state of repair and some of the stones threaten to come down. The floor of the house is paved with big, flat stones from the beach, now frozen tight to the ground. We have been gradually prying them loose. Curiously enough, most of the specimens from the house have come from under the floor. We collected quantities of junk in a very short time. The people who lived here must have been very rich, and very careless.

Mathiassen believes that the new part of the midden and the houses on it date from about 1750 to 1850. It was, of course, a modern culture that we found in the upper layers, but one richer than the present-day culture that we saw at Upernivik, where the natives have many more white men's things and do not make as many things for themselves as the Inugsuk natives used to do. You are probably very impatient with me because I have talked so much about the two cultures which we have been finding here and yet have told you practically nothing about them. I have enjoyed digging in the upper layers, though of course we are impatient to reach the older things. Shall I make a list for you of all the different things which we have been finding in and about the houses?

Among the imported, European things were steel knives, some with the original handles, others with handles which the natives made themselves, hammers, axes, files, nails, awls, scissors, thimbles, saws, a coffee mill, pots and pans, combs, buttons, parts of a type of flintlock which Mathiassen says was invented in 1806 and used in the Danish army from 1808 till 1811, bricks, coffee beans, and bits of woolen and cotton cloth, preserved, of course, by the frozen soil. We found many pieces of clay pipes and of china dishes, some plain and coarse, others with pretty flowered patterns. We could see holes drilled in some of the pieces where the owners had mended broken cups by sewing the pieces together. Mathiassen finds that the pottery belongs to the 1820–50 period, and that a good deal of it was made in England for export to Denmark. I found a piece of a cup with a picture of Kronborg

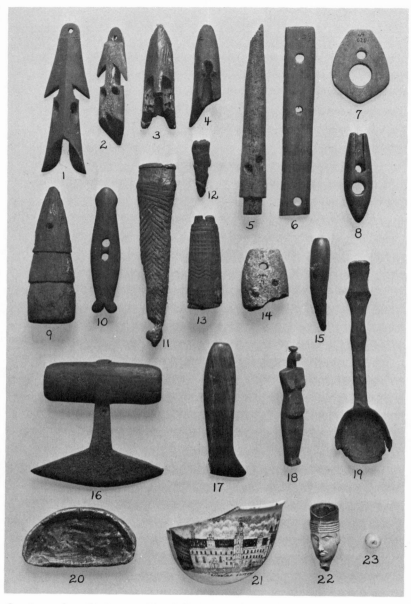

Specimens from the "new midden," Tunúngassoq, Inugsuk
(Photograph, National Museum of Denmark, courtesy of Therkel Mathiassen)

1–4. Harpoon heads. (1 is 11 cm. long.) 5. Harpoon foreshaft. 6. Sledge
shoe. 7–8. Trace buckles. 9. Wound plug. 10. Toggle for towing seals or

Castle, and another with Christiansborg Castle. The latter burned down twice, once in the late 1700s and again in 1884. The picture on the cup was of the building before the last fire. Of course, there were plenty of glass beads. We also found many flints for guns, evidently chipped by the natives. The pattern on some of the knife handles was of a particular type used in Europe in the latter half of the seventeenth century, but perhaps later in Greenland.

The real Eskimo things were, of course, more interesting. We found harpoon heads, all variants of the broad, flat type that is still used, foreshafts for kayak and ice-hunting harpoons, with ice picks for the butts of the latter, finger rests for the harpoon shafts, pieces to hold the line taut, and swivels to keep it from tangling. We found big plugs of wood, used to stopper the wounds of seals so that the blood would not be wasted, and bone toggles to fasten the seal to a towing line. We found part of a bird dart, with barbed side prongs, and two throwing-board handles; one of them had a hole for the first finger, which is an old-fashioned feature. In one of the house walls we got out a sledge runner, almost six feet long, and we also found a cross slat and a few pieces which Mathiassen thinks were upstanders fastened at the back of the sledge. Sledge shoes were very common. These were narrow, flat strips of antler, pegged onto the bottoms of the runners to make them run smoothly and to protect the wood. There were many trace buckles, too, by which the dogs were harnessed to their traces. These were simply bone or ivory rings to which the dog's harness was tied; the end of the trace buttoned into it with a bone toggle. A man could thus unfasten a dog from the sledge without taking off his mittens, or without freeing any of the other dogs. There were fragments of wood which Mathiassen recognized as parts of a kayak "stool" (the harpoon-line rack), broken paddles, and bone mountings to edge the paddle blades. We also found part of an umiak oar.

other game.   11. Knife Handle.   12. Butt of weapon point with screw thread for hafting.   13. Knife Handle.   14. Sinker.   15. Button to fasten the strap of a waterproof kayak jacket.   16. Ulo with tang.   17. Boot-sole creaser. 18. Wooden doll.   19. Spoon.   20. Toy lamp.   21. China cup with picture of Kronborg Castle, Helsingør.   22. Clay pipe.   23. Glass bead.

Among the implements and tools there were iron knives with homemade handles, one with a sort of continuation of the handle into a blade which had a groove along the edge for a thin strip of metal, a type of knife more common in ancient days when the only iron the natives had was small chips of meteoric iron. The ulos, or women's knives, all had a T-shaped handle. This type of handle Mathiassen found to be modern in Canada and in Greenland. There were also a few ulos of the old Thule type with straight handles, which were here probably used as scrapers. The women also had little ivory boot creasers, and boards on which to cut skins. We found all the parts of the bow drill, from the bow itself, the shaft of the drill with a hole at one end for the point, to the mouthpiece made of a caribou astragalus, by means of which the worker pressed down on the drill. We found pieces of antler that had been cut in two by drilling as many as thirty-six holes. There were also pieces of antler with a single hole to stretch and smooth thongs.

We found many pieces of soapstone lamps and cooking pots, and a wooden stand for a lamp. Fragments of wooden bowls, trays, spoons, dippers, hooks for pots, pointed bone sticks for serving meat, native-made tub staves, and wooden shafts for fire drills were very common in the house ruins. We found a pair of snow goggles, made of wood—or, rather, it should hardly be called a pair, for it was only a straight piece of wood with a single horizontal slit for both eyes. We also found *ajagaqs*. The *ajagaq* is a piece of bone, say a dog's shoulder blade, which is pierced with holes. It is thrown up into the air and caught on a bone pin. Points are scored according to what hole is pierced.

These Eskimo certainly loved their children, for we found toys everywhere. There were many wooden dolls. The female dolls all had topknots, curious animallike faces without features, prominent breasts and stomachs, and bodies without arms, ending in a single undivided leg. They evidently represented women about to have children. There were also male dolls, which we identified as such because of their lack of sex. Other toys imitated all the things of the grownups: harpoons, guns, crossbows, kayaks, dog sledges, lamps, cooking pots, and European boats. Besides these, the children had bull-roarers and tops, the latter made of the disk-shaped epiphysis of a walrus vertebra, pierced with a pointed stick. We found two drum handles. Drums were used in shamanistic performances as well as for ordinary singing and dancing. Therefore, the missionaries burned all the drums, and there are no more drums in West Greenland.

Mathiassen believes that this culture of the new midden is really a development of the old Thule culture which was found in Canada and in northern Greenland. This new West Greenland culture, however, has carried the evolution of certain things, for example, harpoon heads, further than the Thule culture did; it has lost some of the possessions of the Thule culture, like the snow house and the snow knife, and has invented many new things, like the boot creaser, the rack on the kayak for the harpoon line, and the thong smoother. Just how this change from the Thule culture took place Mathiassen hopes that the old part of the midden will explain, but I will write you later about what we are finding in it, for every day we seem to find something new, and we are still a long way from the bottom in most of the sections. Mathiassen keeps opening more sections all the time, so when we are through we will certainly have a lot of material.

VI

The Medieval Eskimo

Waiting for the Ship

Inugsuk
July 12– July 27

DEAR FAMILY:

While we were working hard cleaning out House II, three "white" Eskimos from Kingigtorssuaq, the runic stone island, paid us a visit. They were not nearly as pleasant as the full-blooded Greenlanders. I do not like the almost-white natives, but this may be a mistaken prejudice.

On July 13, Dr. Falkenberg stopped here on his way back from the north. He brought some skins to Mathiassen for *kamiks*. He arrived in style, sitting in an armchair in the very prow of his motorboat with one of his dogs lying at his feet. This was a dog which he had loaned to a man at Tugssaq. The last time he loaned that man a dog, all he got back was the skin, so he was pleased to have this one returned more or less intact. The doctor stayed to lunch, and we had music again, though in the tent, for it was cold and overcast outside.

Sunday, July 14, was a perfect day. We lay in the sun all morning and had a leisurely lunch. Then Mathiassen got his shotgun, camera, and digging tools, while I got together my camera, films, and a few things to eat, and we set off in the little boat to row around Inugsuk. We left at about four o'clock. I rowed for the first part of the way. We had great difficulty in getting through the ice, which had formed a solid pack in front of our tents. The north wind, which brings the fair weather, always fills our harbor with icebergs.

We rowed first to the far side of Sangmissoq. It was the first time we had seen our camp from this angle, and we laughed to see how tiny our island was and what a pitifully small and forlorn camp we had. The tents seemed to snuggle together for comfort. It looked completely cheerless.

We went south down the fjord to the southwest point of Inugsuk, which is visible from the top of our island. We waited here, hoping to get a shot at some birds, for they always fly from point to point. Mathiassen shot at some auks, and thought he hit one, but though we hunted for a long time, we could not find the body. After we gave up, and I began to row to the west up the fjord south of Inugsuk, Mathiassen finally did shoot a bird. We thought it was an auk, but it was a much smaller bird, a *teist*, or rock duck, completely black except for white patches on the wings and red feet. He was such a tiny fellow, and was still alive when we took him out of the water. We felt like murderers. We did not know what to do with him. Mathiassen supposed that someone should cut off the head, but he would not do it himself, and so passed the bird to me. I felt that we had to do something, so I laid the bird on the seat beside me and took out my knife, but when it came to the point I was as helpless as Mathiassen. So we sat loking sadly at the bird and guiltily at each other, while it quietly died in my hands. It was the first bird that Mathiassen had ever shot. He does not like to hunt. Later in the day, however, he shot an eider duck, and as this one died at once, we did not feel badly, for we needed the fresh meat.

We rowed farther up the fjord, close to the shore of Inugsuk, until we saw what we thought was a grave and went to examine it. While I was landing the boat, Mathiassen discovered that the empty shell had jammed in his gun, and he worked over it for a full quarter of an hour before he got it out. Though he was able to use the gun again, he had the same trouble the next time he shot. Mathiassen is waiting until we go to Upernivik to get a new piece put in it. It is Robert's fault; he does not know how to care for a gun. Mathiassen had been using my knife, and I put it into my *anorak* pocket, instead of in my trouser pocket. When we stepped ashore, there was a splash. Luckily, though the water was very deep, I could see the knife lying on a ledge of rock, just within my reach. I rolled my sleeve up to the shoulder and, lying on my stomach, was able to rescue the knife. The grave was a disappointment, for when we had scaled a little cliff in order to come to it, we found that it was only a fox trap, of the same kind which we had mistaken for a grave above the coal mine.

We re-embarked and rowed on a little farther. Above a narrow strip of sandy beach we found several graves, of which we opened two. In one was the skeleton of a woman with a bit of a wooden bowl under one stone, and a fragment of a wooden dipper behind another rock outside the stone coffin. Probably someone had already opened the grave and robbed it of what good things it may have held. In the second grave we found the skeleton of a man and a piece of arrow shaft. The woman we put into my pack, after taking out the things for tea, and Mathiassen wrapped the man in his coat. We ate our bread and chocolate on the beach, and rested for a little time on the fine sand.

After tea we rowed on again. There seemed to be an interminable succession of points. Finally we passed the last one on the southern side of Inugsuk and came out into the ice-packed fjord between Inugsuk and Kingigtoq. Behind Kingigtoq was the high, dark mass of Kingigtorssuaq. Now we had to face the bow to row, in order to steer between the icebergs. It must have been very cold, for the water between the pieces of ice was beginning to freeze, yet we were not uncomfortable, for it was absolutely calm, and the sun was shining brightly, though it was late in the evening. We were beginning to be rather tired, especially after we had fought our way through the ice for an hour or so. It is a labor to try one's patience, for it is impossible to move without bumping into a cake of ice. It becomes annoying after a short while to have one's oar constantly scraping and catching on the ice. Mathiassen tried to vary the work by standing up and paddling. This was good for a while, because he could get a view ahead and better dip in his oar, but the oar was too heavy for me to manage in this way for very long.

Mathiassen told me how, during the Fifth Thule Expedition, he and Olsen had tried to escape from Southampton Island to the mainland, where their headquarters were, and how they had fought for hours to get their heavy boat through the thick-packed ice in Frozen Strait. At last they reached a little island only a few miles off the shore of Southampton Island, where they landed to rest and look ahead at the prospect. They climbed a hill, from which they could see that the water between them and the opposite shore was even more covered with ice than that across which they had come. It was impossible to go farther, either with the boat or on foot over the treacherous floes. They could almost see their comrades' camp on the distant shores. They turned back toward Southampton Island, where they were to spend that terrible winter of darkness and hunger, among the unfriendly Eskimo. Mathiassen named that hill on the little island "Mount Tantalus."

At last we came round the northeast point of Inugsuk and knew that we were headed for home. We rested, ate the last of the biscuits, and smoked a cigarette. I would have given a good deal for a photograph of what we saw. We were walled in by monstrous bergs, towering high above us, and carved into fantastic shapes. Where the water was not actually covered by the small fragments of ice which had fallen from the bergs, it mirrored their reflections so perfectly that one could scarcely tell which was reflection and which was true ice. Under the water the huge feet of the icebergs shone pale green; reflection and submerged ice swam together. The only land which we could recognize was Qaerssorssuaq to the southeast and Qagsserssuaq to the northeast, but the mountains were so far away that they could not tell us where we were. We felt that we had journeyed a great distance, and wondered when we should reach home again. There were few birds here.

As we rowed south, we kept thinking that we must soon see the beacon, and were constantly deceived by glacial boulders. The land was totally unfamiliar. It was not only empty and desolate in the extreme, but completely without meaning. It was impossible to "compose" it into an intelligible picture. I had never realized how completely uninhabited it was. When there is no tent or ruined house, not even a fox trap or an old grave to give it some significance, it is only chaos in the midst of the waters. There is nothing on it, people never go there, there are no paths, even the birds do not fly over it. It is only a confusion of rocks, the refuse of a dead glacier.

We came in sight of "our" iceberg, stranded among other monsters of its kind. There was no mistaking it, even though it had been badly broken by the storm. It was like finding a signpost. We were immensely cheered, and felt very close to home. Almost at once we saw the beacon on the hill, and then at last our own little island with the Eskimos' dingy tent behind its big rock. We shouted, but they did not hear us until we had landed and I ran up to their tent. They were much impressed with the eider duck, and with the other little bird, which they assured us was good to eat. We did not try to take the boat through the ice around to its usual place near the tents, but got the men to help us pull it up on the rocks at the north end of the island where we had landed.

How good it was to see our tents again! They no longer looked comfortless and forlorn, but radiated a sense of human presence and the promise of warmth and shelter. I felt then that I would be content to work on our little midden and not to wander more than a few hundred feet from my own tent.

It was eleven o'clock. We had been gone seven hours. I was hungry and insisted on a good dinner. We had fried eider duck's breast, a can of peas, and even French-fried potatoes, the first I had ever attempted.

The next day we dug over all the fields, though there were

only three of us. Mathiassen had to let Karl go hunting, for the Eskimo camp was out of food. My arms were dreadfully lame from rowing, and at times it seemed all I could do to lift the digging stick, but pride was stronger than fatigue. It clouded up in the afternoon, and we were glad to see Karl coming, for there was bad weather looming in the southwest.

It was this morning that I discussed with Mathiassen the idea which obsessed me. I wanted to stay on with him till the end. Long before we even arrived at Upernivik, I was already grieving because the time was so short. In the colony I had him ask if there were any way for me to stay on until the *Hans Egede*'s third trip late in August, and whether there were any way of my getting to Ūmánaq to catch her there. Every time anyone came to the island, there was an agonizing wait for me while Mathiassen asked if there were any favorable news. No one could say. The governor finally sent word that there was no chance for me to catch the *Hans Egede*, and when the doctor came, he brought the more dismal news that the *Gertrud Rask* had sailed early from Copenhagen and would be in Upernivik by July 21. All my joy was gone when I had to say to myself, "This is the last week." And still we had not opened all the fields Mathiassen had planned.

On July 17 it rained so hard that we had an enforced holiday. I took courage, then, to write to you and to D—— in England that I could not leave now, that I must stay here until the *Gertrud Rask*'s last voyage home in October. I put my letter to you in a special envelope so that you would read it at once. It was not an easy decision to make, for it meant postponing my visit in England, and it is a bad thing to break one's word. Mathiassen would not help me, indeed he could not. He told me that he would be glad to have me stay on but urged nothing. It was hard to know what to do, but as soon as I had written the letters, I felt as if a heavy weight had been lifted from me. [See the letters on pages 156 ff.]

The next day the sun shone again. We opened what we planned to be the next to last field, but always Mathiassen wants to dig more and more. After coffee I tried to learn some Eskimo from Karl. We began with the names of the fingers and the numbers. I tried to write down the words in the proper phonetic system. Robert was watching, and he did not at all approve of my spelling, for Eskimo, as taught in the Greenland schools, has spelling rules just like any other language, and I did not know them. I found that the Greenlanders do not use the native numeral system for numbers over twenty, they use the Danish numbers instead. Their own numbers run: one, two, three, four, five, one-on-the-other-hand, two-on-the-other-hand, etc., one-on-the-foot, two-on-the-foot, etc., up to four-on-the-other-foot (for 19). Twenty is rendered by an expression meaning "the whole man." I found it very tiring work, but fascinating.

We are getting into the lower layers now. There are many pieces of baleen which have been well preserved in the frozen earth. The lower layers are sticky with blubber. The very bottom of the midden is on glacial gravel, the top layer of which has been glued by the blubber into a very tough conglomerate. In one place I found some seal ribs with bits of the flesh still sticking to them. We often come upon wads of dog hair, caribou hair, or scraps of sealskin. We also find little wisps of human hair which have evidently been trimmed off.

On July 19 I found a perfectly preserved mitten of sealskin. It was so caked in rotten blubber that at first I did not recognize what it was. Mathiassen had me wash it in salt water, and after it had been painted with the mixture of carbolic acid and glycerin that we use as a preservative, it was so soft that I could put it on. It was made in exactly the same way that my new sealskin mittens are made except that it is smaller, being intended to be worn next to the skin, and not over pair of woolen mitts, and it has a cuff of the natural skin, instead of the band of red leather which Ane sewed on mine. There is one piece of skin for the back of the hand, and two for the palm, one of which covers the upper part of the palm and the inside of the thumb, and the second piece the lower part of the hand and the outer part of the thumb. It had been quite a new mitten when lost; the hair on the skin was still unworn. It was wonderful to think how many hundreds of years it had lain there in the midden.

We also found a big platform mat of baleen. These mats were

like mattresses, laid on top of the stones of the platform to keep the
bed skins from the cold, damp platform. Long, thin strips of baleen were folded into a chain of figure eights, or linked S's, and
the bands thus formed were fastened together along the sides, until
a large mat was made. We got out only a part of the one which we
found. It broke, and the rest is still frozen in the ground. The
pieces still in the ground have to be covered with wet moss, for the
baleen splits as soon as it gets dry. We paint all the baleen objects
with the glycerin mixture. This keeps them from drying out. They
will all be treated again at the museum.

That night we drank the last of our coffee. Our slender supply
had been increased at the last by the Eskimos, as soon as we began
to give them afternoon tea instead of coffee. I saved the grounds,
and for a few times used them to make "second-hand" coffee, but
now they are totally used up, and we will have to be content with
tea. Still, we could celebrate the accumulation of 1,630 specimens.

The next day, July 20, it stormed in earnest. We did only a
little digging. It is almost impossible to see on account of the tears
which the cold wind brings to one's eyes. The wet, barely thawed
earth is far from pleasant to the hands. In a few moments the
fingers are numb and painful. We did not like the storm to come
at this time, because we are planning to go to Upernivik to meet
the ship, and she is due to arrive any day now. They will not be
able to send a motorboat to fetch us in this bad weather. It was a
thoroughly miserable day. I had indigestion. The tents leaked and
flapped in the wind. The canvas sagged on the windy side and
water dripped into the cooking pots and the boxes of provisions on
the south side of my tent. Luckily, my bed is on the north side.
The Eskimos' tent finally blew down, and they had to move over
to the north side of the island to get out of the wind. They left the
pups tied in the old place, and the poor dogs, thinking they were
deserted, finally broke loose and ran all over the island. They visited our camp in the night, cleaned out the W.C., and ate the last
auk in our cache. We had been saving it for our Sunday dinner,
and so did not discover its loss until we told Robert to clean it.

Karl offered to give us another bird, but we could not take it when we discovered it was the only one they had. Robert told us that he would go out in his kayak (in that storm) and soon he would bring us another!

The next day it was still raining, but we were able to work a little. I found an ivory doll with an X scratched on the breast and on the back. Mathiassen tells me that it represents the strap on which amulets were worn. The Thule culture dolls wore amulet straps, so this find furnishes the missing link between the Canadian Thule culture and Angmagssalik on the East Coast of Greenland, where such straps are still worn. We also found a doll with a line indicating the ivory brow band which Thule Eskimo ladies used to wear. Our list of Thule types is already in the sixties, so we know that the lower layers here on Inugsuk represent the Thule culture, but Mathiassen is still uncertain as to just what phase of it we have.

This weather is impossible. It cleared in the morning, and then began to rain in the afternoon. I have almost forgotten what the sun looks like. Ane claimed she heard the ship whistle at Upernivik, and the cannons answering her, but thirteen miles is a long way for the sound to travel, even with the wind. We tried to get the rest of the baleen mat out by pouring hot water over it, but not even two kettlefuls had any effect on the ground. We also found a new mat in the third layer of one of the fields in our cross trench. Since the swamp is draining out over it, there is no danger of its drying up. I felt quite badly during the afternoon and drank a lot of water and took some pills. My theory is that we do not get enough water. Often there is none melted in the ice pail, and so we have to wait until we have a meal, and what water there is is so cold that one does not care to drink much. Besides, in cold weather one is not very thirsty, even when working hard.

Mathiassen and I were digging after tea when a very wild-looking man arrived in a kayak. He was the half-breed Thomassen from Tugssaq, whom Governor Otto had suggested we take instead of Karl. Mathiassen invited him to dinner, and while I was cooking it, he got out his maps and the man told him all he knew about old ruined places. The man had a very keen, intelligent face, and though he had a very ragged beard, and long hair almost down to his shoulders which made him look like an Italian bandit, he was really not a bad fellow. We had only oatmeal and stewed prunes for dinner, because we had no fresh meat and felt we ought to go light on the canned stuff. Our bread, too, was gone, and so was our hardtack. Thomassen was most appreciative of the meal, however, for it was quite out of his usual line of eating, but he was most sympathetic when Mathiassen told him, "*Kaffe nungupoq, brød nungupoq*" ("Coffee all gone, bread all gone").

He had brought with him some skins which he had intended to sell in Upernivik. Mathiassen bought them from him. There were a small dogskin, minus the tail, and a rug of dogskin edged with gray sealskin. The price of the latter was twenty *kroner*, but he was willing to take a piece of our ham for fifteen of it. (Our poor ham! It had molded on the boat, and smelled vile, though Mathiassen had peeled off the worst. I would not keep it in my tent, so he had to keep it in his.)

That night was a perfect hell. It was storming so badly that Thomassen had to sleep with the Eskimos; he was afraid to go farther. The wretched pills got in their deadly work, and if there is anything more disagreeable than having to get up, pull on cold sealskin pants, boots, and slicker coat, to venture out into a howling rainstorm several times in the night, then tell me what it is. I got thoroughly chilled. The wind was blowing a gale, and I was afraid the tent would blow away. The tide was very high, and washed up to the tent door. At last I dozed off, though the noise of the flapping tent and the surf on the rocks was like thunder. In the morning Mathiassen appeared looking very haggard. He had been afraid to sleep all night. Three of the ropes on his tent had broken, and he had not dared to take off his clothes. He had also been up to the Eskimos' tent and had helped them to haul the boat up higher. Thomassen's kayak was carried away by the tide, but luckily it was discovered, still undamaged, in our harbor, and he rescued it with the rowboat.

The storm lasted all that day. Mathiassen offered to be my

nurse, so I did not get up. We were all shut inside, of course. I was still sick and could not eat anything. The tent leaked, but fortunately not on my bed. Mathiassen cooked himself a big pot of oatmeal and lived on it all day. He read aloud to me Dr. Thomsen's article on Greenland archeology, but it was hard work for him to make his voice heard above the storm. He had to go out often to fix his tent, and once when he was away a rope on my tent broke and I thought that the whole thing was coming down on top of me. That was a terrible moment. While I lay there, feeling so helpless and uncomfortable, I thought to myself, Suppose I could go, just by wishing, back to my own warm, safe bed at home, with Mother to take care of me (for there comes a time when one is sick that one simply wants to give up and be sick, and be properly taken care of), would I really want to go? It was a tempting thought. But even as it occurred to me, I knew that I would not want to accept that wish, should some good fairy offer me the chance. To rush home in the twinkling of an eye was too easy; it is part of the charm of Greenland that one is so completely cut off from home, and though I was thoroughly miserable at the moment, I was really having the best time of my life.

Our poor Eskimos had nothing to eat, so Mathiassen gave them some oatmeal, lard, and potatoes. This is the second time that we have had to save them from starving. I wonder how they manage when there is no white man to take care of them. We have had to lend them one of our Primuses quite often, for in wet weather they cannot use heather fires, and Karl has caught only two seals all the time we have been here, so there has been practically no blubber for their lamp. It seems dreadful to think of them in their leaky tent with nothing to eat and no fire. So little is necessary to change from plenty to want. Karl told Mathiassen that he did not mind going hungry but that it was bad for the children. They often come to our tent at mealtimes and wait until we give them something, and they eat all the scraps that are thrown out, though of late we have had less to throw away.

That night was again miserable. I could not get to sleep for a long time. Mathiassen did not dare to go to bed, for the tide was rising and he was afraid for the tents. He spent the time—tireless worker that he is!—in digging, while I tossed, listening to the waves beating in front of the tent and wondering if the ropes would stand in the wind. Mathiassen says that the water broke down the bank of earth around the midden which has been built up by the slow accumulations of our shovelings, and that even part of the midden was washed away. The waves washed up over the big rock in front of House II, which I always find so hard to climb from the beach, and invaded the entrance passage, where we keep the tools. It was two o'clock in the morning before Mathiassen finally decided that the sea would rise no higher and that the tents were safe. I, who had lain uneasily for hours, unable to sleep and envious of him, fast asleep as I thought, heard him come past the tent and call good night to the Eskimos. I told him to come in and get a cup of tea, but he poked his head in only to say, "It's safe now. Go to sleep!"—which I obediently did.

The next morning the sun was shining. It is impossible to tell you how bright and radiant the whole world was. Even the somber rocks have life and color in the sun, and the landscape is so beautiful that one can't understand why it ever rains and wastes such precious days. Mathiassen was up early and out digging again, with Thomassen to take my place. When I looked out of the tent, I saw the beach strewn with great ropes of kelp, the kind Ole uses for whipping his "dog teams," and there was an iceberg as big as a bureau inside the wall of shoveled earth. Mathiassen offered a biscuit for each specimen picked up from the beach, and the children made quite a thriving business.

I was able to get up to prepare lunch. The tent was in a terrible mess. After a fried auk's egg, which is worth two of any hen's, and a cup of tea, I felt equal to the task. There was even more than the usual accumulation of junk, scraps of food, and semi-"officially" dirty dishes on the table and in the "storehouse" behind it. The bags of flour and oatmeal had burst in the box and the rain had leaked into it, so that, as Mathiassen put it, "there were pancakes already mixed." All this stuff I took outside and sorted, throwing away what was no longer fit to keep, and spreading the rest on rocks to dry. In the bottom of the hardtack sack there were still a

Objects of the Inugsuk culture from the "old midden," Tunúngassoq
(Photograph, National Museum of Denmark, courtesy of Therkel Mathiassen)

1. Baleen cup (11 cm. long). 2. Baleen bowl with seal meat (18 cm. long).
3. Coopered tub or bucket (13 cm. long). 4. Soapstone pot (24 cm.
long). 5. Drum with baleen frame and stick (28 cm. long).

few edible scraps of biscuit, and in the bottom of the ex-bread-
basket, under piles of junk, were some bigger pieces of biscuit,
and—three cheers!—a crust of bread which we had thrown away
three weeks before. We had it for dinner that night. It had been
burned and was hard as a rock, so I naturally preferred the hardtack, but Mathiassen cherished his crust and made it last three
days. I also rearranged the boxes in my tent to make more room
and added a few more paving stones to the floor.

Meanwhile the diggers returned with some really fine things.
There was an enormous platform mat of baleen, the biggest piece
Mathiassen had ever seen, and quite interesting because it had a
rim of baleen around the edge. They also had a drum frame of
baleen, which is a very unusual material for a drum frame, with a
wooden handle. There was a baleen thong in a groove around the

outside of the frame, by means of which the skin head had been lashed in place, and beside the drum was lying a rough, unworked stick, which Mathiassen kept because it might have been the drumstick. The drum came from the cross trench, and near where it was found we unearthed several other frames of baleen for drums, and some baleen cups and dishes with oval wooden bottoms—everything glued together in a solid mass of baleen shavings, feathers, filth, and blubber.

That evening we celebrated the return of the sunshine with an eider duck which Karl had just shot, mashed potatoes, and apple cake. It was a magnificent meal in spite of the lack of bread and coffee. After dinner I was able to type out of doors. The mosquitoes were beginning to appear, but they were not very troublesome. They hung on the tent walls and did not move when we went to swat them. They were too apathetic to bite. The rain had melted most of the snow on the hills.

We expected that the motorboat would soon come to take us to Upernivik, and were beginning to get quite anxious because we had had no word from the colony. We were sure that the *Gertrud Rask* had already come. In anticipation of our return to civilization we heated up a lot of water and bathed. I had one Primus going full blast to warm my tent, but Mathiassen scorned to use the other. Taking a sponge bath in these latitudes certainly makes one feel naked.

The next morning the miracle of a perfect day was repeated. Still no boat came. My hands were sore from the washing. I gave Mathiassen his breakfast in bed while I mended his pants. The seams which had been sewn with sinew thread are still holding well, but the seams sewn with cotton thread, which Ane seems to have used when she had no more sinew, are forever breaking. Our precious sealskin trousers, which looked so beautiful when new, are no longer very lovely. Working in the damp ground has been very hard on them. They are worn bare on the sit-downery, which gives us the appearance of chimpanzees, and they are bare on the knees, too, with bald patches already appearing on the tops of the thighs, where we rub across when swinging our digging sticks.

We sent Karl out hunting, and saw him return with five eider ducks, four auks, and two gulls, which was quite a bag. The gulls went to the dogs, and two of the eider ducks to us, so all were happy. I spent a long time after tea playing with the children. Ole was making a toy kayak. He had taken his mother's cutting board, a piece of wood about twelve by four inches, and had cut another scrap of wood, one by two inches, with a hole in the middle, to represent the extra keel. This he was trying to lash onto the cutting board, near one end, just as the false keel is lashed under the stern of the real kayak. The cutting board was not shaped at all, not even the manhole was drawn on it. I was interested to see that what Ole considered essential should be the keel and not the outline of the kayak, but perhaps that was because his mother would not let him cut her precious board. His sister had helped him to tie the keel on with some thread, but they had not made a very good job of it.

Ole then appeared with the stomach of one of the gulls. He tied one end as tightly as he could with thread, holding the end in his teeth while he cut off the extra length with an enormous butcher knife. The manual dexterity of that child is amazing. The knife looked pretty dangerous so close to his face, but that is the ordinary Eskimo way of cutting. Their mouths are like a third hand. Mathiassen says they give their children knives to play with at a very early age. He once saw a year-old baby playing stark naked with a knife on the platform of a snow house, and the child tumbled off the platform, knife and all, onto the icy floor without seeming any the worse for it. The parents said it was a good thing to give the children knives, for then they would soon learn how to use them. Malia, however, does not share this pedagogical theory, and had a hard time keeping the baby, Peter, away from Ole's knife. The small boy tried to inflate the gull's stomach, but the thread was not tight enough, so all the air came out as fast as he blew it in. To blow up his toy bladder, he had to put the raw gut into his mouth. He made a face to show he didn't like the taste and soon gave up the attempt.

It was now July 26, and we began to worry because we had

seen no boat. We thought that the ship must have come and gone without anyone's thinking of us. Accordingly, Karl was sent to Upernivik in his kayak to take a letter to the governor and was given money to buy us bread and coffee. He came back the same evening. The ship had arrived during the day, and the people would send the boat for us at once. Rasmussen and Freuchen were on board the *Gertrud Rask*, and might come out to see us. Karl also brought us some bread and coffee. The beans were unroasted, but Ane roasted them in a frying pan over the Primus and ground them with a round stone in a skin, so we had real coffee for dinner, and were very happy. While Karl was away, we had chocolate in the afternoon to celebrate the first two thousand specimens.

We went out to work as usual the next day, while waiting for the boat to come. In the fifth layer of one of our best fields I discovered a perfect little tub, almost small enough for me to encircle with my two hands. The sides were made of small staves, with a groove at the bottom into which the oval wooden bottom fitted. The staves were flat, not bulging as are our barrel staves. They were lashed in place by a hoop of baleen about the top and another about the bottom. Two of the staves were somewhat longer than the others and were pierced at the ends to hold a little handle, which had been lost. The tub was frozen fast in the ground between two big stones, which had evidently served to hold up the weight of the midden and keep it from crushing the delicate object. Inside was a solid mass of ice. Thank goodness I had sense enough to call Mathiassen at once, and did not spoil it by careless digging! We cleaned it up as best we could and covered the baleen parts with damp moss, and left it to thaw out. We are all tremendously excited about it, for it is our best specimen.

While we were poking about the tub, we heard the chugging of a motorboat, so I raced off to get washed and to put on my brand-new blue *anorak*. Mathiassen put on his civilized pants, but I refused to change from my warm sealskins, knowing the trip would be cold. We ran up to our lookout rock. Soon the motorboat was near enough for us to see a white man standing in the bow.

"It's Freuchen!" cried Mathiassen joyfully. "There's only one man in Greenland as tall as that. I'd recognize him anywhere."

But the man proved to be the fishmaster from Prøven, and although we were very grateful to him for coming to fetch us, we could not help being disappointed that he was not Freuchen, Mathiassen's old comrade. Mathiassen escorted him around the diggings while I finished getting together the things I wanted to take with me to the colony. He had brought our mail, so finally we left him to amuse himself while we retired into our tents to read our letters. The mosquitoes, which the warmth had emboldened, got in a few good bites while I devoured my mail. I would have been completely happy if my conscience were not troubling me about D——— in England whom I was disappointing and who had written to me. Everyone seemed to think I was terribly brave to come to the Arctic, and imagined that I must be suffering incredible hardships. It is certainly fun to have them think so. Fortunately, they had guessed that I might be out of reading matter and had sent me several magazines.

We had the fishmaster to lunch and then set off for Upernivik, taking everyone with us but Karl and the pups. Ane and Malia had on new *anoraks*, and Ane even had some new red boots. They looked pretty fine.

We went first to the ship. As we drew alongside, there was Rasmussen himself just stepping into a rowboat to go ashore. Mathiassen waved to him and said we would soon follow. Then we went to see the captain. Through some mistake he understood that he was to take both Mathiassen and myself back with him on the return trip, so you can imagine how surprised he was to discover that I did not want to go back now, as had been planned, and that Mathiassen had never intended to go back at this time. He distressed me terribly by insisting that all the room was taken up on his next voyage home, the one we want to go on, but Mathiassen at once radioed to our old friend the inspector of North Greenland, telling him that I was absolutely essential to him in his work and asking him to tell the captain to take me back on the next trip. Of course, the inspector wirelessed back the necessary order, so everything is all right. The captain was very nice. He gave me some apples and oranges, and has invited us to spend the night on the boat, and to come back for supper at five. We are going ashore now.

Exchange of Letters [1975]

My mother had written:

Greensboro, Vermont
June 19, 1929

DEAR FREDDY:

. . . It seems so strange to be writing to you on your barren Arctic island while I sit at the spot so full of memories of you. . . . Your last long letter came the morning we left Bryn Mawr, and I've thought and dreamed of you daily and nightly ever since. . . .

It is very good of you and D—— to be willing to change your plans and be married over here. Let's not decide just yet. It may be that we can manage to go abroad with you in June and you can be married over there. It would be preferable in many ways. But we can't decide now. . . . One reason I have in mind for wanting you to be married here is that it would bring D—— here where he could see Prof. T—— again. Just a vague idea an interview might lead to something. But if D—— came over in August and just had time to be married, it wouldn't do much good. T—— probably wouldn't be in New York at that time of year and D—— wouldn't see him. . . .

Lots of love,
MOTHER

A letter from my father:

Greensboro, Vermont
Wednesday, June 19, 1929

DEAR FREDDY:

. . . I suppose when you get this you will be pretty nearly ready to start for home. I can't get the time-pattern straight in my head. Maybe you'll be full of triumph. Maybe you'll have had a lot of disappointment. But in any case it will have been a great adventure—something to remember when you are a happy *Hausfrau*. My Philippine wanderings have been like that to me. I am such a *very* domestic person! And yet I can think of sailing along in the moonlight over a tropic sea; I can think of coco-palms and mipa-thatched huts; I can think of brown men and women and brown little boys and girls, and brown babies, who, as I told their mammas, cried in English. And I can think of riding over a lonely trail in a heavy thunder-storm, and wondering how it could be the same I that was living through that, and that had always lived such a narrow, starved life in Oakland, California.

It's nice to have had some young wanderings.

Much love
DAD

[My father had been among the very first schoolteachers sent by the United States government to the Philippines. His two years on Mindanao, where he was the only white man for miles and had to learn Visayan, as well as the visit to Japan which ended his adventure, made a profound impression on him, and had, in fact, led to the initial suggestion that I study anthropology.]

Of course, as soon as I reached the *Gertrud Rask*, I gave her radio operator messages for my family and D——, explaining my change of plans, and mailed the letters to them which I had written on the island.

I wrote home:

Inugsuk, Upernivik
July 17, 1929

DEAREST FAMILY:

I have a very difficult decision to make, which I hope you will approve. I have already made up my mind unless something in the letters I hope I will receive from you or from D—— will alter it.

You see, we came here to the island on June 27 and have been here only three weeks tomorrow. Any day after the twentieth we may expect the *Gertrud Rask*. She is the second and last ship to Upernivik this year, and by some ill chance will be here long before she was expected. It was intended that I should go back on her. Dr. Mathiassen is staying until the middle of September, when he is taking a small boat to Jakobshavn in South Greenland, where the *Gertrud Rask* is touching on her next trip. I was trying to see if I couldn't possibly return in late August, but there doesn't seem to be any chance. It is now a question of going in three days or waiting until the middle of September. Up to now we have only accomplished enough in our work to see that this midden will furnish very important clues for the chronology of Greenland culture types. It is, moreover, the first properly conducted excavation in Greenland.

There are two cultures represented: a modern (perhaps eighteenth-century) "whalers" culture and a [modified] Thule culture. I feel that to leave now would be to leave before we had really got to the worthwhile bit. We have been able to reach the bottom of the midden only along the edges. The fields [squares] we have opened in the middle have still a lot of work to be done on them. It is fascinating work, and M. is very good about explaining things to me. He has Eskimo archeology at his fingertips, so I am learning a lot.

To stay would give me the chance to see this place finished and to do some exploring, both at the "Old Ships' Harbor" and also to accompany M. on a motorboat trip to the north, almost to Melville Bay. This would be a marvelous experience, for the people there are really primitive.

But to stay would mean that I could not get my degree this coming year. . . . The great advantage I have in staying here is that I am doing my first real work in the field. Three weeks of it seems hardly enough to count, and if, as I intend, this is to become my profession, I should not give up this unique opportunity. I would feel like a fool to return before Dr. Mathiassen. And besides, I am not sure anyway that I could get my degree this next year. Boas, I feel sure, would want me to stay.

The whole trouble is with D——. He, poor boy, is counting on spending his vacation with me in September, and now that will have to be postponed until October. Then, too, it will mean that I must leave him for a while that first year that we are married to finish my degree.

I hope that my decision to stay here has not been too influenced by the fact that I am thoroughly enjoying myself, in a way that I have never experienced before. Dr. Mathiassen is an ideal companion and we get along splendidly together. Although the work is very hard, I am feeling very fit. Besides, everything is so new and exciting. I love to look out of the tent and see the ice in our little harbor, and I love watching our Eskimos and joking with them. So far, I feel that I have only got started, and that the best lies before us. It will, of course, be rather grim and cold here by September, but I think I will enjoy even that. It is all such a splendid adventure.

I should like when I leave to be so trained that I could conduct an expedition like this. I'm making full notes on our equipment, etc., and on our methods, and some briefer notes on the results of our finds. It would be good for me also to have a longer time with Dr. Mathiassen, for when everything is so new it is hard to assimilate all one's impressions, and I haven't learned the different Eskimo archeological types we find here, by a long shot.

This has been a very hard decision to make. I have lain awake for nights worrying and wondering what was the best thing to do. Mathiassen has been very good about letting me make up my mind alone, though he has let me discuss it all with him. He seems to think that if I am to go on with this sort of work at all seriously, three weeks' experience will not cut much ice, and I agree with him. He seems to think there would be many chances for me to get a job as Eskimologist in the United States or Canada, and especially to do excavating in Alaska. Dr. Mathiassen seems to be the only real archeologist in the Arctic field [I did not then know of Diamond Jenness or Henry B. Collins], and I'm his first assistant, aside from the half-breed Olsen when he was in Canada in 1921–23. He would like to have me stay, for he says that I am really useful to him. I am doing all the cooking, except breakfast. He serves that to me in my bag, and besides, I work in the field, too, though I can only stick it as long as the Eskimos, while he goes back to work after our afternoon coffee when the Eskimos go hunting birds and seals. We [Mathiassen and I] take the fields by the edges of the midden which are the most easily spoiled by digging too deeply at the edges where it is most thawed and where one can mix up the levels. Often he gives me one of the men and lets me take charge of a section. Besides that, I always help a lot in the labeling and packing—so I am very glad to be useful and quite proud that he thinks I'm worth my salt.

I wish I knew what D——— and I were to do. I can't bear the thought of giving up all my intellectual work and living in Wales all my life. If only he would come to America! We must have it out when I see him again. I don't want to put undue pressure on him, but I don't see how I could be happy in England. Especially now that I can see openings for continuing this sort of work in America, it seems like a cruel sacrifice to give up all chances by living in England. I am dreadfully afraid that D——— will have gotten into a rut and will not want to pull loose and leave his old mine. I wish he would decide to come to America without my urging, for I should hate to think I forced him to do so against his will, especially if it shouldn't work out as I hope. . . . It seems to me that D——— and I have too much in us that is worthy of something better than a coal mine. . . .

To this I added:

Upernivik
July 26

DEAREST FAMILY:

Your letters from Greensboro have just come. They seem like the nicest letters I have ever got from you. I'm glad I can picture you in Greensboro. If Greenland were not the most wonderful place in the world, I would be homesick for America. I do wish you could share in this. . . . I feel sure now that you would have approved my decision though it was hard to make alone, especially since D—— was counting on our vacation together in September. How I hate to disappoint him! He writes that all he needs is for me to be happy in Wales. But how can I be happy there when I can't go on with my real work? By that, I mean this. I can't bear to think that this is the last time I shall ever dig in the Arctic. If you knew how lame my back gets and how blistered my hands, and yet could see my enthusiasm, you would understand that it is a real love. . . .

You are the best and dearest family and I love to think of you all together there in Greensboro. I am just bursting over with happiness. It is a wonderful world.

All my love,
FREDDY

P.S. I may need more money on coming back to England. Could you send me some—say $200?

Although the answers to these letters did not reach me until much later, I include them here. My mother wrote:

Greensboro, Vermont
August 22, 1929

DEAR FREDDY:

We had a letter from D—— about ten days ago saying you had radioed him that your return was postponed until October.

. . . It must have been some good reason, else you wouldn't have disappointed him about his September holiday. He didn't say much about it in his letter, but one could read between the lines that he was disappointed, for even if you spend as long a time in England when you do get back, it will not be pleasant outdoors weather.

The forty-two-page journal of your voyage arrived a day or two after your father's birthday. It was glorious reading—like a breath from another world. It came just as we were starting over to the Whiteheads for dinner [Alfred North Whitehead, the famous philosopher, and his wife, who had a summer home in Greensboro, too], and I took it along and after dinner read the first part aloud—with expurgations. Everyone enjoyed it immensely. . . .

You know you wrote that you felt as if you were writing from another world in which all the values had somehow changed. Well, your letter gave that sort of impression. It was as if you were changed yourself; all the way through it seemed as if you were half intoxicated. . . .

Love,

MOTHER

My father had been sick but was finally well enough to write:

Greensboro, Vermont

September 1, 1929

DEAREST FREDDY:

Your second batch of diary, with the accompanying letters, came to hand last night, and I have just finished reading them. . . .

You did perfectly right about staying on. To have come home after only three weeks' digging would not only have been missing a great deal of actual profit, but would have given you the stamp of a halfhearted amateur for good. I am not sure but that the expedition is worth more to you than a doctorate—though you ought to have both.

I will send you the extra two hundred dollars when we get back to Bryn Mawr.

[But the letter also contained sober hard truths.]

Your mother and I most earnestly hope that D—— will make up his mind to come to America. . . . Of course, for our own selfish sakes we hope so, for we have not so much in the world that we want to lose you to the extent that your residence in England would mean. But altogether aside from that, it seems to me that the chances for you both having an interesting and happy life are greater on this side. On the other hand, you must not forget that his career must necessarily take precedence over yours if there has to be a conflict. It is he who will have the responsibility of supporting the family, and with that responsibility go some clearly defined rights. He has the right to choose his work and your common residence as he sees fit. Of course, it is his duty to consider your interests and happiness in this as in any other decision, and no doubt he will do so. But the ultimate responsibility in the matter is up to him.

Do not underestimate the value to him of his own work. A dirty coal mine may have something of the same professional interest to him that a dirty midden has for you—not the same romantic interest, to be sure, for there is not the ever-vivid possibility of finding something new and strange. There is, however, the sense of doing a serious and important job as efficiently as one can; and that is a good deal more than many men have.

Nevertheless, when I look at the matter as objectively as I can, it seems to me that it would on the whole be clearly better for you both, if he adopted an academic career and if he followed that career in this country.

In the first place, he has a real interest and talent for research; and that is a very precious thing, not only for the world but for the enrichment of his own life. . . . I think he feels this too.

In the second place, it [an academic job] allows one a free control over a much larger part of one's time. It is not simply the long vacations . . . but the working months too.

[While my father pointed out that, for some, the academic

life cuts one off from practical affairs, this would not be true in engineering. Although the career of mine superintendent would be safe, one probably pays for that in the long run, and there is no doubt that D—— would be a success as a university man. He was disappointed at his first offer, but with his practical experience, he could get a much better offer now.]

There is another matter about which I want to say a few words to you, though. You should realize that, especially in the first years of your married life, you will have immediate duties that must take precedence of any professional ambitions. It is a hard problem, I know, for a woman to reconcile the claims of scholarship with those of motherhood; but your own mother has shown very brilliantly that it can be done. She is now a person of a good deal of distinction, widely respected in her profession. And she has never in any way neglected you or your brother.

Any man who is worth having as a husband wants to have children, and he wants a real home. You can be a mother and also go on expeditions to Greenland and Alaska; but your first obligation is to be a good wife, and that means also a good mother. I am using the word *first* literally. You may very well develop interests and incur obligations which are entirely separate from your husband or your children. But in the early years of married life these must to a great extent yield precedence to the responsibilities of your home.

Don't think that I am advising you to curtail your ambitions. I am urging you to let them expand to the limit. Don't give up the old for the new. Claim both.

Now I am going to stop sermonizing altogether. . . .

Much love,

THE OLD MAN

My mother wrote shortly after their return from Vermont:

221 Roberts Road
Bryn Mawr, Pennslyvania
September 28, 1929

DEAR FREDDY:

It is time to get a letter off if it is to catch you at Copenhagen on your return. . . .

I realize you and D—— have a difficult problem to solve about your residence, and it seems to me he probably feels settled where he is. He should, I suppose, stay there until he gets his Manager's Certificate, in any case. And when he does, of course he will have an assured future with a good salary at once in England against the uncertainty and poorer salary over here. All you can do at present is to let him know how you feel and prevent his settling down to regard the matter as decided. If he can only keep an open mind. If you had definite prospects over here it would make the situation seem different to him. . . .

[Then news of my father's illness, probably the first symptoms of the stroke that was to take him from us in a year's time, though we were mercifully spared that premonition.]

With a great deal of love,
MOTHER

Digging Again

Inugsuk
July 27–August 14

DEAR FAMILY:

I had a good time in what Mathiassen calls "the big city." When we went ashore to see Governor Otto, we found Rasmussen and Freuchen at the house. Freuchen is enormous, with a regular Forty-Niner's beard. He is peg-legged, having lost his foot on the Fifth Thule Expedition. He got two toes frostbitten on an exploring trip. Mathiassen says that he might have saved his foot if he had let an old Eskimo woman cut off his toes, as she wanted to do. He insisted on waiting until summer when he could get to a doctor; by that time his whole foot had rotted, and so he lost it all. He has lived for a long time in Greenland, mostly among the Polar Eskimo at Rasmussen's Cape York trading post. His first wife was a native woman. His present wife was with him on this trip. The Greenlanders call him "Peterssuaq" ("the big Peter"), and it's a fitting name.

(1930: He has just written a splendid novel about the Canadian Eskimo, called *Eskimo*, which had been translated into English. I was surprised, for I had always thought of him as a man of action, not a writer.)

Mathiassen went off to talk to Rasmussen while Freuchen took me to see about my laundry. He took me to Sofie, the best-dressed Eskimo woman in Upernivik. She has a fine house, full of things, and wears skin mosaic on her boots as well as on her pants. When we came back, Mathiassen and I went to the store and bought a lot of things. I bought a pipe. I did not tell you that I have learned to smoke one. I have always wanted to see what it was like. My other pipe was only a clay affair, and I bit off the stem one day when I was digging in a very tough patch of midden. My new pipe is wood, and cost me all of twenty-five cents. I have had to ration myself to three cigarettes a day, so you see a pipe is pretty useful. It doesn't satisfy me as a cigarette does, but it's a cheerful, cuddly thing to hold in one's fingers on a raw day. I also bought some presents for our people; knives for the boys and men, and handkerchiefs for Ane and Malia.

Rasmussen's daughter, Inge, is with him, and there is another girl in the party. They are all going with him on the *Søkongen*, his schooner, to Cape York, where he will collect the year's fox skins from his trading post. It is his daughter's first trip to Greenland. She is just out of school. She was wearing silk stockings and a light summer dress, and seemed very civilized. Can you imagine the contrast we made, sitting in the governor's parlor and chatting, she in her pretty clothes and I in odorous sealskins with chapped and

The *Hans Egede* from above Qutdligssat, midnight, June 15–16

Kayakers and the *Hans Egede* at Umánaq

Kayaker with auks, Ūmánaq

Eskimo children, Ikerasak

An Eskimo woman entering her turf house, Upernivik

Eskimo women, Upernivik

Upernivik church

Our tents from the cliff, Tunúngassoq, Inugsuk

Washing in the sea: myself and Mathiassen

Ane Møller dressing Peter while
Malia watches

Robert washing our dishes

Ole and the pups

Removing turf from below House II

It was a perfect sealskin mitten

Mathiassen painting the baleen mat

The Geodetic Survey visits us. *Left to right, back row:* Lt. Gabel-Jørgensen, Thomasen, Emil, Mathiassen; *middle:* Dr. Christiansen; *front row:* Stenør, Birgette, Sørensen, myself

Karl and I go kayaking. Photo by Mathiassen with my camera

Eskimos, Kûk

House with old-style gutskin pane, Kûk

Old-style skin tent, Kraulshavn

A Greenlander with his young dog, Kraulshavn

Old woman with a pipe, sewing, Kraulshavn

Martin Nielsen and his family, Ikermiut

Man and daughter with new-style skin tent, Kraulshavn

Skin tents and sod houses, Ikermiut

The Devil's Thumb,
Quvdlorssuaq

The *Natarnak* at the Devil's Thumb

Eskimos watching us dig, Holms Ø, the Devil's Thumb

Mathiassen asking the men of Quvdlorssuaq about ruins

Hobbled dogs beside the umiak, Ituvssâlik

Abel Danielsen carries his kayak past his umiak, Ituvssâlik

Caspar Petersen, two girls,
and a youth stop at Inugsuk on
their way to Tasiussaq

Umiak and kayak from Tugssaq

Robert and Mathiassen opening a grave on Sangmissoq

The interior of the grave on Sangmissoq
(*Meddelelser om Grønland*, vol. 77 [4], 1930, fig. 17)

grimy hands! It gave me such a funny feeling to find myself the more experienced person. Up to now I have always been the novice in any group. Mathiassen and I invited Inge and her friend out to spend a night on our island—she has never slept in a tent— but her father was expecting his ship at any moment and was afraid to divide the party. Crossing Melville Bay to Cape York is a terrible undertaking on account of the ice, and he did not want to waste a day.

I had a good talk with Rasmussen. He certainly seems more in his element here than he did in Copenhagen. He is the perfectly charming and witty hero I have always imagined him to be, with the enthusiasm of a small boy and the understanding sympathy of the veteran. I opened my heart to him, and he reassured me that no one ever came to Greenland just once. He insisted that I should write a book about my experiences and lecture before women's clubs about the Arctic, but I only laughed, and would not let him pull my leg. Freuchen was surprised when he learned that I was not the "queen of Inugsuk," as he put it. I told him I was "only one of the boys." Karl had told someone that I dug harder than he did; Freuchen had heard this, and repeated it to me, much to my gratification. Our conversation ended when Freuchen went over to join Mathiassen. Rasmussen and I joined in singing my partner's praises. Rasmussen called him one of the finest men he had ever known, and a bang-up archeologist. I told him that I was grateful to him, Rasmussen, for bringing me to Greenland, since it was he who had given Mathiassen his chance, a debt of gratitude which he had repaid by doing the same for another youngster.

Freuchen now came over to announce that the natives were having a dance at the warehouse, and that we must all go down and join them. Ruth Otto was going, all dressed up in native costume. The dance was in the warehouse at the harbor, and the room was packed to the doors. How the natives laughed at me in my man's dress! They were dancing to a concertina propelled by the captain of the *Hvalen*, a man whom I never know whether to class as a white man or a Greenlander. The dances were old whaler's dances, and how I thanked Miss Applebee and May Day at Bryn Mawr, for the steps were just like the old English country dances that we had learned at college. I danced with Thomassen, and another little Eskimo whom I had never seen before, and with Rasmussen, who was far the best dancer of any in the room, and who did ten steps to the others' five. Freuchen collected our wraps, as we peeled them off in the heat of the dance, and stood holding them like Santa Claus at one end of the hall. I was very sorry that Mathiassen does not dance. I wanted him to try, but he absolutely refused. He wanted Robert to dance with me, but Robert would not, either because he was too shy to dance with a white woman, or because he was ashamed to appear with a girl in man's trousers. It was very curious to have the "wallflower" feeling with Robert, and have him rank as a possible partner, i.e., as a social equal—or, rather, as a superior. After a time Mathiassen and I left the dance. It had become very hot and crowded, and, to tell the truth, I was not sorry to escape the gibes of the little girls, who thought my costume very funny.

We walked to the top of the hill. It was no longer covered with snow but with yellow Arctic poppies. I asked Mathiassen why he still called me "Miss," and if he would not use my first name, but he was quite shocked. It seems that people don't call each other by their first names in Denmark unless they are extremely intimate. The most informal title he has for me is "partner."

The next day we finished our shopping and got off our mail. The captain gave a luncheon party at which Freuchen made a long speech, a custom to which the Danes are addicted, and to which they yield at the slightest excuse. It must have been a funny speech, for everyone was convulsed, and told me afterwards that he had complained about Mathiassen's and my unwashed condition.

Everyone urged us to stay another night, but Mathiassen was homesick for his midden, so we left at four o'clock, as per schedule. We did not see Rasmusseen or Freuchen again in Greenland.

Our voyage back to Inugsuk was very cold. Ane had little Jens with her, the nine-year-old boy who has been sick with tuberculosis at the hospital. Freuchen says that the whole family is tainted with the disease and that Karl used to be very sick and for several years was unable to hunt. That explains his labored breathing and his need for frequent rests, though Robert calls him an old man (he is only forty-five). Jens was wearing the beautiful new clothes which the people at the hospital had given him. He was clean all over, and looked very civilized compared to his little brothers and sister. We wondered how long he would stay that way. The whole family was exhausted and fell asleep on the deck. I wonder if they had as good a time as they had expected? They certainly had the "morning after" look; Ane's new red boots had burst their seams; Ole and Malia were dirty again, and Robert, who had bought a new pair of pants at the store, in which he had proudly strutted all over the village, was back in his rags again. I am afraid their trip to the colony was not altogether a success, for they were poorly dressed in comparison with the others there. But Robert, at any rate, now owned a shotgun, bought with his first wages.

It was with a glad feeling of homecoming that we sighted the tents and the black midden. We were happy to be back on our own little island.

That night we were out to dig at the edge of the bank. I was really tired, more tired than I would admit to myself, and in consequence did a foolish thing. Mathiassen does not really approve of digging along the edge of the midden, because it is much more difficult to dig without hurting specimens, especially long baleen objects whose other ends are frozen fast in the bank. One's natural inclination is to grab the end sticking out and give a heave, which is not at all the thing to do. This was just the mistake which I made. I came to the end of a flat board, about two inches wide, and not thinking much about it, tried to pull it out. The end broke off, and I tossed it carelessly aside. I was terribly chagrined when a few minutes later I got out the other end, only to find that it was one of the wooden handles which have for so long mystified Eskimo archeologists. We have already found a good many of these handles, but most of them are broken off just above the grip, so Mathiassen was very anxious to find as many examples of the complete implement as he could. And now I had broken what would, perhaps, have been our best specimen. I could have cried. Of course, I hunted everywhere for the end, but though I looked for it that night and the next morning, and though we set the children to work with promises of biscuits, it was never found.

These wooden handles are very interesting. Mathiassen found them in the Thule culture villages of Baffinland and they have been found in ancient sites on the now uninhabited coast of Northeast Greenland. They all have a well-made grip, with a place cut out for the fingers and for the thumb to encircle the shaft, and a depression on the upper side for the fingertips. They are about a foot long, and end in a rough point, or blunt tip, on either side of which is a notch. Something has evidently been lashed on here. All we know about this implement is that it was very important in the life of the people, because we have found so many examples of it; that it was something the children loved to play with, because we have found many of them fitted to a child's hand as well as miniature models for dolls; and that it was something which received hard use, since so many of them are broken. The careful carving of the grip means that it was an implement which required accurate manipulation. The style of the grip is like that on some of the throwing boards. Of course, we are forever handling these implements, and trying to guess what they could have been used for. None of our Eskimos, of course, had ever seen anything like them. Some archeologist suggested that they were used as meat sticks, and that the handle was made to prevent the stick from slipping when covered with blubber. But this explanation did not suit us for several reasons. I was convinced that it must have been some kind of throwing handle, and tried to prove my point by making one and attaching a sling to the end, but as I am not skillful in that kind of thing, my attempts to demonstrate the sling theory were not very impressive. The boys laughed at me. Mathiassen did not say much, either.

(1930: I was very pleased to see that in his report Mathiassen does consider the suggestion which I made that these handles may have been used as sling handles. Slings are known to have been a very important weapon among the Eskimo in former times, but since no example of them has ever been found by an archeologist, we do not know what they were like. It seems, however, that the Chukchi, a tribe in northeastern Siberia, neighbors of the Eskimo and related to them in culture, used "whip slings" with handles. The Icelandic-Greenland sagas mention a sling, which they called *valslaungur*, to which a handle was attached. They compared it to the *fustilabus* of the Romans, which was also a stave sling.)

[1975: Henry B. Collins, who read this manuscript, wrote me: "By the way, if you need proof of your original theory that these were sling handles, we got it at Resolute, in 1953. One complete example, a toy, had part of the leather thong attached. H. B. C." (Collins excavated a number of Thule culture sites at Resolute Bay, Corwallis Island, in Arctic Canada.)]

On July 29 we got out 120 specimens, including the little tub. We painted the baleen parts, wrapped the whole thing in toilet paper, and poured plaster of Paris over it before we lifted it from its icy bed. Then the inside had to be stuffed, and the outside swaddled in cotton wool. We packed it in a biscuit tin, along with a few other precious objects. Mathiassen calls it "the baby."

Late in the afternoon we heard the rapid chug-chugging of our old friend the *Umarissoq*. It brought Sørensen and the other geodeters, Gabel-Jørgensen and Stenør, and Miss Christiansen, the Ūmánaq doctor, who just came for the ride. They refused our invitation to dinner, but had us on board to a swell meal. I took my picture of Sørensen in his dogskin *anorak*. We traded some of the twenty eider ducks we had just brought from Upernivik for some pork, a paper sack of new potatoes, and a hunk of seal meat, which they advised me to fry with onions. They were on their way to the Devil's Thumb, one hundred miles farther north, and would not spend the night with us. They left immediately after dinner.

That night we had a lot of packing to do, especially of long and fragile baleen things—sledge shoes, snow-beaters, mats, etc. I don't like the job of painting them late in the day: my fingers get too cold.

The next day we found 130 specimens, a new record. These included a louse-catcher, our second one, made of a baleen strip folded over a tuft of bear's fur. Our first louse-catcher was just an ordinary one, a tuft of white bear's hair wound about the end of a stick. The Eskimo are terribly troubled with lice, and manage to catch a few by poking a louse-catcher down the back of their necks and pulling the lice from the white fur. Mathiassen says that the Canadian Eskimo like European underwear because it is white and they can see the lice on it.

It was Jens' birthday, and we were invited up to the Eskimos' tent after lunch for coffee and white bread, which Ane had baked at home in Upernivik. We gave him a red kerchief full of candy. Ane had moved the box in front of the platform and had covered it with a white cloth and a few sheets from a magazine I had given her. Mathiassen and I were made to sit behind the table in the place of honor, and the meal was conducted in the most solemn fashion. Since they had no milk for the coffee, we drank it Greenland style, that is, nibbling at a lump of sugar between sips. The handkerchief seems to have been much appreciated, for Jens appeared in it, tied around his head, as I wear mine. I was astonished to see that he would imitate a woman, but perhaps he thought that I was following a man's style of wearing a bandanna, since I tie mine at the nape of the neck, while the Greenland girls wear their kerchiefs tied under their chins. Malia and the baby also wore Jens' bandanna.

That night we had fried cod and seal meat. Niels had caught the fish at Upernivik. I fried the seal meat with onions, and it was magnificent—tender, rich, and black with blood. It was a delicious meal.

The sun was so warm in the morning, July 31, that I had to lie in the grass, but was roused when Mathiassen announced the discovery of a stone floor in the old midden, near the big house ruin. We could not uncover all of it that day, for the stones at the back were covered with frozen earth. We found fragments of a baleen net there, which we called a fish net. It is not certain if the Eskimo used fish nets before the coming of the Danes. Mathiassen does not know what this net was used for, since we also found a drying frame of baleen, a hoop with a net across the bottom.

Today was Niels' birthday, though his parents were not sure whether he was fourteen or fifteen. He is very small for either age. We gave Ane the remains of the seal meat and told her to cook it, so we joined the Eskimos in their tent for a real Greenland dinner of boiled seal meat and black coffee. Mathiassen does not care for seal meat, but I found it not so bad, only rather curious. It tastes very "fishy" boiled, though "fishy" is not the correct expression, for the meat does not taste like fish, but like eider ducks or auks that eat fish. I like the rich, gamy taste, though the seal is rather strong. I am told that when boiled it should be soaked for half a day to get some of the blood out, or it will taste very rank, but that spoils it for frying. When it is fried, it should be full of blood, and black. I hate the idea of going back to eat our pale, washed-out meats, after living on this rich food. I am sure I will be hungry, and though our diet is now a little monotonous, I know I will remember it longingly. Our Eskimos have no plates, so we ate the meat with our fingers and a knife. The ribs are considered the best portions, though I like the meat next to the bigger bones. One is supposed to eat the blubber with the meat as it comes, but there is too much of it to suit my taste. Mathiassen dared me to eat a mouthful of pure blubber. It tasted like an old rubber boot flavored with cod-liver oil, to which as you know I have a profound aversion. Blubber mixed with meat is not so bad, for the meat is dry without it. Eating without plates or forks is, of course, the most interesting way of eating seal meat, but by far the messiest. A whole new system of table manners is required, which I have not yet learned. We gave Niels a few presents. Mathiassen gave him a little notebook and pencil, and I gave him a pocket comb which a classmate at college had given me. That afternoon we served chocolate, not coffee, in our tent. We were hungry all day, for there had not been enough meat for so big a crowd, and our European appetites feel cheated if there is nothing but meat.

The *Umarissoq* stopped on her way south, and again they entertained us for supper, this time on boiled seal meat with pickles and mustard. But we were still so hungry that at 11:30 we cooked ourselves a fish supper.

After the *Umarissoq* had gone, a kayaker arrived from Augpilagtoq. He introduced himself as Enoch Petersen, and when he heard my partner was "*the* Tikile," he gave us an enormous hunk of seal meat and refused all payment. He told Mathiassen that he had read of him in Jacob's book in Eskimo about the adventures of the Fifth Thule Expedition among the Akilinermiut ("people of the other side," the Canadian Eskimo)—Jacob was Mathiassen's assistant. I was tremendously impressed by this gesture, and as proud of my teacher as Kim of his. All white people in Greenland have Eskimo nicknames, but Mathiassen is one of the few people who are openly called by their Eskimo names. Freuchen, "Peterssuaq," and Rasmussen, "Kununguaq" ("little Knud"), are also called by their Eskimo names. I must have a nickname, too, but we have never found out what it is. We invited Enoch in to pancakes and coffee, the first pancakes he had ever eaten, I suppose, for he seemed to have a dreadful time controlling his knife and fork, and would not venture on a second.

The next day, August 1, we again found 130 specimens, which meant a lot of work packing. That night when we were in bed, we heard the sound of oars, and saw a big whaleboat, with the priest from Upernivik, row between our island and Sangmissoq. They landed on the nearest point of Inugsuk, just north of us. The next morning the priest called on us, and we gave him tea. He, his wife and three daughters, and six rowers had all camped in one tent. Already the place began to look inhabited, with a new midden, consisting of last night's bird bones, scattered down the bank. I took a color picture of the crowd lying and sitting in the sun. We invited the priest and his wife to lunch with us. We had eider duck's breasts, fried in margarine, and a washbasin full of mashed potatoes. I am glad to say we gave them more than they could eat, which is the standard of a good meal in these parts. But when they had left, I felt that I never wanted to see a potato again. I suppose I should not call him a priest. The Danes are Lutherans, not Catholics, but Mathiassen always calls the ministers "priests."

It froze during the night, but only a little, and the ice in the water pail broke easily. Robert slept until lunch, which meant that the rest of us had extra work to do in order to finish the half of the fields which we usually dig over before eating. I dug over five fields and cleaned off the stone floor near the big house ruin for photographing. In order that they might show up properly, I scrubbed off each stone, and pressed the dirt away from it. Mathiassen drew sketches in case the pictures failed, while I set up his big camera, focused, deliberated over the exposure, and finally took the pictures. I enjoy taking pictures, and Mathiassen does not care much for it. Mathiassen does not use a table for exposures, but his guesses usually check with my elaborate calculations, so he has confidence in my exposures. We will not have any pictures developed until we go back to Copenhagen, so we can only do our best and pray that we are not making some terrible mistake.

The tide was very low that afternoon, so I went across to Sangmissoq to dig in the remains of a turf house just above high-tide line. I found nothing of any interest except a few scraps of the "Royal Copenhagen" pattern and the flowered china which we have been finding in the younger midden on our own island. Mathiassen figures that our young midden once extended across to Sangmissoq and that the land has sunk two meters (a little over six feet) since the house ruins were built. In the church records Tunúngassoq and Sangmissoq are called "Qeqertaq," which also shows that they were one island. The last record of the village here was in 1855, and Mathiassen believes that the sinking of the land and the encroachment of the sea was what caused the people to move away. The oldest house ruins at the bottom of the old midden are dug into the moraine, and they are now below the high-tide line. The land has been sinking at about the rate of one meter a century, so it may have sunk six or seven meters since the first people came here. The midden that is left now must be only a scrap of the great deposits here in former times.

After all this digging I was so exhausted that I could hardly eat any supper, and Mathiassen scolded me for working so hard. We packed after supper, and by that time I was rested, so we went across to Inugsuk in the evening "afternoon" and climbed to the highest top of the island, a hill about 250 feet high, and almost due north of us, but hidden from Tunúngassoq by a lesser summit, which we have named "White Hill." Inugsuk is made up of gneiss or granite of two colors, one light gray and the other red. The rock is very much contorted, and I have not been able to discover which rock has intruded into which. The view from the top is glorious. To the north is Upernivik Icefjord, with the Qagsserssuaq massif blue in the faint sunlight and a series of unknown islands behind Tugssaq. The bays and fjords are packed with ice. To the east rises the chaotic mass of Târtoq, whose red rocks are so split by joint planes that it looks like a Cubistic nightmare. The islands to the south are dominated by the majestic white pyramid of Qaerssorssuaq.

We built a beacon on the top of Inugsuk and so were not in bed until two in the morning.

The next day, August 4, was Sunday, which means harder work than ever. We slept until noon, when we had "lunchfast," and then rowed over to Inugsuk, where we climbed to the beacon and took several photographs and made sketches of the harbor. Mathiassen is anxious to have a good collection of sketches from all possible angles, to help him make a map for the publication. Unfortunately, he was no surveying instruments; otherwise it would be easy. We walked north from the beacon to a second hill and built another cairn on top of the ruins of the fox trap. The land at this part of the island is incredibly bare—nothing but polished granite and boulders. Of course, if one looks, one finds a number of small mosses, lichens, and little flowering plants, but they count for nothing.

We also went over to the point in back of Sangmissoq, to a ruined settlement called Qamaneq. There is a long stone house here, and two newer houses, one of turf and quite modern, and the other of stone and square like our own *iglorssuaq* (House II). We poked about and found a few pieces of junk at the modern house ruins—scraps of iron, china, and a few glass beads. There is no midden in front of the long house, for the sea is washing against its walls. It is about eight by three meters, with the long side parallel to the shore, and the door passage running out of the northeast corner. We began to dig in the house just inside the door. It was very hard work prying up the stones and turf and heaving them over the wall. The rewards were slight, moreover, for there was only a scanty cultural deposit inside. The specimens we found were badly rotted. We decided to come back another day and finish the work. Mathiassen thinks the house dates from Hans Egede's time, when several families shared a long house, as they now do on the East Coast. Our backs were very lame that night.

Karl saw a seal next day, so we sent him off hunting. We dug after dinner until the rain came. In all we had 150 specimens to pack, counting our Sunday's finds. We had a comb with a high, narrow openwork handle, with a border of alternating spur lines running around the hole. Both the style of the comb and the spur-line decoration are typical Thule culture features. We also found a wooden doll representing a man at the W.C. The squatting attitude and the tense, expectant expression of the whole body made the artist's intention quite evident. It was very cleverly carved, and very funny.

On August 7, Mathiassen started a new method of digging. He selected a narrow field near the cliff, and had us save all the bones in each layer. There were tons of bones. In the afternoon we gave Karl all those from the top layer and asked him to divide them up into piles, one pile for each kind of animal. It was wonderful to see the skill with which he classified, to us unrecognizable, fragments, and to hear the reasons he gave for his choices. The animals were: caribou, bear, dog, whale, and, in larger numbers, white whale and narwhal, bearded seal, hooded seal, Greenland seal, and especially the little fjord seal. Unfortunately, there did not happen to be any bird or fish bones in this section, nor any bones of fox or hare, though Mathiassen has recognized them in other parts of the midden. We counted the bones in each of Karl's piles, and saved samples to check his guesses. We did the same thing for all the other layers of the section, though we have not yet got to the bottom of it. The bone-collecting job was not very interesting, because there was very little else in the section. The same species of animals seem to be represented in the lower layers that were found in the upper, the bones only dwindling in numbers and increasing in rottenness. There seem to have been more whales killed in former days, however, than in the later periods of habitation. There do not seem ever to have been many walrus about, for we found few things of ivory, and there are no walrus here now. Mathiassen saved *all* of the animal bones from Naujan in the Canadian Arctic. He was hoping, I suppose, that there had been some important change in the animal life that would help in dating his finds. But even though nothing much comes of all the work of saving and identifying bones, it is the proper thing for an archeologist to do.

One of the most interesting things we have found so far was a baleen dish with a wooden bottom, containing blubber and seal meat. Mathiassen found it under a stone, where some ancient Eskimo had hidden it. We packed it very carefully. It will make a fine display in the museum. I am very much amused that our Eskimos have taken to collecting the more blubbery bits of turf from the midden and are burning them. They burn slowly, for there is much moisture in the turf, but it makes a very hot fire.

We have achieved 3,000 specimens!

For several days we have been suspecting that the caramels which Dr. Bertelsen gave us are disappearing too fast to be natural. We counted them to make sure if anyone were stealing them. Mathiassen suspects the children, who may come into the tents when we are at work. Mathiassen drew a line around the few remaining caramels in the box and wrote beside them: *"Tigdligtut piumangilara Inugsukme, Tikile"* ("I don't want thieves on Inugsuk, Therkel"), in the hopes that this would stop the petty thieving, which we cannot afford. But if the little children took some candy, who can blame them?

One afternoon an Eskimo man came to visit us and to sell seal meat and dogskins. It was Cornelius from Tunorqo. He and his family were camping on the far side of Inugsuk. Mathiassen bought a fine dogskin from him, complete with ears, tail, and paws, which he put under his sleeping bag. He is going to give it to Mrs. Otto. We also bought some meat, including the liver, which is fine, but the piece was so big that it spoiled before we could finish it. I gave the rotted piece to Ane for the dogs, but I believe the Eskimos ate it. Why is it that rotted meat gives us ptomaine at home but that the natives seem to be able to eat it here and enjoy it?

The weather that afternoon was magnificent, with bright sunshine and no wind, so I asked Karl if he would take me kayaking. He thought it was a good joke, and brought Robert's kayak down to the water. I got into it and at first paddled very slowly around the harbor, and then, growing bolder, went down to the southern point of Inugsuk, rounded the point, until before I knew it we were well on our way to visit Cornelius' family. Karl stuck close beside me. He seemed to be favorably impressed with my skill in the kayak, and joked with me, telling me I might paddle all the way to Upernivik. He afterwards spoke about it to the doctor. When we passed the place where I had lost my knife in the water the afternoon Mathiassen and I went exploring, I tried to tell Karl, but I know too few words. I evidently used the wrong local expression; there are any number of words: *uwani, dawani, pawani,* meaning "near me," "near you," "over there," etc. Karl tried to explain to me, by pointing in different directions and saying the different words. However, I thought he was trying to explain which word to use for the near places and which for the far places. Really he was saying "in the north," "to the south," etc., for the same words are also used for the different points of the compass as well as for up and down.

Cornelius' family were camped under their umiak, at the head of the bay on the south side of Inugsuk. They had built a low wall of stones and turf upon which one side of the boat rested, and they had fitted turf about the other side, which rested on the ground. There was a gap in the middle of the wall, covered by a skin hanging from the gunwhale, which served as a doorway. It must have been very dark and uncomfortable inside, for there was hardly room to sit upright. The woman was cooking over a heather fire in the shelter of a rock. There was an open meat cache and seal meat spread in the sun to dry. We were given some of it. It is tasteless, tough stuff, like shreds of leather, and eating it was thirsty work. There were three young dogs tied up behind the camp with lumps of ice to lick. The children were unusually unattractive. Some of them looked like the bastards of a moronic white man.

We stayed only a short time at their camp, for I was afraid that Mathiassen might be anxious if we did not return soon. I should have liked to go on around the island, and tried to ask Karl which was the quickest way back, but since I understood him to indicate the way we had come, we returned by the same route. A little breeze had sprung up and my progress was quite wobbly. I got well splashed about the arms, and was very lame before we got home. Luckily, Mathiassen had been so hard at work that he had not noticed how late it was.

That night Thomassen from Tugssaq paid us a short visit and was entertained at supper.

Karl came down to us after supper to tell us that Robert was suffering from a badly infected finger. He had complained of it several days before, and I had examined it. I could see no break in the skin and so concluded that it was sprained. I had washed it in disinfectant and wrapped it up with a bandage to keep him from using it, but now it was so swollen and painful that he could not sleep. We found him sitting beside a little fire, swabbing his hand in hot water. Mathiassen decided that he must go to Upernivik, so he sent him and Karl off at once in their kayaks. It was lucky that Robert was able to paddle.

The next day, August 8, it rained a little but cleared again. With only Niels' help we dug over all the fields. It was hard work, especially the shoveling. Niels also had to take Robert's place at the dish-"*vask*-ing," which he did not seem to enjoy. We rewarded him by inviting him to supper. That night we had a feast to celebrate the 3,000 specimens and Mathiassen's twins' birthday. We had ham, new potatoes, our last can of asparagus, and Tokay. (I seem to say a great deal about our food. You are probably bored with hearing what we had to eat, but it is a matter of intense interest to us, especially to me, who have such a vigorous appetite, and to whom this food is still so delightful and strange. Ordinary days, when we don't do anything unusual or find anything exciting, I keep track of in my mind by the menus.) This birthday dinner lasted until 9:30, and we were up till 1 A.M. packing specimens.

August 9 was a red-letter day. We began by finding a perfect little dagger of baleen, with a baleen cord to hang it. You probably wonder that baleen was used as a weapon, but when new it is surprisingly tough, though springy, of course, and can be cut to a very sharp edge. We have found many blades for harpoon or lance heads of it. Mathiassen also found another baleen drum frame in perfect condition. The most spectacular find was a wooden doll, which I came upon. It was only about two inches high, and had unfortunately been burned about the feet. It was armless, and had no features, after the fashion of Eskimo dolls. The waist was very small, the hips flaring, so that it must have been a woman with a garment fitting closely about the waist and full at the hips. The headdress was the most curious of all, for it was apparently made of a separate piece of material which fell below the shoulders in front and behind, giving the woman the appearance of a nun. If anything was clear, it was that the woman was not an Eskimo at all! I announced my discovery as "Gertrud Rask," but of course the doll was older than that. Mathiassen believes it to represent a Norse woman, for the costume looks very much like the wonderful dresses excavated in the Norse churchyard in South Greenland. Unfortunately, no women's headcloths were found there, though there are old paintings with which to compare the doll. The old style of headcloth is still worn by nuns, which accounts for the religious look of the doll. The more we think about it, the more wonderful it seems that such a thing should have been found. Now this will give us a method of dating the old midden. (1930: In his report Mathiassen suggests that the doll may represent a man and not a woman, since the style of dress was very similar for both sexes. If it is a man, the length of the frock shows that it was of the same style as men's dresses in Norway between the twelfth and the middle of the fourteenth century.)

We have also found two other objects which suggest contact with the Norsemen. The first was a lump of metal, which looked like silver and was quite heavy, but which, unlike silver, had a greenish tarnish. Mathiassen thinks that it may be the same metal as the alloy out of which the Norsemen made their church bells. (1930: A chemical analysis showed that this lump was an alloy of copper and tin, of the same kind that was used for bells. Many lumps of bell metal have been found in Greenland, in the old Norse colony at Gardar, and also at Itivdlilik in Upernivik District, which we later visited.)

The third object which may show contact with the Norsemen was a little wooden carving. On one side of the wood was a face— that of a woman?—with long pointed chin and narrow nose. On the forehead is a thick band, which at first we interpreted as a brow band, but Mathiassen decided that it must be the brim of a hat or cap. On the other side of the wooden plaque is a carving in low relief of a twisted scroll or knot. We saw at once that it was not an Eskimo design, but until we found the Norse doll a few days later we thought that the design of the plaque might be Indian. It is probably a crude imitation, however, by an Eskimo artist of the elaborate scroll carving of the Norsemen, examples of which have been dug up in the ruins of one of the Norse churches in South Greenland.

These three objects were all found at about the same relative depth of the midden, that is, about one-third of the way up. We cannot help wondering how they got here, and whether there may not be some basis of truth in the old Eskimo legend. Perhaps the Norsemen who left the runic stone on Kingigtorssuaq were the ones with whom our Inugsuk Eskimo came in contact. If these finds can be dated by the runic stone as belonging to the thirteenth century, then this checks nicely with Mathiassen's estimate of the age of his Thule culture villages in Canada. The land there has risen twenty meters since Naujan was built, and estimating the rate of the rising of the land there by that in Scandinavia, he finds that Naujan must be about one thousand years old. Our village, then, is perhaps some seven hundred or eight hundred years old, which leaves about the right lapse of time required for the migra-

Objects showing intercourse with Norsemen, from the "old midden,"
Tunúngassoq, Inugsuk
(*Meddelelser om Grønland*, vol. 77 [4], 1930, pl. 22)

1. Lump of church bell metal (6 cm. long).   2. Fragment of woven woolen
cloth.   3–4. Eskimo dolls representing Norsemen.   5. Eskimo carving of a Norse
face and scroll design.   6. Eskimo spinning top made from a Norse piece for
checkers.

tion of the Thule Eskimo to North Greenland and down the West Coast to Upernivik, and for the development of their culture from the original Naujan phase to the Inugsuk phase.

There are several other things which suggest contact with the Norsemen, though that contact may not have been direct. We have found several harpoon heads with metal blades, and several heads and knife handles with very thin blade slits, evidently intended to hold metal and not stone blades. The metal seems to be iron. The Eskimo, we know, had access to natural iron in the form of meteoric and telluric iron, which are very pure forms of the metal. They did not know how to work it, however, but used to chip off tiny flakes and haft them just as they would a piece of flint or any other stone. It is possible, however, that the iron we have found at Inugsuk, or some of it, was obtained from the Norsemen, either directly or through trade with Eskimo tribes to the south. (1930: An analysis of the iron blades in two harpoon heads shows that the iron is the same kind of damascened steel, on the border line between wrought iron and true steel, which the Norsemen made. It is the type of iron used in the early Iron Age in Europe.)

We found some knife handles with extension of the bone handle into a sort of blade, with grooves along the edge to hold a metal blade, or a row of metal blades. It was evidently an attempt to imitate the steel-bladed knives of the Norsemen, but the Eskimo did not have enough iron to make the whole blade of it. (1930: My little baleen dagger Mathiassen believes to be an imitation, in baleen, of a Norseman's steel knife.)

Mathiassen believes that the tubs and pails which our Inugsuk Eskimo made were patterned after the Norsemen's tubs and barrels. The Eskimo have always been very clever in patching together small pieces of wood to make something large, but it is significant that it is only in Greenland, where they had a chance to learn from the Norsemen, that they mastered the principle of coopering.

We have several blades of baleen, notched along one edge, which Mathiassen believes are saws, imitated from the saws of the Norsemen.

We have found many pretty bodkins, some of wood, and others, usually larger and better made, of bone and ivory. They have decorations of different kinds. On the top of one ivory pin is a face; on a smaller antler bodkin is a little knob like a woman's topknot; on another is a hanging link carved from the same piece of ivory. These were something that women used or wore, for they have been found in women's graves, but we are not sure just what their use was. All of the bodkins have what we should call a "turned" decoration, consisting of rows of raised bands around the pin near the head, something like the rings about chair legs or banister pillars. These bodkins are very common in old West Greenland sites, but do not belong to the Thule culture of Canada. Mathiassen wonders if there is not some connection between them and the styli with which the Norsemen used to write on wax tablets, though, of course, the Eskimo did not write and must have used their bodkins for some very different purpose.

The style of decoration of the spoons, with their narrow, oval bowls and pretty openwork handles, is just like that of medieval spoons, or like the old-fashioned antler spoons used by the Lapps today.

So in many ways, you see, the Inugsuk Eskimo must have learned from the Norsemen.

It was a really hot day and the water looked tempting. After we had stood about and admired the wooden doll, I went in wading, to the astonishment of the Greenlanders. I climbed onto a cake of ice that was stranded on the beach. It felt like a hot stove burning the soles of my feet. I had to run out of the water and rub my numb toes to get them warm again.

We got Karl to draw a map of Inugsuk. At first he refused to try, but when we gave him paper and pencil to take to his own tent, he succeeded in making quite a fair map. We did some rough surveying of the island and found his map to be pretty accurate for the main outlines, though the lakes in the interior, which have no sense to them anyway, he had hopelessly confused. He had also omitted several obvious little points and bays in the harbor across from our island.

The next rainy day we started something which I had been

wanting to do for a long time—we made an index of all the types which we have found, indicating for each the specimen numbers and the locations where they were found. It is astonishing to see how many different things we have found and what are the most common types, and also what belongs in the old midden and what in the new. Of course, we have not yet been able to finish this index; we will probably be working on it for days. Mathiassen reads the information to me out of his notebooks, and I make the cards, one for each type, and jot down the specimen numbers in their proper places. Mathiassen has been telling me which types are common Eskimo, which belong to the Thule culture, which are found only in Greenland, which are very modern, and which have never been found in Greenland before. We are very proud of our list of "never-before-found." Quite a few objects are unique in the Eskimo world. We are also keeping a separate list of all the objects made of baleen. These people used baleen for many purposes, so much so that Mathiassen calls this a baleen culture.

We also beguiled the rainy day by drawing pictures. I drew cartoons of us all: Mathiassen in his bald, shabby pants, Robert out hunting in his kayak with only the little *teist* behind him to show for his trouble, and Malia with the baby, her old boots full of creases and sliding down over her knees. How the Eskimos laughed when they saw the pictures! Ane felt a little ashamed that I had noticed Malia's shabby boots, for a day or so later we saw Malia appear in a new pair. Karl was much impressed with my artistic ability and told Mathiassen that the women of his people could not do such things. This put Ane on her mettle, and she demanded paper and pencil at once. She drew pictures of Mathiassen and myself beside our tents, and also cut out and drew figures of an Eskimo woman and an Eskimo girl in party dress.

The next morning I woke up to see three little birds wading in front of the tent. They were black and white, and about the size of robins. I do not know what they were. I would have called Mathiassen to look at them, but I was afraid of frightening them, and they had gone by the time he was awake.

It was Sunday again, so we dug only until noon, and then

Paper dolls of West Greenland woman and girl, by Ane Møller

started to make a survey of Inugsuk. We used the measured line along the back of the midden for a base line, and with my compass sighted to various points on Inugsuk and our own island. Because of the masses of magnetic ore all over Greenland, we eventually had to abandon this method, and learned never to trust the compass.

While we were working, Cornelius and his family stopped by on their way home to Tunorqo. I think our children must have been sorry to see them go, for they have been rather lonely on the island, and while Cornelius' children were on Inugsuk they had company. Our children used to row across the harbor, where the other children met them, and then they would all come back here, to play till all hours of the night.

It was a very hot day, so after we were finished with our surveying, I took out the last of our lemons and made some lemonade. Mathiassen was very anxious to see how it would taste—I don't think he had ever tasted American-style lemonade—but alas, the stone on which I set the pitcher was not steady and it all was spilled. Instead, we had to make coffee, to which we invited "Gunila" (Cornelius). Later that day his brother Pelle came. There are three brothers living at Tunorqo with their families. We have now seen all the brothers, but we have never met the old father.

We noticed that there is no longer any midnight sun, but just when the sun began to hide itself for a few moments behind the Inugsuk hills we cannot say.

We had marked out a field inside House II, far enough inside the walls so that they would not collapse, and now, August 12, we arrived at the bottom, forty centimeters below the level of the first floor. There have been a whole series of stone floors, with moss growing between the layers. The specimens, however, all belonged to the new midden, and did not show any development in type. About thirty centimeters below the lowest floor of the house we came upon another floor, this one belonging to a house of Thule times. Evidently, the later Eskimo built right upon the ruins of the medieval house, probably using the old stones as building material.

For some days I had been collecting all the scraps of wood I could find. Most of them came from the midden, and had been discarded by Mathiassen because they were not good enough to be specimens. I wanted to cook over an open fire. I have the feeling that I do not understand a strange food until I have prepared it myself, and that I do not know how meat really tastes until I have broiled it over an open fire. Mathiassen cannot understand my love for picnicking and open-fire cooking. In Denmark there are no woods where people can go to build little fires for lunch. Like a man, he prefers his food at a comfortable table. By August 13, I had enough wood for my fire. I had not enough paper for kindling, and even when we poured kerosene on the fire it would not burn properly. I blew and blew until I was exhausted. The wood, filthy with ancient blubber and goodness knows what other stuff, gave off a deadly smoke which made the tears stream down my cheeks. Mathiassen tried to dissuade me from this torment, and all the Eskimos laughed at me, but I was determined to eat my meat broiled. So I stuck to the job, while Mathiassen slipped inside and started the Primus. At last I had a very dry piece of meat, smoked, not cooked, and very raw inside, which I ate. As the auks had already begun to rot a little, it was not very good. Mathiassen stuck his head out of the tent and called me. Bless him! He had a fine dinner all ready for me, with fried auk breasts and our last can of peas.

After dinner we surveyed the southeast part of Inugsuk, measuring the angles with my compass, and building beacons on two hills back of Qamaneq. Then we took Niels and rowed north up the fjord to a little island next to Inugsuk, called Tortlarpiq, where Karl thought we would find house ruins. It was the first time we had rowed north along the east side of Inugsuk. The sunset colors in the sky were magnificent. Niels and Mathiassen rowed and I sat curled up in the stern, doing nothing, and quite happy. There were no house ruins on the island, only a few graves, which we did not touch.

When we were in Upernivik, Mathiassen made all the arrangements about a trip to the north. There are many old sites between Upernivik and the Devil's Thumb, one hundred miles to the north, which he wants to explore. He finds that he can hire one of the fishing boats from Prøven, which will not be used at this time of year. He plans to take it for two weeks. We cannot have it longer, because it will be needed for the white whale hunting, which begins September 1, when the white whales begin to migrate south.

On the morning of August 14, the day before we expected the motorboat, I woke up with the most vivid dream that I have ever known. I dreamed that Mathiassen and I had gone home to Bryn Mawr for a weekend visit and that I told my family all about our proposed trip north, even giving the Eskimo name, Quvdlorssuaq, for the Devil's Thumb. I also discussed with Mother whether or not I should buy skins for a fur coat while I was north, but decided not to do so. Then we came back to Greenland. The scene of our boat forcing its way through the ice was very clear. The dream was so real to me that when I woke I found it hard to believe that I had been quietly in my bed all night. I ran out of the tent as soon as I was dressed and was surprised to find everything just as we had left it the night before, and that the midden had not thawed more than its usual two or three inches. I had a happy feeling that I had really been home and seen you, but I was glad, too, that I was still in Greenland and that my adventure had not been made commonplace by a weekend in civilization.

It was a cold day, so I wore my pajamas, in default of other long underwear, under my sealskins. They are very warm and have the advantage that one does not have to get bare before jumping into the bag at night.

After a very early afternoon coffee we opened the grave at the back of the midden. There were four skulls in it and any number of seal bones and other rubbish which had fallen in. The grave belongs to the old midden, and the new midden has grown around and partly over it. Below the grave is more of the old midden. The grave itself seems to have been built on the ruins of a very early house, for some of the stones that form its walls are frozen deep in the ground, and must have been there at the time when the grave was first used as such. In it we found several things which were buried with the bodies, or which had fallen in through cracks in the cover. These were part of a sledge upstander, an arrow shaft, the wooden bottom of a baleen bowl, the blade of a snow knife, and a broken throwing board. The skeletons were very much disturbed. Did I write you about finding a skull in the new midden which had come from the grave? The grave was never big enough to hold four or five bodies at once. It must have been opened several times over a period of years.

We can expect the motorboat *Natarnak* from Prøven any day now. The summer is already half over. I'll mail this if I have the chance.

VII

Farthest North

DEAR FAMILY:

August 15 was the day we began our journey to the Devil's Thumb. It was such a cold day, with wind from the southeast threatening a storm, that we did not believe that the *Natarnak* could possibly come to us. We were very anxious to leave at once, for we knew that we should not be allowed to keep her beyond the first of September, when she is used for white whale hunting. We had talked of spending the first two weeks in September, after our return from the north, at the "Old Ships' Harbor" near Upernivik, but now Mathiassen has decided that Inugsuk is such an important site that we ought to excavate it properly. We are still not to the bottom in most of the fields, and have done little work on the other sites nearby. So he arranged that when we went we should make a cache on the island of our tents, the three boxes of specimens which had not yet been sent to Upernivik, and the supplies which we should not need in the north.

Much to our surprise and delight the *Natarnak* arrived just after lunch. Robert was on board, his finger almost healed, and so was Peter Møller, Karl's brother, and two other men. Mathiassen made quite a break by greeting Peter, who is a big, imposing man, as Joseph Christiansen, the skipper. The latter is a small, curly-headed Greenlander, like an Italian. There was another man on board whom we left on the island to help Karl and his family row back to Upernivik. We gave the men coffee and then set about sorting our possessions and packing up. We were not ready, of course, for we had not expected the boat till the next day.

Thinking that this was to be our last night on the island, we had invited our own Eskimos to our tent for a dinner of white men's food, and now the invitation had to be extended to the whole crew. There were thirteen of us who crowded in, the tent seeming to expand like rubber, though truth to admit, Robert, who was at the door, could only be said to be technically indoors. We began with a pot full of barley, to take the edge off the appetites, and then proceeded to a washbasin full of potatoes and two of the large "expedition" cans of corned beef. There were not plates or table utensils enough to go round, so Ane and the children had to wait their turn while the important people ate first. The Greenlanders were tremendously pleased with the dinner, though one could see that they did not know quite what to make of the curious food. Some of them saved little bits of the meat to take home. Mathiassen's tent had already been taken down and all the things we were taking with us had been carried down to the rocks. It began to rain while we were eating the barley, so Mathiassen sent the men out to put the stuff aboard. We omitted the coffee which should have been the end of the meal because we were in such a hurry to be off.

In no time at all my tent was down and folded up. What a change that made! Only a few minutes before we had all been sitting warm and comfortable inside, and now there was only the stone floor left and the flat rock on which I set the Primuses. Our camp had ceased to exist. The natives went around collecting all the junk which we had thrown away, and seemed to set great store by such trifles as scraps of paper, or worn-out Primus needles. We put the boxes and my trunk, etc., on the floor stones of Mathiassen's tent and covered them with our two waterproof bed sheets and my tent. Mathiassen's tent we were taking with us. Then we went down to the motorboat. Our midden looked very queer and desolate as we looked back at it. If we had not planned to come back, I should have been heartbroken. I did feel rather sad when I said goodbye to Karl and his family, for we were not certain that we should see them again.

Then we looked at the boat. What a wretched, small, dirty craft! Though Governor Otto had had it washed for us, it was still black with sticky blubber from one end to the other. It was only twenty-four feet long, with most of the space taken up by the fish hold in the center. Only a tiny triangular cabin was left for us in the bows. This cabin was crammed with our things, which the men had thrown down the hatch. There were two bunks, one on each side, exactly six feet long. They were about two feet or so wide at the stern end but narrowed down to a common six inches at the bow end. They were a little lower at the wider end (where we put our heads), so it was always uncomfortable, and Mathiassen and I were always kicking each other at night (with our feet at the narrow end). Mathiassen chose the port side, for there was a little stove at the head of his bunk, and by tucking his head behind it, so to speak, he was able to stretch out a little. There was a cupboard at the head of my bunk. The worst thing about the cabin was the smell. It reminded me of the W.C. on the *Hans Egede*, with stale Eskimo and blubber added, and we have never been able to get rid of it entirely.

Our first job was to clear out the cabin and spread out our bags for the night. Our tents seemed like palaces compared to the cabin. The rest of the boat was not much better. The cargo hold was filled with all sorts of junk. One of the bunks was piled with stuff, and Robert and Peter had to sleep on top of each other in the other. Joseph, who was fortunately very small, curled up in the engine room. The men did their cooking in the hold and, as the days went by, it became more and more messy, for they used to shoot birds as we chugged along and toss their carcasses down below. The deck was taken up with our little rowboat, coils of rope and the anchor chain, our dirty dishes stacked for Robert to wash, and two blubbery pups. When we came on board, they were curled up together in a dirty heap just forward of the cabin hatch. They belonged to Joseph. They were hardly more than round, fat, fuzzy, downy lumps, and were perfectly adorable.

We headed for Tugssaq, only about an hour's run, on the north side of the Upernivik Icefjord. It was a cold, wet trip and rather exciting, especially when we chugged past the end of Inugsuk, where we had toiled in the rowboat. There was little ice now, only big, scattered bergs, and nothing happened to delay us. There seems to be very little difference between one outpost and another. There is the village of turf houses, the great red, wooden storehouse, and the smaller frame house of the post manager. I did not get any definite impression at all of Tugssaq, except that the post manager gave us coffee and some of the same sweet biscuits which we had on Inugsuk. While we were being entertained, his wife, a Greenlander, was feeding our Eskimos in the kitchen. The Greenland wives of white men always seem to stay native, and very rarely do they come in and share in what they offer to their husbands and to the guests. The post manager's wife was most obviously pregnant, and never have I seen a woman so distorted. Her tight-fitting *anorak* came down as far as the middle of the bulge, and below that was an expanse of the white undershirt, stretching down to her tight-fitting trousers. It was the worst possible costume for a woman in her condition. The Greenland woman's dress is only pretty on young girls. When the skins are soft and the red leather or white leather boots are new and stiff, and the *anorak* carries out a color scheme in good taste, then such a costume is becoming to a young girl. But the skinny little girls and the fat old women ought to wear something else.

After calling on the post manager, we went to see Thomassen. His wife had sewn Mathiassen a sealskin bag to hold his *kamiks*. She appeared very shy and could not be made to say how much she wanted for it. That is the usual Eskimo trick, which means that the unwary white man, who wants to pay a fair price, usually offers too much. Thomassen's wife served us seal meat. I had some, but Mathiassen, as usual, refused it. I hate to think how much he must have suffered on the Fifth Thule Expedition with nothing to eat for months at a time but seal meat and walrus meat, which is like seal meat, only more so.

We passed the night tied up to the dock, and we all slept on board. Since I was already wearing my pajamas, I did not really have to get undressed, but the proprieties were observed by Mathiassen's waiting on deck while I pulled off my sealskins and hopped into my bag. Then I looked the other way while he did the same. We had an evening pipe, while Mathiassen read the last of his newspapers from home (he has religiously rationed himself to one a day), and wrote in his diary, and I read a little of *Anna Karenina* and wrote in mine. Then we pulled off our *anoraks* and sweaters, rolled them up for pillows, and lay down to an uneasy sleep.

Our motorboat started off at seven next morning, and we were up soon after. Mathiassen got dressed first and went up on deck while I dressed. Of course, there is no toilet on board, so he passed down a pail for me. Then we rolled up our bags, and made breakfast on one of the Primus stoves. Later we did not bother to undress in relays, since our pajamas and underwear are the same, and we neither of us really got undressed. Our boots had a habit of sticking, and we usually had to help each other off with them. I was often quite helpless when I was wearing the fine new pair with sealskin socks which Ane made for me, and which seemed to shrink on my feet. As the days went by, it became too dark to read in the cabin at night, for we had only two tiny portholes, and it was too cold to have the hatch open.

When we came on deck the first morning, I soon made friends with the two pups. They were great fun to play with, but rather a nuisance, for they made dreadful messes all over the boat, and ate everything in sight. One was black and white, the other bigger and darker. I called them both "Puppy" indiscriminately, which the Greenlanders have corrupted to "Puppik." It is curious how they change names. Joseph is "Yosepik," Robert "Robertsia,"

Peter is something like "Pitair," and Karl is "Kahli." The puppies were always under my feet and obeyed me far better than they did their own master.

The theory is that dogs will not make good sledge dogs unless they are severely disciplined and in general kicked about to make them feel the futility of their existence.

One never sees an Eskimo making a pet of his dog. White men who bring revolutionary ideas about dog driving have notoriously poor teams, it is said, because their dogs never learn that it is not all a joke. But perhaps that is because the sentimental white man hasn't the guts to thrash the life out of his team on those occasions when things have gone too far. The Central Eskimo, however, are forever thrashing their dogs, Mathiassen says, with heavy, cruel lashes, and the animals are so terrified that they are not much use and have to be whipped the whole way. The Polar Eskimo, though they are cruel to their dogs at times—as, for example, when they break off the points of the dog's teeth so that he will not be able to bite through his traces—make the best dog drivers, because they use the whip only when it is proper and encourage their dogs with sympathetic shouts, so that the dogs love to travel and pull enthusiastically. Mathiassen said the Polar Eskimo who were with his expedition in Canada could drive circles around any Central Eskimo team.

It seems extraordinary that Joseph and the others were not attracted to the fat and foolish pups. To me, they were irresistible. Joseph was never really mean to them, but he and the others would kick them aside with a too ostentatious display of human superiority. Yet they always ran gaily to meet him. Once or twice I have seen him try to play with them—this was after they had become my devoted slaves—but they misinterpreted his advances, and shrank from what they thought must be the intended punishment.

That first morning Joseph stepped on the bigger dog. The poor beast yelped loud and long. At first we did not think that Joseph had done more than bruise his paw, but it was evident that he had really injured the leg, for the dog could not walk on it.

One could not judge by the yelps, for Eskimo dogs are dreadful cowards and yelp over anything. Joseph sat down with the pup on his knees, and felt all over the leg, rubbing the puppy gently until he stopped crying and allowed his master to bend his leg. It did not seem to be broken. Joseph bandaged it with a piece of sacking. He did not seem to be the least distressed because the animal was in pain, but it was wonderful to see how skillfully he handled the dog, and how the puppy trusted him. Meanwhile, the other pup, not understanding in the least what was the matter, tried to get his little brother to play with him. I have noticed that the big dogs are not very sympathetic to the cries of pain of the others. Still, the injured puppy did get a lick on the nose when he was set down. He has been lame ever since. Perhaps he will never recover. Often when the puppies were lying together, the other would roll over on his sore paw. He never seemed to pay the slightest attention to the injured dog's howls.

That first morning was clear, but windy. We were chugging up narrow passages, between absolutely deserted islands, whose shores sloped so steeply down into the water that there was no room on the banks for any habitation. We felt that we could travel like this forever.

We came, however, to Tasiussaq at eleven o'clock in the morning. Just in time for lunch, we thought, which our friend the "King of Northern Upernivik" will be sure to offer us. He came down to the shore to greet us. It was amazing how much better he was able to get about among the rocks and swamps of his own home than on Inugsuk. He took us up to his house. It was a big frame building. In front was the usual midden of bones, rubbish, half-finished carpentry work scattered about, tools, old cans, etc. As is customary, there was a little front porch with a railing about it and a gate at the top of the three or four steps, not to keep babies from falling off, but to prevent dogs from wandering up. Inside was the entrance hall, with pegs for hanging heavy clothing, dog whips, harness, etc., and then, inside, the bedroom, with Eskimo platform, wooden chests well polished from the seats of sitters, and the inevitable tin bedroom pot without which no Eskimo establishment is complete. The living room beyond had table, chairs, desk, bookcase, etc., like any ordinary living room.

Sitting on the platform in the bedroom was a young girl, gorgeously dressed in Greenland clothes, but with the blond hair, white skin, pale washed-out blue eyes, and statuesque proportions which constitute that ideal of female loveliness of which the Teutonic races are accused. She had the saddest face that I have ever seen. She was holding a very blond baby in her arms. These were the "Old Man's" granddaughter and grandson. The mother of the baby, a rather attractive, but completely effaced Eskimo woman, was there also, as was the father of the baby, the present post manager, really a half-breed, but showing hardly a trace of native blood. The "Old Man's" wife, a substantial Eskimo woman, full of dignity, padded about setting the table in the living room. I did not see the father and mother of the young girl. Her mother was the red top-knotted woman whom Mathiassen had seen eight years before at Ūmánaq, but of course it was not the girl herself whom she then carried in the *amaut* on her back. The "Old Man's" blondness seems to be of so indelible a color that even two generations of Eskimo blood cannot efface it.

We came in, sat down; cigars and cigarettes were produced; the table was set. Now for lunch. We were hungry. Instead, only coffee appeared. It was a blow. Then a flood of Danish followed. I grew restive at last and went outside. The blond girl detached herself and followed me. She was miserable and very lonely. But she could not speak a word of Danish. It seemed impossible that she, with her blondness and her stature, could be anything but a Danish girl. Yet she was really a Greenlander. I went to the W.C. An expectant cur shot around to the back, and the girl waited for me. Then I went to the house, fetched my camera, and, closely followed by the girl, who was evidently reluctant to let me out of her sight, went over to the church. We climbed the hill with the flagstaff on it, and then I took a picture of the girl standing by the pond in front of the church among white, feather-tufted grass (Alaska cotton?). I invited her down to the boat and gave her a piece of chocolate, and took her picture with a color film. I tried to talk to her in Eskimo, but of course that was beyond me. I was relieved to go back to the house again.

The "Old Man" invited us to stay until three o'clock. This surely means lunch, we thought hungrily. Instead, more tobacco and a sip of Madeira, which his wife shared with us. The "Old Man" told us that he had some fine skins of young Greenland seals (*ataq*) and proposed that I get his wife to make them up into a coat for me. The skins were really very beautiful, silver with soft brown spots, and the price he suggested absurdly low. The coat was to be trimmed with dogskin, the soft reddish brown fur called *singarnaq* that looks very much like fox. We thought this was a wonderful idea, and had the women measure me for my coat. The coat was to be ready on our return from the north.

We all went out for a walk to see the church, and then the "Old Man" took Mathiassen down to see the harbor, which is quite a distance from the village. It is completely landlocked, and gives the village its name, "like a lake." The girl had me stop at the house of some fishermen from Jakobshavn. They had been brought up here by the post manager who wanted to test the possibilities of starting a real fishing industry. The women in the house gave me some coffee. Though I did not know it then, their house was really very big and very fine. They had no end of nicknacks on shelves and on dressers. There were dolls, and miniature furniture, etc., perfume bottles, cheap vases, and such truck, stuff that one would expect to find in the room of a little girl at home who cannot resist the five-and-ten. I wondered how such junk could ever have come here. The girl insisted on my seeing everything. She evidently thought the nicknacks were wonderful.

At last it was three o'clock, and we rushed on board. The anchor was hardly up before we had begun to pump the Primus. I don't remember what we had, but we wolfed it.

We arrived at Kûk just after dinner. Kûk means "stream," for there is a little stream dividing the village into two halves. There were quite a number of houses, and it was a very large village for a purely native settlement. It was the first real Eskimo village I had seen. About half the households had moved out of their houses and were camping in sealskin tents. All of the men had gathered at the landing rock, and some of the women were bunched a little behind them, but most of them came no farther than their doorways. No one said anything. I felt rather shy, though my smiles were cordially returned, especially by the women. We stepped ashore, and Mathiassen shook the first man by the hand.

"I am Tikile. We are people from Inugsuk. I want to see old houses. Are there any old houses here? Who are you?" (*"Uvange Tikile. Piumavera dakusarama igluqut. Igluqut perapit? Kinavit?"*—or something to this effect, though I am not sure of the forms, and much less how to spell the words.)

This is the usual formula. It is always a mystery to me how Mathiassen manages to pick out the most important man, for except for the mistake with Joseph, he is always right. All the men look alike to me as I see them lined up at the landing place.

Soon we had set off, following a guide, and followed by the entire population, including the children and dogs. One man was lame, but he hopped along on one foot with surprising agility, even hopping across the stream on the rough stones. Just across the little brook was the ruin of a house built of stone. On top of the ruin was a modern meat cache. The high tide washed about the walls and had carried away the midden. Mathiassen sent Robert back to get the digging sticks. While we were waiting, I went to take a picture of a skin tent, and a house with a gutskin windowpane. The pane, made of strips of translucent gut sewn together, was the kind of window the Eskimo had before the white man came. Now all the houses have glass windows. The people were very willing to pose for me, and the small boys fought for the tabs torn from my film pack.

A girl came out of the tent and, to my joy, invited me in. Over half the space inside was taken up with the platform, a raised wooden floor across the back. On the platform and on the ground were piles of junk, dirty dishes, scraps of food, pots and kettles, worn boots, a bowl full of black tasteless berries which are now very plentiful, scraps of skin, etc., etc. The housewife, a cheery old dear, with her topknot all awry over her bald temples, welcomed me to a seat on the platform beside her. A blubber lamp made of a tin plate tilted on one edge gave a luxurious warmth, and when the tent flap had been carefully shut, the tent savored of well-nourished humanity. I was a little disappointed to see Peter in his pale blue *anorak* sitting grandly on a box, for I felt that he was watching me critically. On another box by the door was the husband, and crowded in the remaining space were the little children, a half-grown boy, and an older daughter. A little girl, dressed only in a dirty cotton shirt, tumbled about among the featherbeds piled on the platform.

The woman set about making coffee and chattered to me gaily, evidently giving me the whole family history, for she pointed often to the children and shook her head in the loving, scolding way mothers have. She might have been just any dear old lady, instead of a fat, dirty old Eskimo in ridiculously inadequate fur pants. I fell in love with her at once and did my best to keep up my end of the conversation with grins and "A*p*" ("yes"). Another daughter came in with a steaming plate of seal meat, which tasted good. Seeing that I had no knife, my host loaned me his, a courteous attention, and the woman passed me a bandanna on which to wipe my fingers when I had eaten. Then she poured out black coffee, which we sipped between nibbles of sugar. How pleased the old soul was with my thanks as I rose to go, explaining that I had to go to Tikile!

"*Qujanaq. Assut mamaqpoq.*" ("Thank you. It tastes very fine.")

"*Ivtitlo. Ivtitlo.*" ("And you. And you. You are welcome, and thank you for coming.")

I found Mathiassen and the entire population assembled at the house ruin. Dirt and stones were flying as they had never done on Inugsuk. The tide was so high that one could hardly cling to the ruin without getting wet, and at every moment one had to duck out of the way of the stones which the energetic diggers were throwing down. They had already found the usual miscellaneous scraps of soapstone, fragments of wooden bowls, a Thule harpoon head, a double-handled scraper, so that we might have thought we were back on Inugsuk, in the old midden. Each new discovery provoked a roar of laughter. What funny things had been hidden here under their noses, the people must have been thinking, and no one dreamed of their existence, until these quixotic white people came and introduced this new game!

Mathiassen went away after a time. I was invited by another girl to have more coffee. I went after her into a house and found Mathiassen showing the Visitors' Box to the chief man and the other important people. All the people here seem to be related in some way to Eskildsen, the old man of the village, who rules over his happy family, a benign and venerated patriarch. His numerous daughters and granddaughters typify the merry spirit, the radiant health, and plump good looks of his clan. The doctor at Upernivik had told me that I should like the people at Kûk, that he himself was always glad to go there, even when, as it happened last winter, there was no place for him to sleep and he had to curl up on a couple of boxes, but I was not prepared to find such an open-hearted, unaffected, and uncivilized happiness and good nature. I was particularly attracted to one young couple, one of the daughters and her husband. She sat in his lap, with her arm around his neck, laughing and whispering in his ear, and seemed proud and glad to share her happiness with everyone. Mathiassen said it was the first time he had ever seen such a demonstration of conjugal affection between Eskimos. There was a fiddle hanging on the wall, and before we went, one of the old men got it down and played us a tune, with considerable scraping, I confess, but in splendid rhythm, and with such enthusiasm that I wanted to dance.

When we went back to the ruin, we found the people still at work. Since they had done all they could without imperiling the meat cache on top, Mathiassen called a halt and showed them the Visitors' Box. These people know how to laugh! It was too late in the day to take a photograph, but I should have liked to have a picture of the little crowd gathered about the mound where Tikile sat, their eyes shining with mirth and interest.

Before we went to bed, we climbed a hill in back of the

village, to a beacon about three hundred feet above the water, and
sat for a while to watch the red sunset color rock and Inland Ice.
There was too much spread out, we had already seen too many
new places, for me to remember everything that we saw from the
hill, but as we came down the hillside, slipping over dry heather
tufts, we felt rather than saw the quiet, empty expanse of both the
moving and the frozen seas.

The next morning, August 17, at seven-thirty, a barbarous
hour, the anchor was raised, the chain rattling onto the deck
above our heads, but we rolled over and went to sleep again.

In the middle of the day we came to Kraulshavn, the most
northern outpost in the Upernivik District. It is in a magnificent
harbor on the south side of the great peninsula, Nûgssuaq, which
divides the northern part of the district into two parts. [The name
is the same as that of the peninsula north of Disko Island.] A
strong wind was blowing from the north and roared through the
valley into the harbor. This is the most desolate place we have
seen. The other side of the bay was so far away that we could not
see whatever vegetation might have been leading a stunted existence. There appeared to be only the hills of red schist, cracked by
the frost into sliding rocks and boulders, and the deep valley, leading up into what inland desolation we could not imagine. I would
have given anything to have been able to set off along the valley,
with a pack on my back.

The son of the "Old Man" of Tasiussaq is the post manager at
Kraulshavn. He gave us coffee and invited us to dinner that night.
He was full of praises for the place. He told us that on the other
side of the point on which the outpost was built there was an
Eskimo village (there are only two families living at the store), and
that we might find house ruins there. We took a path leading
along the shore of the harbor and turning up to the right, to cross
the ridge of the point. The people of the village were mostly living
in skin tents, made of sealskins with the hair turned out. I was
delighted to find one tent built in the old-fashioned way, with a
single peak at the front, and the poles resting on the ground in
back. The ordinary tents are now built in imitation of the white

man's wall tent, with a gable at each end and a ridgepole. I suppose that in the old days the limited supply of wood prevented the natives from devising a more roomy type of tent than the kind they used.

We met an old man at the village who showed us where the house ruins were. They had been so robbed of their stones to furnish building material that I could not see any house ruins at all, and even Mathiassen was baffled. A woman sold us a string of beads which she had found in one of the houses. They were very big, and dated, so Mathiassen thinks, from the days of the Dutch whalers who used to come to Greenland in the seventeenth century. The man who was our guide was followed about by a beautiful white dog, which he caressed. She was very privileged, and had to be kept out of a kettle of seal meat which was cooking out of doors. Usually the Eskimo don't pay much attention to their dogs.

We went back to the tents, where some women were cooking over a heather fire. Another woman was scraping the hair from a sealskin with her ulo. One old lady, with spectacles falling off her nose and a pipe in her mouth, was mending a skin. One girl had to fetch her sewing things, another fill her pipe, and a third thread her needle, and when the thread broke the old woman would not sew any more. While we sat around, the men from our boat came up, escorting a blond-haired Greenland beauty, painted and perfumed with the vilest cosmetics. Their coming rather spoiled the fun, for they felt themselves superior to the simpler people, and put on airs.

In honor of the occasion, we had a thorough wash on board before going to dinner. I had forgotten to bring my tin mirror with me, so we had to rely on mutual inspection. Mathiassen even shaved himself. Only the post manager ate with us. His wife and their fifteen-year-old daughter, a fairy princess with golden hair and a pink chintz *anorak*, waited on table. We had seal meat and a few canned *paalæg* (things like sardines, etc., out of which you make sandwiches). The meat was only boiled, but it was so good that we asked how it had been cooked. They told us it had been soaked for half a day and boiled in half fresh and half sea water. I have since followed the recipe to the letter, but the results have never been as successful. We gorged. Our host wanted us to spend the night, but we left right after dinner.

If the weather had been better, we would have traveled all night, but since it was so foggy we took shelter at Ikermiut, a village on a little island to the north of Nûgssuaq, and halfway between the point and Holms Ø, an island which also sticks far out into the open sea. It was quite late when we came to Ikermiut, so we just went ashore for half an hour, met some people, were barked at by the dogs, and saw some ruins which we decided to investigate in the morning.

After breakfast we were ashore with spades and cameras. There were about five house ruins, of the small round variety of the Thule culture, and of the derived type called the "clover-leaf" house, which is really three of these small houses set together with a common doorway. Mathiassen began measuring the ruins while I went off with his camera to take pictures.

When I came back, I found Mathiassen had started to work on one of the clover-leaf houses. There were many stones to be moved, and the place seemed much disturbed. It is Mathiassen's principle never to poke in a house ruin if he cannot excavate it properly, unless it has already been tampered with, or unless the sea is washing it away. There was little to find here. While I was digging, Mathiassen had his camera already set up to get a picture of the best-preserved house ruin when the chief man of the village, Martin Nielsen, the catechist, came up and told him not to take the picture, because his mother's grave was on the ruin. Without letting him see what he was doing, Mathiassen snapped it anyway. The people here did not help us with the digging as they had done at Kûk. But Martin Nielsen invited us to dinner. His house was very big and clean, and his wife gave us a basin of water and a piece of soap to wash our hands. We had seal meat and coffee. There was one boy in the family who looked almost white and rather solemn. I took a picture of them all and hope that it will show the curious contrast between the merry, intelligent Eskimos and this poor little misfit. After lunch, people brought us specimens which they had dug up from the houses at one time or another. Among them was a Thule harpoon head, and one of the finest snow knives I have ever seen. It was from a village site near the point of Nûgssuaq. Mathiassen bought the specimens, paying from fifty øre to two *kroner* apiece, the price depending on the archeological value, but the natives were not always satisfied with his valuation.

We had intended to leave after lunch, but there was too much wind, so we did not lift anchor until about nine-thirty that night.

The sky was overcast and it was bitter cold. We had to move slowly because of the ice, which lay in bands of crushed berg fragments. One of our men stood in the bow and signaled to the helmsman and to the motorman. Whenever we passed through a patch of broken ice, the motor had to be thrown out of gear, and of course we tried to avoid the worst places. Robert took the post of lookout for a time, but the others laughed at him for his excess of caution. It seemed to me that we would never reach Holms Ø and the Devil's Thumb. After a time, of course, we did get past the small berg pieces and steered through open and rougher water. From the size of the swells we met now we could imagine how strong the wind had been during the day. We passed great icebergs, of monstrous shapes that seemed to ape animals or buildings. It was interesting to see how long the illusion of these resemblances could last as we came past the icebergs and the viewpoint shifted. I had on my warmest clothes, with a fur cap on under the hood of my sheepskin-lined soldier's coat, sealskin mittens on my hands, and my legs were down inside the cabin hatchway, wrapped in a blanket, yet I was frozen to the bone. I have never been so cold. I knew that at any time I could go below and crawl into my sleeping bag, but I wanted to stay up until we had passed Holms Ø and could see the Devil's Thumb. Even the Eskimos were chilly, too, and had put on their sweaters. It was a long wait.

Holms Ø looked more and more barren as we approached. From a little distance any Greenland coast looks like a desert, for the scanty vegetation makes but a poor show among the rocks, but

Holms Ø was really bare. A little black lichen, which Robert calls "crow feed," and a little moss was all that grew to soften the jagged outlines. The land lay in alternating masses of the crumbling red and the hard blue-grayish gneisses which we have seen on our own Inugsuk. We chugged boldly under towering cliffs, stained black by the rusty drippings from rotting moss. It was close to midnight, and the thick clouds cast a gloom which was the nearest approach to real nighttime we had yet experienced. It was a reminder that the happy summer was nearing the end, and my thoughts were sad as I sat huddled in the bow, shivering with cold.

At midnight we chugged around the point of Holms Ø, and the Devil's Thumb, enormous, impossibly realistic, lifted its specter finger before us. It was the North Pole of our expedition! I stayed to watch a minute, then dived below into the protecting warmth of my bag. I was afraid I was going to be sick with a chill, and cursed myself for not having given up sooner, but Mathiassen gave me some hot tea, and I went happily to sleep. Two hours and a half later Mathiassen woke me, and I hopped in my bag to where I could look out. The Devil's Thumb was out of sight behind the shore where we lay at anchor. Before us was the north slope of Holms Ø, dripping icebergs, and the water about us was so packed with ice that I wondered how we had come through. A few snowflakes were falling.

"It looks Arctic, doesn't it?" said Mathiassen.

VIII

Home to Inugsuk

DEAR FAMILY:

The bright noonday sun welcomed us when we came up on deck the next morning. After a hearty breakfast we went ashore and walked over a slight ridge to the Eskimo village. Asleep in the heather was an Eskimo who did not budge when we stepped over him. We wondered if he were drunk, and where he could have obtained any liquor. Quvdlorssuaq is a village of about five or six families; the head man is Vitus Jensen, a short, energetic man, whose legs are bowed by too much kayaking. He is a great hunter, but not too scrupulous a trader. They tell this story about him: Once he came to Tasiussaq with two fine narwhal tusks to sell. He was paid, according to custom, by the weight. After the "Old Man" had had the tusks in the house for a day, he noticed that they had been filled with ice to make them heavy, and the ice was now melting. In order to punish Vitus, he took back the money he had given him, and paid him according to the weight of the tusks, not when the water had first run out, but after they had become

very dry in the oven! The "Old Man" wanted the people to remove Vitus from his office—he was the local representative to the
assembly (*Kommuneraad*) at Upernivik—but they refused.

Quvdlorssuaq is the newest of the northern settlements. In
1900, Kûk and Mernoq were the most northerly villages in West
Greenland south of the Polar Eskimo country. There has been a
steady migration toward the wonderful hunting grounds of the
north, and now Governor Otto talks of opening an outpost at the
Devil's Thumb because Kraulshavn is too far away. Upernivik itself is one hundred miles away, and a trip to the "great city" is the
adventure of a lifetime for the bold kayaker.

They were flensing a seal on the rocks when we came over
the hill. All about the village were animal bones, some whole skeletons with the sinews still holding the parts together, and great
lumps of blubber. This was indeed a land of plenty where the dogs
were too full to eat blubber. According to Mathiassen, it is axi-
omatic that an Eskimo dog is always hungry.

As soon as we appeared, Vitus took off his fine black and
white checked *anorak* (the favorite pattern in the north), and
dressed in his kayak jacket. He was evidently waiting to show us
some stunts. The kayak jacket is made of waterproof dehaired sealskin, and fits tightly about the top of the manhole and is lashed
around the face and wrists so that no water can come in. Vitus was
a long time about his preparations, stuffing something up his nos-
trils and ears, and paddling about until he found just the right
spot. Then with slow deliberation he laid the paddle close along
the side of the kayak, and turned upside down. Equally slowly he
righted himself, the paddle at right angles to the craft and held at
the extreme end of one of the blade tips. This performance he
cautiously repeated several times. The people were much impressed, and so was I, for the water must have been very cold.
Mathiassen, though, said this was poor stuff compared to the
stunts of the South Greenlanders, who are all but born in the
kayak, and live in it the year round. When the king came to
Greenland, for instance, thirty kayakers met the ship at Godthaab,
and at a signal all turned over in a twinkling. While Vitus was per-

forming, I climbed out on a rock to take pictures of the show and was nearly nosed off into the water by the curious dogs that followed me.

There were five house ruins in and just north of the village. Some of the houses seemed to be of the clover-leaf type, others were too overgrown for us to be able to see much. One seemed to be a simple round house, and another, where we found a big piece of a sledge runner and some poles, had a storehouse built onto it. In the morning we dug in the two most northerly ruins, which had already been disturbed and were being attacked by the sea. We found some bits of ivory there, but what the specimens were I can't remember. While we were at work, a big iceberg just opposite us dropped a fragment and turned over. Enormous waves rushed out from it, and crashed on the shore. We had to jump up the bank to save our *kamiks*. Mathiassen says that such an iceberg wave washed away a house from Erqodleq, and another destroyed the whole village of Sarfaq. People were asleep in the houses, and many were drowned.

After lunch, sometime in the middle of the sun's afternoon, we dug in one of the clover-leaf houses in the center of the village. A lot of people gathered to watch us, and the dogs were all on hand, too, for they loved the taste of the blubbery earth we shoveled out, and we even had to protect the few miserable specimens we found from their ravenous jaws. Afterwards we gave a coffee party on board the *Natarnak* to the men who had helped us dig. Mathiassen showed them the Visitors' Box and asked them about house ruins.

It was six o'clock when we decided to climb the hill back of the village; Vitus said he would go with us, since he had already been thinking of going there. He put on his *Kommuneraad* cap for the occasion. It was white with a black visor, on which was a polar bear emblem, the official West Greenland crest. He lit his pipe, and off we started. I had the impression that I was taller than he, and wondered how his short bowlegs could keep up with us. I am ashamed to confess, however, that he was more agile than I, and it was we who followed. The land rose in a series of gneiss terraces, sloping in toward the hillside, that is, to the north, so that one was always scrambling up a six-foot cliff only to find that the top lay beyond the next. The hill was about a thousand feet high.

As we came up over the shoulder, the Devil's Thumb rose up before us. It is truly a giant thumb, carved in stone, complete even to a vertical cliff to represent the nail as seen in profile. It is impossible, and terrible. There is nothing else in the world like it. The thumb part of the island is almost separated from the part on which the village stands by a low *itivdleq*, in which is a lake. To the north, behind the fleshy part of the thumb, we could see the true magnificence of the Inland Ice sweeping in a majestic quarter circle to the north, falling sheer into Melville Bay. Quvdlorssuaq itself really lies within the bay. We could not see the eternally drifting ice pack for which Melville Bay is so famous and so dreaded, but the water was well filled with glacier fragments. Only a few small nunataks broke the circle of the glacier. The farthest of these, already halfway to Cape York, was Cape Seddon (Tugtuligssuaq), famous for polar bears, once the southernmost dwelling place of the Polar Eskimo. I felt contempt for all the distance we had come and the land that we had seen as I looked out across the ice and water and sky toward that wonderful country in the north.

On the way down I saw a caterpillar drowned in a little pool, and we picked up a caribou antler. It was not many years since caribou roamed over this part of the country, passing from island to island over the winter ice.

When we returned to the village we had a fine appetite. Mrs. Vitus Jensen was busy at a pot over a heather fire, and we thought that we would be invited to partake. Her children were running around in fancy crepe-paper hats—where on earth did they get them? Since no invitation was forthcoming, however, we invited Vitus to share our meal. We had the breasts of two eider ducks fried in onions (delicious but scanty), some boiled seal meat, and Mathiassen excelled himself in pancakes. Vitus ate very little, certainly not because he was overawed by us, but probably because the food tasted strange. Here in the north, coffee is the only store food that is known.

We had told our men that we should leave early in the morning. When we came on board for the last time that night, we found that the fellows had loaded fourteen seals onto the boat. They were unflensed, though a few had been stripped of the skin and outer layers of blubber. Two of the seals belonged to us. One was a young one which Vitus had sent in return for our hospitality, the other was a gift from an old gentleman with a beard, whose name we can't remember. This shows the wealth of the little community that could afford to dispose of fourteen seals at the same time. Robert and the others had traded stuff they bought at Kraulshavn for their seals, and they also got skins here and at Ikermiut. The seals were piled up on either side of the boat, and were covered with canvas. Of course the pups discovered them at once, and from that time on their little snoots were always more or less red with blood, and the blubber acted potently as a laxative, so that one could barely move on deck without stepping or sitting in filth. It was about this time that Mathiassen perfected his oatmeal and prune combination. He cooked both together at the same time. On one occasion the dogs got the prune pits, in fact fought over them as if they were a great delicacy, and we wondered somewhat anxiously if their little guts were big enough for such heavy traffic. It seemed like a long time until little contributions to the general mess evinced unmistakable signs that all was well.

We were off at eight o'clock the next morning, August 20, with our rowboat still bloody from the seals it had transported, the two pups, our fourteen seal carcasses, and three kayakers with their kayaks who wanted to go to Kraulshavn. The only place on deck where we could sit down was on top of our cabin.

We stopped at some ruins on the south side of Nûgssuaq point about four in the afternoon. Mathiassen, Robert, and I were put ashore with things for tea while the others were told to go on to Kraulshavn, where there was a good anchorage, and to fetch us at eight o'clock. There were two house ruins for us, both of the long, rectangular community type. One was undisturbed and overgrown with grass; the other, some little distance away, was half washed down by the sea. We excavated the remains of the latter. It dated from the days of the whalers, for we found some large glass beads of the type imported then. We also found quite a few dolls. Altogether, we obtained a good number of specimens, the best of which was a large and almost complete wooden bowl, found by Mathiassen. We interrupted the digging with coffee and sandwiches. To my horror and shame, I found that I had forgotten the sugar!

The next morning, August 21, after an early breakfast at Kraulshavn, we sailed southeast to Ituvssâlik. It was only a short run, and when we stepped ashore at the village, we found the three kayakers whom we had taken to Kraulshavn the day before. The great man of this place is Abel Danielsen. We had coffee in his house and also in the house of another famous hunter. At this place I do not remember any house ruins, though Mathiassen has recorded two small, poor ones in his notebook. Here there was an enormous umiak, the largest I have yet seen, set up on two supports out of the reach of the dogs. It belonged to Abel. Some of the dogs here were hopping about on three legs, for one of the forepaws had been tucked up in their harness—to keep them from running away, Mathiassen explained.

When Abel heard that we were going on to Tikerarssuaq and Kitsorsaq, he said that he would come with us. He has houses at both of these places, though his real home is at Kitsorsaq. The other man who had entertained us came also. Both brought their kayaks, of course, and dressed all in white for the trip, even pulling a piece of white cotton underwear over the tops of their black caps, to be ready for seal hunting.

We touched at Tikerarssuaq for a half hour before lunch. Most of the house ruins were quite modern and were made of turf. On the beach we found several things, most of them modern, but I found a broken toy ulo handle which may have been older. We were especially interested in the ulo, because out on the beach were the very much disturbed ruins of a house which was certainly much older than the others, and which we suspected of belonging to the Thule period. On the beach in front of the modern houses were some toy houses built of stone, charming little things. In one we found a toy gun, which we put carefully back again.

In the afternoon we re-crossed the bay, going this time to the southwest, and stopped at the old, deserted site of Kitsorsaq, on the north side of an island. The modern village is on another side of the island. At the old village there are three house ruins. One of them seemed to be modern, and is well preserved. We went on to the other two, while our Eskimos dug at this house and got the usual assortment of "civilized" junk. On the other side of the point there were the ruins of a house just at the high-tide level. A very thin, poor midden in front of the house yielded only a flat harpoon head of modern type. To the right was a thicker, older midden, which had been cut into by the sea. This midden contained some stones which looked like the back wall of a very old house, the rest of which had been washed away. On the beach in front we picked up several things, including a Thule harpoon head and a double-handled scraper made of split animal leg bone. On the beach we found half of a wooden doll, and what was our surprise and delight when I found the other half of it in the old midden. Our impression was that this old midden belonged to Thule culture times. (1930: This doll, like those we found at Inugsuk, proved to be a representation of a Norseman, dressed in a hood and short jacket.)

The modern village of Kitsorsaq is one of the prettiest spots we have seen. The village is built on a narrow isthmus which connects the two halves of the island. Abel's house is built on the highest point of this bridge of land, and commands a glorious view in both directions. The only thing that is lacking is a view of the Inland Ice. There are quite a few house ruins here, of assorted ages—square, long, and groups of older, overgrown roundish ones. There is also a midden about one meter thick which the same Dr. Andersen who discovered Inugsuk had partially excavated. There is still much of it left. We dug there for a while, but it was not very old. We found a wooden wound plug (younger than the bone or ivory wound pin of the Thule culture), snow goggles, beads, etc. This midden probably dates from the time of the long stone house at Qamaneq on Inugsuk.

We stopped for half an hour the next day, August 22, at a little island which lies quite out in the open sea, west of Qugdelsorsuit. It has a wide, flat meadow just above the beach, with only one house ruin on it. It was a beautiful double round house, undisturbed and buried in luxuriant grass. There seemed to be a midden before it, though it was so far back from the beach that no part of the midden outcropped there. We did no digging.

Late in the afternoon, just after our lunch, we passed under the auk cliffs of Cape Shackleton (Agparsuit). For a little distance one cannot see the ledges where the birds make their nests, but the cliff is stained white with their droppings. At this time of year most of the older birds had apparently gone south; only the young ones were left. We ran quite close under the cliffs, and swarms of the young birds and some gulls who were living with them flew out but refused to be lured within range of the Eskimos' guns, though Joseph whistled and whistled in imitation of the gulls. Then the men did a dreadful thing. The boat was headed straight for the cliff, and we came right up to it, so close that we could see the little birds sitting side by side on the ledges. When the prow was almost touching the rock, Robert fired. The wretched victims, either dead or wounded, fell back into their nests, or tumbled down to be caught on the ledges below. Only one fell into the water. Robert fired again, with no better success. After each shot the little birds flew out, but immediately returned to their perches to wait for the next. In the end the men did not pick up the bird that was in the water, probably because they did not think it big enough to be worth the trouble. This seems to be a typical example of how heedless of animal suffering these people are, natural enough for men accustomed to and dependent upon the cruel harpoon, and how wantonly wasteful of their food supply. I felt that they were only savages after all.

In the afternoon we stopped at the deserted island Qeqertaq, due west of Kûk. There were two ruins with a midden below them. I was trying to pry out a hunk of turf, using a big boulder as a pivot, when the handle of my geological spade snapped off. It was a disaster! Mathiassen had often warned me not to put the stick to too great a strain. I was very much surprised, for the turf had been moving, and I was not conscious of using much force, when the handle broke. I was very much ashamed and very much afraid of Mathiassen's unspoken anger. This was the lowest point of my whole summer. It was hard to have to tell Mathiassen that I had broken one of our four precious shovels. I hardly dared look at his face. He was not angry, however, only regretted the loss, and explained again to me how I should work. It was with timid reluctance that I took another spade and went back to work. Fortunately, since Karl did not come back to Inugsuk, we did not miss the fourth spade. That night over coffee I told Mathiassen how frightened of him I had been, and how grateful that he had not been cross with me. He had a good laugh, and still pokes fun at me when we speak of Qeqertaq.

Mathiassen decided to save time by pushing on south to the twin villages of Ikerasârssuk and Nutârmiut, which lie halfway between Kûk and Tasiussaq. Ikerasârssuk is on a tiny island, Nutârmiut on a slightly larger island, separated by an extremely narrow channel. We tried to sail down this channel, and were almost through when we came to a stranded iceberg blocking the way. It was very annoying to be forced to turn about, and go back and way around the smaller island, before we could finally anchor in the mouth of the channel, only a very short distance from where we had been stopped.

We went ashore at first on the larger island. There were two houses near the mouth of the channel, but no ruins at this place, and only the women were at home, so we pushed on across country to Nutârmiut, about a half mile to the west. This was one of the few walks on a path that we experienced in Greenland, and it was a delightful change after riding in the little boat. We found some very old ruins at Nutârmiut, but they were so overgrown with turf that we could not see much of them. It was a good mosquito-breeding place, for there were large patches of swampy ground, green with the wiry swamp grass tufted with feathery balls. One of the houses at the village had a curving turf entrance passage, one of the first that I had seen, though Mathiassen says they are not rare. I stopped in front of the house to look at the passage, when all the dogs rushed out to bark at us, and the people came out to see what was the matter. The man of the house was out hunting, but his wife, a very pleasant woman, invited us in to have coffee. She, too, had heard of Tikile. He is famous all over Greenland. That is real fame.

After a brief visit we walked back to the boat and were ferried across to Ikerasârssuk. People from the village had come out of the houses and were sitting patiently on the rocks, waiting for us to come to them. There was something unpleasant about this place, but I can't say just what it was. The people did not seem quite as friendly, and there was also the pitiful figure of a hunchback girl, with the shrunken, wistful, and cunning expression common to cripples. There was also a man here who had fallen down thirty meters on the cliff at Agparsuit—into the water, I believe—but had miraculously escaped with his life, though he had broken almost every bone in his body. Our Dr. Falkenberg from Upernivik and Dr. Christiansen from Ūmánaq had visited him, and the prevailing medical opinion was that eventually he would be as good as new. We saw him sitting in front of his tent, smoking his pipe. He was quite a young man, and rather fine looking, though thin and pale. He had a pair of rough crutches by him, so doubtless he was already well on the road to recovery.

Here, for the first time that summer, we saw the moon. It was in glorious completeness, not "smiling sulkily" at all, and we welcomed her as an old friend, though I could not make myself realize that, even as I looked up shivering at that impassive disk, she was shining down equally impassively on steaming, choking Philadelphia streets at home.

From Ikerasârssuk we went on to a place called Augpilagtoq (not the outpost near Upernivik), where there is nothing left but four house ruins, just above the rocks where the sea breaks at high tide. The hillside slopes southeast, so it caught all that was possible of the yellow sunlight. The little terraces into which the venerable gneiss was broken were each filled with a profusion of late summer flowers, the most beautiful of which is the Arctic "fireweed," a well-proportioned plant, crowned by three or four flaming blossoms. Mathiassen identified the beautiful flower which I brought him as *Chamaenerion latifolium*.

We called at Tasiussaq, and this time our hopes for a substantial meal were not disappointed. While waiting for dinner, I paid for my fur coat. It was a little too small across the front, so an extra skin had to be added. The blond girl and one of the "Old Man's" daughters-in-law sewed it while we watched. The girl sat on the platform, her legs straight out in front of her, holding the material between them, her right leg on top. She sewed an overhand seam from right to left, pushing the needle in toward her, with the thimble on her forefinger. This method seems to make for greater speed and precision than ours, though I have not learned to master it. She used sinew thread, which is ideal for sewing skins, though the pieces are very short. The other woman sat on a chair beside her and began in the middle of the seam. When it was finished, the fur was pressed flat and "ironed out" with the thimble until the skins lay flat, and not a sign of the sewing was visible, so well were the skins matched and the work done.

So now I have a fur coat for only twenty *kroner* (about seven dollars). Never mind that it smells like a dead seal when dry and like a wet dog when damp, and is as stiff as a board. It is beautiful, shining like silver. Thus was my dream prophecy fulfilled. (1930: I should have been warned by my dream, however. This coat was the only warm coat I had to wear when I got to Copenhagen, and it certainly was a little queer in style, and decidedly queer in smell, as I discovered when I returned to the commonplace odors of civilization. I had to have the skins cured and the coat recut. In all, it cost me eighty dollars and much anguish and bother. But it is still a handsome coat.)

After paying for the coat, we went down to the harbor to watch Joseph repair the local motorboat. The "Old Man" joined us, and we went with him to the store to make sundry purchases, stocking up with margarine, flour, oatmeal, and a tooth-cracking variety of hard bread, especially designed for the subjugation of the Greenlander. Mathiassen also bought a copy of Olsen's book on the Akilinermiut, the Central Eskimo, among whom he lived while on the Fifth Thule Expedition. It was wonderful to see what literary Eskimo looks like. I could recognize about one word in a hundred, and then it was usually part of an impossible combination. One can see the wisdom in Porsild's practice of sending all his radio messages in Greenlandic, whereby he can swindle the authorities by compressing a whole paragraph into a single word. Mathiassen also bought a pair of "store pants," for we had observed through holes in Robert's sealskins how he defied the elements with an extra pair of trousers, so Mathiassen thought it wise to copy him.

We came to Ivnarssuit in the late evening. It was really dark, for storm clouds were blowing up from the southwest, and the light shining from the tiny windows of the house was grateful. There are only two houses at this place. In the larger, which boasts two rooms, lives the old man, Vale (pronounced "Wali," really Valdemar Christiansen), and one married and one unmarried son. In the other house lives another son and his family. The old man has four sons altogether; we have now seen three of them, and they have come to visit us at our island. The family in the big house seemed to live in only one room, for the window in the other was broken and the empty frame stuffed with rags.

I do not remember if this incident occurred here, but I may as well mention it, for it amused me. Usually wherever we visited, the natives were sophisticated enough to observe the white man's etiquette of passing the coffee cup first to me, if there were only one, while Mathiassen had to wait. This custom does not apply to the Eskimo women, who are always served after the men, even when the ordinary polite rule that the person who serves must wait did not seem to apply. On one unique occasion the solitary cup was passed to Mathiassen first, who drank it off absently, and then was quite embarrassed when he saw it refilled for me. I was very much amused. I have often wondered what these people thought of me, especially since I went dressed as a man, and was obviously neither wife nor daughter. Mathiassen told me that at Ikermiut someone had asked if I were a *kivfak* (servant), but he had told them that I was an *agbara* (comrade).

Vale has a particularly attractive family. The sons, especially the two who live in their parents' house, have a very sweet expression, and lack that somewhat brutish masculinity that so many

Greenland men have. There is no subtlety about the sex of an Eskimo. These young men were very shy and one could hardly get a word out of them, either at their home or ours. The old mother, however, allowed no gaps in the conversation. The young wife, who lay on the platform nursing her baby, was one of the loveliest girls I have ever seen. She had soft dark hair and large dark eyes, a fresh complexion, and a sweet innocence of expression that matched that of her young husband. The baby, a little girl about a year old, had actually curly hair, brown rather than black. The child refused to suck when we came in, and both mother and baby lay watching us, the mother not bothering to rearrange her shirt with an appealing lack of self-consciousness. The girl was as lovely in her body as her face. Her husband hardly took his eyes from her, and it was charming to see that the tenderness of their first love had not been lost in the publicity of their life in the parents' house.

The next morning, August 24, I was awakened at a very early hour by the dismal howls of our pups. It was raining, and they were drenched and shivering. At last I went up on deck to see if I could not find some shelter for them, but there was nothing to be had except my own raincoat. The pups ran to me so trustingly that I had not the heart to refuse it to them. I put a shovel and a digging stick across the gap between the cabin roof and the hatch of the cargo hold, laid my coat across it, and pushed the pups inside. That silenced their whines, and I was able to sleep again, though, as I had foreseen, my coat was filthy when I came to put it on later.

At Ivnarssuit we found a small part of a house ruin by the water's edge; on top had been built a meat cache as at Kûk. We dug here for a time, and the material seemed so promising that we engaged the two young men to finish the work and bring what they found to us at Inugsuk. This place is indelibly impressed on my memory, for hundreds of large, horrible white worms lived in the midden. I have no horror of snakes, I am fond of mice, but everyone has some phobia, a shrinking, a dread, an overpowering dislike about which it is useless to chide or to argue, and mine is associated with wriggling, slimy creatures, with or without legs. To dig we had to pull the dirt *and worms* down upon ourselves, and I shudder still at the recollection of that ghastly sensation when one fell down the back of my neck!

Our collection, when finally completed by the finds of the young men, showed a culture belonging to the same period as that of the long community house at Qamaneq on Inugsuk. There were glass beads of the kind imported by the whalers, and a "winged" needlecase with the alternating cross-line decoration. Both the needlecase and the pattern belong to the Thule culture, so it was interesting to see how long they had lasted. Of course, our estimates of the ages of the finds we have made on this trip have to be very rough, for none of these collections is very big, and we have only three fixed points against which to measure them: "Older Inugsuk," that is, late Thule culture with round or clover-leaf houses; "Qamaneq" or long house period; and "Later Inugsuk" with square stone houses, probably only a hundred years old.

Our next stop after leaving Vale's home was to be at Igdlulik, on an island close to the Inland Ice. But the fjords about Igdlulik were packed with ice, and though I was all for pushing ahead, more authoritative judgment was against the risk. We landed on another island, and I saw what looked like an old dwelling place on the southeast shore. Mathiassen and I set off overland while the others followed in the boat. We found a camping place with the frame of a kayak, a sledge, two harpoon shafts, a *kamiut*, or stick on which to soften *kamiks*, and other things which the people had left behind them. The *kamiut* was broken, so I took it, for we had none for our own *kamiks* now that Ane was gone. Nearby were a couple of house ruins. One was a large square stone house, the other was quite modern. We did not dig. We were interested, however, because we had found this place though no one had told us of it. Several times we have found ruins in places where none were known, though as a rule the people know their country well. We were able to identify the place by the abandoned sledge. The camping place is called Nunako.

Because we dared not push farther up the fjord to the east, we went on south to Naujait ("the gulls"). The village is divided into three parts by two low cliffs that face each other and run back from the beach to the hillside. Several houses are built on each of the two headlands, but there is only one house in the valley between. Only one woman was at home in this lower place. She was living in a tiny sealskin tent; the others had gone *puissemut* ("seal hunting") in an umiak. She was the catechist of the village and had once been a servant in a white family, which accounted for the extreme neatness of her person. She invited me into her tent and gave me seal meat and coffee. The Eskimos from our boat came also. She had only three pieces of fresh seal meat, as far as I could see, but she offered it to me, though she served dried seal meat to the men. Of course, I could not refuse to taste, but I was careful not to take much. When the men went out, she showed me some things belonging to a little girl, probably her granddaughter. There was a doll with a china head and homemade body, and there were also some clothes which the old woman was making for the child. She had already finished the two strips of skin mosaic for the trousers and had embroidered her a guimpe. For company, I suppose, the old lady had a pup in the tent—this was the only time I saw a dog inside a tent or house. He was very fat and insolent, and yapped at me when I tried to make friends with him. The old lady had a blubber lamp, made from what looked like half a boiler. She was very proud of the lampstand, which her father or grandfather had made. I think we saw only half a dozen lamps in use during our trip, though Mathiassen says that there would be more in the winter. In summer the lamp is only a luxury to heat up the tent a little. The only stone lamp we saw was at Ivnarssuit.

While we were visiting the catechist, two women from a house on the south cliff came to invite us in to have coffee. One of them was of low intelligence. She was dirty and ragged; no one paid any attention to her mutterings. The old lady came up with us, taking my arm white-man style, and remarking that we looked like a man and his wife, because of my clothes.

There were only two house ruins at Naujait, and although we dug in the midden in front of the older, we found nothing.

That evening Mathiassen went to bed very early to smoke his

pipe and read the last of his Danish papers. I went for a walk by myself, the first time, I think, since I have been here that I have ever gone far alone. In fact, I doubt if I have ever in my life been very far away in woods or fields or wild places by myself. It gave me a curiously nervous and excited feeling that was quite delicious. Coming back across the empty hillside, I came to a place where women had collected piles of heather. Down in the fjord, almost at my feet, were two kayakers fishing. They sat motionless, not a ripple disturbing the clear reflection in the water, except for the quick, sharp jerks of their wrists. They were evidently fishing without bait. I sat on a rock and watched them for some time, and they pointed out to me the best way back to the village. Beside the path was an old grave.

August 25 was the last day of our voyaging. We stopped at the village of Qagsserssuaq in the morning, though we stayed only an hour. The village had been abandoned recently. There were many turf ruins, and the heavy stone walls of the post manager's house. The priest's house, a large building of turf, was pointed out to us. There were some older ruins, but these were very poor and much blurred by age. The people from Naujait were camping here in skin tents. Somewhere in the grass about the houses is the shutter release of my camera. I lost it while taking a picture of the graveyard.

At two o'clock we were back at our own island, and the great trip was ended. How wonderful to swing down the fjord, the landscape shifting itself back into the dear, familiar profiles, even more exquisite than we had remembered it, the hillsides greener by contrast with the bleak northern islands we had just left! Now we were in Inugsuk harbor, now we had touched the big rock in front of our camping place and were jumping ashore! Everything was as we had left it, the picture was complete except for the tents. We had come home.

IX

The End of Summer

DEAR FAMILY:

The sun was shining brightly and it was really hot as we unloaded our stuff and pitched the tents. Peter and Joseph helped us to establish camp. We tried to have our tents exactly as they had been, but when they were up, we discovered that we had unconsciously improved on the previous arrangement, for they stood a little farther apart, thus giving more room for the ropes, and they were set back a little from the very edge of the midden. The interior of my tent was the same as before, but Mathiassen had to change his quite a bit to make room for Robert.

Robert, we discovered, had no blankets or cover of any kind and seemed quite indifferent as to where or how he was to sleep. Mathiassen gave him one of the long rifle boxes Governor Otto had sent us. It was just big enough for Robert to squeeze in, though there seemed to be no room for turning. We fitted him in and were very much amused. Robert laughed, too, and said it was just like a coffin. Mathiassen's bed had been on the south side of the tent next to mine, but he put Robert there, and moved to the north side, for experience had shown that this was the more protected side. This was not out of regard for himself, but for the box of specimens, which could find a place only at his feet. We gave Robert our raincoats, the rubber sheet from my bed, and three sacks. When we began to open the graves, we had to take back two sacks for the bones, but as Robert was using them only for a pillow, he did not miss them much. Mathiassen reported the first morning that Robert had actually taken off both pairs of pants when getting ready for bed—and we had thought he would freeze! We kept asking him from time to time if he were cold, but he insisted to the end that he was quite warm.

When the hardest part of the work had been done that first afternoon, I asked permission to take the pups ashore. They had grown so fat that they could hardly walk. The first place they headed for was the edge of the midden near my tent, and tumbled down onto the half-excavated field, biting the blubbery earth with ecstatic growls. I had to take them away, for I was afraid that they might destroy some precious specimen still in the ground. The midden had a rich smell that afternoon, for the sun lay hot upon it. Always now I think of particularly nasty bits of it in terms of pup enjoyment.

We all had coffee together in front of my tent, but it was almost too hot to enjoy it. Then we waved goodbye to the *Natarnak*, which took with her our three full boxes of specimens. After we had finished arranging the tents, we went out to dig a little and found the earth well thawed. That night we could eat our supper in the tent without our heavy sweaters on and with the flaps open. This was almost a record. I was constantly astonished to see how green Inugsuk was in comparison with the more northern islands we had seen. Ground willow, dwarf willow, heather, *empetrum*, and caribou moss grew so thick that it was hard to say which gave the land its color, the rocks or the green plants.

One of the first tasks we gave to Robert was to build a meat cache for the three seals. He built one of stone in the approved style just beyond Mathiassen's tent. After a bit, when the meat had rotted, the north wind would waft the odor all over camp; but as it was pretty cold weather by this time, the smell seldom troubled us. It was curious that the meat kept fresh as long as the animals still had the skin or the thick layer of blubber on them, but once opened up they spoiled in a very few days.

The next four days after our return home it rained. One was not really uncomfortable, but I hated to have the beauty of the place, which depends so largely on the bright sunshine, spoiled by nasty weather. We were thankful, however, that we had had such a perfect day for our return. Now we could no longer use our rain-coats, for Robert needed them for his bed. Luckily, we did not have really drenching downpours; it was chiefly overcast and cold, with scattered showers. The *kamiks* were quite a problem, espe-cially for Robert, who had only two pairs, and those full of holes. To work, one was always sitting in the mud, though we had each a favorite slab of whale bone for a seat, which we carried about with us from field to field. Gradually, however, in spite of our efforts to keep track of them, they were shoveled under and lost.

Robert kept a little box just outside Mathiassen's tent in which he had all his worldly goods. He would sit beside this box when not working, in spite of the rain and cold which drove us in-side. Sometimes he would disappear altogether, and we would hunt all over the island for him. Then suddenly he would appear from behind a rock where he had been sleeping, just like a dog out in the rain, while we had huddled shivering in the tent.

In spite of the fact that the cross trench had been practically emptied before we went away, the first days at home brought won-derful digging. The first day we got 149 specimens, a new record. These included a large drying rack of baleen with a net bottom, which had been partially uncovered before, and a big mat made of wide strips of baleen, lashed to two crosspieces. We did not know what to make of this, and Mathiassen believed at first that it might be a toboggan, for baleen toboggans are known from Alaska. (1930: This mat turned out to be a house door, the first ever found of baleen. There are holes on one side for hinges of thong, and, like modern Central Eskimo and West Greenland doors, it was probably hung obliquely so that it would close of itself when opened. It measured a little higher and a little narrower than the entrance passage to House II, which we found such a tight squeeze.)

I dug in the field inside the big stone house; we were now well below the level of the floor of the more recent house and were uncovering a stone floor belonging to a much older structure. It was not so much fun to work there, because one could not see what the others were doing, and one could not announce any interesting discovery without climbing up out of the hole and over the stone walls. While I was working there, I came upon a great mass of human hair. It was all I could do to go on digging, for what horrors might not be preserved in the frozen soil! But I found nothing more than the scalp.

We came upon many evidences of house ruins near the bottom of the old midden. There was one long paving of flat stones, running across several squares, which might have been the floor of a dance house, or of a long community house. When we got to the bottom of some of the fields, we found pits which had been dug down into the moraine, and which were now below high-tide level. These pits were about two meters wide, but we could not tell their other dimensions because the outer edge of the midden had been washed away by the sea. These pits were filled with almost pure blubber and contained many good things. It was in one of these that Mathiassen found his baleen dish full of meat and an almost complete soapstone pot. I found two tiny ivory dolls in another pit, just under a stone paved floor. They represented a man and a woman. The female figure was exactly like one of these fat Eskimo women, and the man who made her must have been an artist. She is armless, according to the convention, and the head is missing. Her proportions are more ample in the horizontal than in the vertical direction. Stomach, buttocks, and breasts are well rounded. We call her the "Venus of Inugsuk." The little husband has only a triangle outlined in the region of the sexual parts, probably to represent the *natit*, or genital apron, that used to be worn.

Among other good things which we found in these lower layers were a number of ivory bodkins. Mathiassen's "private field," so called, not because he claims exclusive digging privileges, but because it has happened that he almost always is the one to dig there, is one of the richest for its size. It was evidently part of a house where a man lived who was an expert carver of bodkins.

The first two days we had a great many specimens to pack, and we soon filled the box in Mathiassen's tent. So we had to move the other "coffin" into my tent, thereby straining its capacity to the utmost. It could only fit in lengthwise, and the kitchen "table" had to be shoved up to the far end. My trunk had to be set on the platform at my head, and the flour and biscuit box (the only one left, and, alas, half empty) rested uneasily at my feet. The platform sloped to the door, and I always slid a little in the night, so usually the biscuits were found outdoors when Mathiassen came to wake me in the morning. The "coffin" in my tent made a wonderful table. We let the specimens collect in Mathiassen's tent until they overflowed the top of the specimen box, and then two or three days' accumulation of dishes, etc., would have to be moved from the lid of the "coffin," and the specimens packed in it. The big, flat baleen mat gave us a lot of trouble. The only way it could go in the box at all was diagonally, and we were afraid it would be injured unless it could be protected in some way. It was a problem to decide which of our few remaining smaller boxes we should sacrifice for lumber, and how to fit the small boards together to protect all the projecting corners of the mat.

It was already late in the season. Frost covered the ground with white, the water froze in our pail, and almost in one night the green hillsides of Inugsuk had turned to brown. On August 26 the sun set twice, once behind the hill directly opposite us, then reappeared for a few minutes in a cleft, only to be hidden for the night by the highest summit. This was about nine o'clock, and very soon it was too dark to read in our bags. We had no lantern or candles with us. After the first day's magnificent haul we got very few specimens, for the midden thawed more and more slowly, never deeper than three centimeters a day, and often less.

On August 27 we saw a rowboat coming from Upernivik. The

boat was going to Tasiussaq. The two men in the stern were Caspar Petersen, the "captain," and the brother of old Mrs. Nielsen. The latter was a very white Greenlander and a great man because he is a member of the *Landsraad*. He was taking a white whale net to Tasiussaq, for the "Old Man's" son wants to test the possibility of white whale hunting. This is another example of how a progressive Greenlander can help the natives to discover better methods of hunting. There were a crew of six in the boat, two grown men, two girls, and two boys. One of the girls was very pretty and was dressed in her fine clothes with a bead collar, as if for a dance. The boys looked like girls to me, for they had quite long hair, cut in a Dutch bob. We entertained them all with coffee, and then they rowed off, laughing and chattering gaily, though the rain was drizzling.

That night, according to my diary, we had boiled seal meat, French-fried potatoes, and pancakes—"very fine!"

We began to open new fields, for so little thawed in the old ones that we did not have enough work to keep us busy. We had no hope of getting to the bottom of these new fields, but we expected to get into the old midden, for the top layers would now be thawed for a depth of thirty centimeters or more. On August 28 we opened a new field near the trench. This involved a great deal of preliminary shoveling, for dirt from the trench had been thrown up here. Robert and I did the work. It was the first time that I had attempted such a long job of shoveling. The shovel, of course, was too heavy for my size, and though I kept at the job until it was finished, by the end of the day I found myself so lame and exhausted that Mathiassen nobly did all the packing. This was the first time I ever shirked that job. That day we celebrated the 4,000 specimen mark with apple cake.

We sent Robert out to hunt, and he came back with six baby *teist*. The old birds have almost all gone south, and with the rowboat, the only craft left us, Robert could not get close to the few remaining grown and wary birds for a shot. Our appetite for fresh bird meat was so strong that the slaughter of six tiny birds did not worry us, though there was pitifully little meat on the bones. They were too messy to eat when boiled in margarine—our usual method because it gives off plenty of fat and grease, necessary in this cold climate—so I made soup of them, boiling them in water and peeling all the flesh from the bones. I an very fond of this dish, though Mathiassen laughs at me for taking so much trouble. But I could not work hard at the fields all the time. The work is pretty strenuous, there is not enough to keep us all busy, and it is too cold to sit idle, so I welcome a job that will keep me sitting indoors by the Primus.

We finished off the little field from which we had been saving the animal bones. Robert helped Mathiassen with the identification of the different animals, although he is not nearly as well informed as Karl. The rest of the afternoon we worked on our index of specimens, though there was not enough space in the tent to spread out all the cards.

The next three days, August 30 to September 1, we had fair weather, with sunshine in the day and heavy frost at night. On these clear nights, without the protecting blanket of clouds to hold in the warmth of the earth, the little heat the ground managed to absorb during the day seemed to pour out with a rush into interstellar space in the first few minutes after the sun had set. The sun did not reach the midden until 11 A.M. and was gone at 7:30 P.M. By nine o'clock it was quite dark. One can understand that at this rate the ground thawed very slowly, and we could only scrape away a little mud from the surface, and pry up stones and bones. The pickaxe was much in use. August 30 was quite warm during the day. In the afternoon we went over to the long house at Qamaneq. We had a great deal of heavy work, cutting turf and heaving out stones. Most of the boulders were so big that it took both Mathiassen and Robert to move them, and we wondered how the Eskimo had got them into place. We found little.

The next day the two brothers came from Ivnarssuit with the specimens they had dug for us. We gave them lunch, and by mistake one of the young men was given a spoon as well as a knife and fork with which to eat his mashed potatoes and fried seal meat. He had evidently never eaten with these implements from a plate before, and was so shy he nearly choked with embarrassment trying to control these curious eating tools. That evening we celebrated Mrs. Mathiassen's birthday with chocolate and Tokay.

I think I really must have been getting tired after all these months of digging, for the next day I sat on the bank most of the time, watching Mathiassen dig over the little that had thawed, and talking about how I was ever to come back to the Arctic again and lead an expedition of my own.

An umiak came by with the post manager and his family from Tugssaq. The baby had been born ten days before and they were on their way to Augpilagtoq to get the child baptized by the priest there. We entertained the grownups with coffee and the children with candy. When they left, we decided to go with them to Târtoq. We rode in the umiak, and they took our boat in tow; Robert followed in one of their kayaks. It is a wonderful sight when such a family party travels. The boat is filled with things— birds, fish, or seal meat, cooking pots, coffeepot, dirty cups, coffee mill and frying pan to roast the beans, bags and boxes filled with clothing, and the inevitable tin bedroom pot (why this should be needed in God's great out-of-doors is beyond me), and perhaps a rifle or two. The father of the family sits in the stern and steers. The sons and sons-in-law come in their kayaks, sometimes paddling ahead to hunt, sometimes following lazily behind. In this party the wife with the newborn baby and her two other little girls sat in the stern. There was also a poor woman who seemed to be a servant, and with her were two little girls in ragged cotton dresses pulled over their sealskin pants. There were also two small boys squeezed in between the rowers. The oars were manned exclusively by women, but their relationship to the family I did not ascertain. The umiak is a clumsy craft, not suited to rough weather, and the long, awkward oars require plenty of muscle. But it was a happy and carefree party aboard, and we were glad to go with them. In the bow were four pups, too small to be left behind. No umiak party is complete without a dog. The seal meat was put right under their noses, and whenever they woke up they snatched a bite and had to be thrashed. It did not seem to occur to anyone to move the meat. The wet skin of the umiak was almost transparent, and through the sides I could see the shadows and lights of the water swirling past. [1975: There is not an umiak left in Greenland any more.]

It was only a short ride to the nearest point of Târtoq, and soon we had waved goodbye and the umiak was out of sight behind the icebergs. We had been landed at the foot of a great slanting shelf that runs up the face of the cliff. Here the square blocks are on an enormous scale, and though the climbing was not difficult, we felt like pygmies adventuring into a giant's land. At one place we had to climb through a hole, formed by a huge block that had fallen across the chasm, and I laughed at Mathiassen, for he had a tight squeeze. The view from the top was against the setting sun. We could see everything: our island, Sangmissoq, and all of Inugsuk spread out like a map, and beyond, the dark outline of Kingigtorssuaq against the waters of Baffin Bay. On top of Târtoq there was a cairn which had probably been built by some white man long ago. It had fallen down, so we repaired it. We came down by a longer and less precipitous way.

On September 2 there was rain again, and I woke with a bad sore throat, which I probably caught from Robert, and passed on to Mathiassen. This is very unorthodox for the Arctic, where there are supposed to be no germs.

The next day I lay in bed till eleven, when the sun looked so glorious that I crawled out. In the afternoon we went over to Sangmissoq, and measured the house ruins, etc. I took photographs while Mathiassen made a sketch map. Then we set about opening the big stone grave. We did not ask Robert to help us, because we thought he might have scruples against disturbing the dead, so set him to digging in the thin midden. He soon left that unprofitable work and helped us to throw down the stones. We found the nest of the snow bunting, now long deserted. I was surprised to find it quite clean inside, but Mathiassen told me that some birds teach their babies to go to the W.C. outside the nest, that he has actually seen swallows pushing the baby birds about until their little posteriors were over the edge of the nest.

The inside of the grave was really horrible. It contained ten skeletons, only one of which we could extract as an individual; the rest were mixed hopelessly together. On some of the bones hung shreds of filth and a few wisps of stiff black hair. The bottom of the grave was a muddy mass of rotted bones and a yellow grease that Mathiassen insisted upon calling "corpse fat." He wanted to take a photograph of the grave before we disturbed the contents, but in order to do this the camera had to be set too high for him to see the ground glass. I had to climb on his shoulders and do the focusing, while he balanced on a stone. It was rather scary to be held so high in the air, bending precariously over the open grave with its gruesome interior. We put most of the bones into one of the sacks; the single identifiable individual filled a small box. Under the bones in the fatty clay we found the remains of sealskins, with which the grave seemed to have been lined. Although the grave measured three meters in length and breadth by its outside dimensions, inside there was not room for more than two or three bodies at a single time. At first we had thought that this community grave contained the victims of an epidemic, but it now became evident that it must have been opened and used again and again over a long period of time. We were disappointed not to find anything buried with the bodies.

We had been eating seal meat pretty faithfully since our return to the island, hoping to get most of the meat disposed of before it went bad. By September 3 the remains of our two seals had become rotten, so we asked Robert to open his. He skinned it that night, and left the skin in the salt water to soak. When he went to get it the next morning, all that was left was the snoot by which it had been fastened. A shark had taken the rest. Robert was rather sad. This was probably the only seal that he had ever owned.

There was a raven which hung about Inugsuk, and would fly over our island, cawing loudly. Robert put the seal's entrails on the top of the island for him. We could not understand why he did this—was it to lure the bird within range, or was it only for kindness? We finally decided that he did it because he thought it was amusing to see the raven flying about. Some time later a small brown hawk drove the raven away. The poor old raven was twice his size and could have made a fight, I should have thought, but he allowed himself to be chased away without resistance, though he uttered the most mournful cries. Robert said that the hawk did not like him about because his squawks might frighten away the little birds.

The day of the theft of Robert's sealskin we obtained only 67 specimens, an average haul for these later days. That afternoon we opened one of two graves on top of the island. It did not look very big, and when we got the cover stones off, we were much surprised to find that it contained eleven skeletons, several being those of children. It was very difficult to get the bones out, for the grave was built against a ridge of bedrock and the stones on the other side were too heavy to move. We had to take turns climbing down into the narrow grave and digging in the "corpse fat" with a trowel. The bones were much more decayed than those in the grave on Sangmissoq, for so many bodies had been piled on top of each other that the bones were buried in filth. We found the remains of sealskins and cloth. We also found a collection of little sticks near the bones of a child; one of the sticks was identified as a toy harpoon. We also found a Thule harpoon head, very much decayed, a slate ulo blade, and an ulo handle of a type intermediate between those of the Thule culture and the modern West Greenland culture. These showed that this grave had been in use since the time of the old midden down until the time of the recent house ruins of the new midden.

We began to work at the house ruins on the point of Inugsuk just north of our island, at the site called "Inugsuk" in the church records. Two of these house ruins were modern affairs of turf; the third was a large square house built of stone, like House II on our midden. Just over the little hill behind the village was a gully filled with graves, which I called "The Valley of the Dead." Some of these graves were evidently recent. One was made of turf, and at the village site there was a large bare patch from which turf had been stripped, probably to make it. We excavated only the older stone house, working a little on it every day. It furnished us with a fine lot of "junk," though we were not able to clear it out.

While we were at work on this house, the two young men called on their way back to Ivnarssuit. They had been to Augpilagtoq. They told us that there was a bad throat sickness at Upernivik, and that in consequence the colony was under quarantine. No one was allowed to go there. Was it diphtheria? We were alarmed. In order to catch our ship, we must go to Upernivik by the fifteenth. Our provisions were already running low. The recent guests had drunk up almost all of our coffee, and there was no bread or hardtack left. We asked the young men to order supplies from Tugssaq for us, but were afraid we might not get the food, since the post manager was still visiting the catechist at Augpilagtoq.

That night, September 4, it was 46 degrees Fahrenheit in my tent with the Primus running for supper, and outside it was 37 degrees, which seemed rather chilly.

September 5 was Mathiassen's birthday. Isak, a thin man with a foolish smile, came from Tunorqo. I bought a white dogskin from him. We let Robert entertain him in Mathiassen's tent with boiled seal meat, while I opened the last can of sausages, which I had been saving for this occasion, and the last can of apple cake.

After Isak had gone, we went over to the house on the point. We were busy at work when we heard the sound of distant voices. We jumped up on the ruin and looked all around but could see no one. It was very curious. The fjord was filled with ice but seemed to be quite empty of human life. Suddenly, way across under the cliff of Târtoq, we caught sight of the umiak from Tugssaq coming back from Augpilagtoq. How we had managed to hear the people talking at that distance still remains a mystery, especially since we all had to shout together at the top of our voices to make them hear us. Perhaps they were passing a particular spot from which the cliff threw back echos. They came over to us, and Mathiassen repeated the order sent on by the Ivnarssuit young men—coffee, tea, flour, oatmeal, hard bread, margarine, and sugar. He paid for it in advance, plus fifty øre (a little less than fifteen cents) for kayak delivery. The post manager's wife had a big bowl of *empetrum* berries, some of which she gave to us. Robert ate them with great relish, though I found them full of seeds and tasteless. Robert told us that one of the young men with the party said that his father, Mathias Ling, had lived at the newest house on the point. He had moved there from Kingigtoq on account of some family quarrel. That was in 1897. He stayed only a few years and moved again to Tugssaq.

That night in honor of Mathiassen's birthday we had a grand feast, with dried vegetables, six baby *teist* with a few slices of pork in the soup, and pancakes with plum jam. Then we drank the last of the Tokay and the Madeira. In the afternoon we had also celebrated with chocolate.

The next morning we woke to find heavy frost, lying like snow. It stayed until noon when the sun reached the midden. Even when the sun was shining on the ground, it was so low that frost could still lie unmelted in the shadows of the little unevennesses. At supper it was 45 degrees in the shade, but there was a rapid drop after the sun set at seven, and at night it was bitter cold.

We slept late the next morning, and when we woke, we had been twelve hours in the bag. The return of darkness seems to make a big difference in our ability to sleep. There was heavy frost again, and the thermometer read 32 degrees in the shade at breakfast. It was quite hopeless to dig on our midden until afternoon, so we went back to the house on the point of Inugsuk. There we found quite a collection of clay pipes, most of them with faces on the bowl, and several pipes with the name of the maker, "Barne— Mile End" (in London.) I explained to Robert that Mr. Barne had made these pipes, and he was much impressed, asking if Mr. Barne were not a "very great man" (*inuk angisserssuaq*). Poor Robert's mind is much on pipes. His own pipe, with a metal lid snapping over the bowl, he loaned to a man in Ikermiut, and never saw it again. I gave him the remains of my clay pipe. I had bitten off the stem while digging too energetically, and it had been further broken until only a stub was left. It was a fearful operation to light it, for the bowl was now just under Robert's nose. I still had to keep my wooden pipe, for the cigarettes, even with careful budgeting, were almost gone.

Even the house ruin on the point, which faces south and is

not cut off from the eastern sun, had thawed very little. We chopped lumps of frozen earth out with the pick and set them on the walls to thaw. In one we found a piece of printed matter—in Eskimo! Robert told us it was not the *Avangnamioq*, the North Greenland newspaper. (1930: On his return to Denmark, Mathiassen discovered that this was a piece torn from a catechism, and probably dated from 1830 to 1870. The pipes seem to have come from Scottish whalers, probably in the first half of the nineteenth century.)

While we were digging in the house, a kayaker came from Tugssaq with the things which we had ordered and with change for the money Mathiassen had given the post manager. The food was done up in flour sacks which had to be returned, and the hard bread, ten kilos of it, had just been dumped into the body of the kayak.

We dug on our midden after lunch, though the fields had thawed a bare one centimeter. The bags of skeletons which had been sitting outdoors to dry had to be packed in the "coffin" in my tent. I was not very enthusiastic about sleeping with twenty-one dead Eskimos, and that night, I confess, I slept but lightly. Once I awoke—probably the ice had made a very loud noise—and, half asleep still, thought I saw that the lid of the "coffin" had been pushed a little to one side. I could smell the skeletons! How I had to laugh when I found it was only my dirty fingers! The bones really have no smell, and the dusty, moldy odor that comes from the graves is caused only by the lichens we crush when throwing down the stones. I have smelled it on the cairns, but I always associate it with graves.

Robert no longer collects iceberg fragments for the water pail. They hardly melt at all during the day, and at night they freeze together more solidly than ever. Instead, he takes all our pails over to the stream by Qamaneq and fills them there. He keeps a pitcher in my tent, where it does not freeze so hard during the night, and this makes it easier for Mathiassen to get breakfast. I still have my breakfast in bed. Mathiassen passes Robert's cup and sandwich out to him.

On September 7 we were rudely awakened by shots, and

tumbled out to see Dr. Falkenberg and Karl, who had come by kayak from Upernivik just to see how we were. How clean and pink the doctor looked! I was especially impressed by his long, slender fingers. There was not a speck of dirt on them, and the nails were in perfect condition. He is very fair, and even in Upernivik, where we finally got clean ourselves and became used to seeing clean people again, the doctor always seemed to be cleaner and more pink-and-white than other people. Here on our island he looked like a pure being from another sphere.

The doctor had brought two thermos bottles full of coffee and some delicious *smørrebrød*. We gorged on it, while Robert entertained Karl with seal meat. The doctor told us that the sickness at Upernivik was only mumps, so we were much relieved. What diphtheria would have meant in this isolated community is too horrible to contemplate. After the doctor had looked over the diggings and admired our industry, he went to sleep on Mathiassen's bed, and Karl went out bird hunting, while the rest of us worked as usual.

It was an overcast day, and very cold. There were more icebergs off the island than we had ever seen before. They were "rotten fellows" according to Mathiassen, with high towers and overhanging cliffs, which threatened great waves when they "calved." Luckily, only one of them broke near the island, and then it was at low tide, so no damage was done our camp. We heard a tremendous thunder, dropped our spades, and rushed to the highest part of the midden. A great block of ice was moving away from the mother berg, which rocked backwards and forwards, and finally turned over completely, lifting the blue, water-soaked bottom into the air, with water running down the upheaving sides like a waterfall. A series of waves spread in every direction, rattling the smaller blocks of ice together, and crashing in breakers on the beach. There was a great commotion when one set of waves met an earlier set which had traveled all the way around the island. The surf washed up against the stones for many minutes. Whenever we hear iceberg sounds, we always run to see what is happening.

When the doctor woke, we discussed with him the time of

our return to the colony. The doctor told us that the governor was planning to fetch us in the Upernivik schooner, *Sælen*, which was now going north to Kraulshavn. Before she would pick us up, however, she had to make a trip south to the coal mine on Disko, so we could not expect her before the twentieth. Then we should have to race south again to catch the *Gertrud Rask* at the coal mine, where she was expected on the twenty-fourth. Mathiassen was much worried, for he did not want to stay on the island so long. The digging could not last longer than the fifteenth, for by that time we could expect snow and heavy frost. Besides, he was afraid that Governor Otto was cutting the time very short, and we might easily miss the *Gertrud Rask*. If that happened, we should have to wait three weeks more for the *Disko*, which would not get us back to Copenhagen until the middle of November. We told the doctor that we wanted very much to leave on the fourteenth, and he promised that a boat of some kind would be sent to fetch us.

The doctor and Karl left at three o'clock. Although the doctor was an excellent kayaker, judging by a white man's standards, it was easy to see that he was very poor compared to Karl, who paddled easily and silently, never making an unnecessary movement.

The next day was Sunday, but we worked as usual. It had been overcast during the night, so there was no frost. The temperature did not rise above 36 degrees all day, but since there was no wind it did not feel cold. Mathiassen worked at straightening the walls of the excavations. These always slope in, so by the time we reach the bottom, the field is much smaller than when we started. The walls were the only parts that had thawed decently, for the sun was so low that its rays were more horizontal than vertical. Mathiassen also opened a new field near the grave on the midden, and was able to dig quite deeply here because the warmth had been carried down into the ground by the stones of the grave. While he was working there, I found a long missed Thule type, a cup-shaped fat scraper of ivory. Mathiassen thinks that these scrapers were not used more here because walrus ivory was scarce.

Instead, the two-handed scrapers of split leg bone were developed.

In the afternoon Robert and I found a very indecent doll in the house on the point. Robert was very particular that I should not miss any of its features.

The next day brought the same dull weather, and a little rain, too. Mathiassen was tremendously excited over the finding of a tiny square of woolen cloth deep in our midden. It was woven over-two-under-two, just like the woolen garments found on the dead Norsemen from South Greenland. It must have come from the Norsemen. Mathiassen also found a fishhook of baleen, without a barb—a new type.

On September 10 the thermometer stayed low all day, reaching only 40 degrees at 3 P.M. There was no wind, and we felt cold only when resting. Of course, it was hopeless to dig in our midden in the morning, so we went on to Qamaneq, to open a grave on a rocky point between the stream and the long house, a beautiful spot where we had once picnicked early in the summer. The grave was very fine in appearance, and seemed to be quite old, judging by the thick growth of lichens. It was substantially built, and there were many heavy stones to throw down. We rolled them down into the water below with glorious splashes. When at last we had made a hole and could look inside, what was our disgust and disappointment to find that the bones were quite fresh, horribly so, and that the grave could not be more than a hundred years old. We had to collect more stones and cover the opening.

Behind the long house we found another grave, very poorly preserved. It had been built in the middle of a gully where water runs in the spring, and all but a few bones had rotted away. Fortunately, the skull and jaw were in fine shape. The teeth were worn down almost to the roots, so we judged they must have belonged to an old woman who had spent a long life chewing skins to soften them.

After lunch Mathiassen worked on the midden, while Robert and I dug in the house on the point. We had been very anxious to bring the number of specimens up to the 5,000 mark, and now, to our delight, we had achieved 5,042, and could celebrate with the last little bit of chocolate. We had just made it when, to our disappointment, two fellows came from Augpilagtoq, bringing with them fish and birds. We were delighted to get fresh meat, for the seal meat was now past eating, but we did not have enough chocolate to share with them, so had to make coffee, and save the chocolate till that evening.

Robert is quite useful. He not only washes dishes, but peels potatoes, and can cook a little. He also keeps our *kamiks* in repair.

We opened a few fields near the north end of the midden, behind the little turf ruin that I call "my" house, because I excavated it all myself. The midden is only thirty centimeters thick here, and the top of the old midden reaches a mossy layer only ten centimeters above the bottom. Mathiassen cut a section of the turf from the top of the midden to the bottom, which we packed in the now empty margarine can, marking with a peg the line between the two levels of the midden. This is for a friend of his who is making a study of climatic changes in Greenland, and for whom such a tiny bit of turf with pollen, even less well documented and dated than ours, is of great value.

The nights were getting increasingly cold. I had great difficulty in keeping warm. I found that I had to pin my spare blanket to my soldier's coat to make a kind of extra sleeping bag of it, and when I crawled in, I had to wrap my dogskins about my feet. If the coverings did not fit tightly, the little pocket of air would get cold very rapidly, and I would soon shiver.

September 12 was the first really cold day. Ice formed in the water pail as soon as it was broken. Strong cakes of the new sea ice floated down the fjord. It was nasty working, and my feet ached with cold all day. All we could do was to open fresh fields, for though the frost lay thick on the turf, it had not penetrated into the ground. Stripping the turf, however, was a miserable business for bare hands. In the house on the point, where Robert and I again worked in the afternoon, I found a little pocket behind the stones of the entrance pasage in which were crammed a few fragments of the same dear, familiar blue Willowware china that we have at home. You can imagine how surprised and happy I was to find this, and how it *almost* made me homesick. Soon I will have been eighteen months away from home. I think the finding of this china behind the stones shows that the house was rebuilt at some period. The china must certainly have come from England on some whaler.

September 13 was such a dull, overcast day that we decided we would not dig, but would go for an exploring walk on the other side of Inugsuk. Just as we were about to set off, a kayaker arrived who told us that he was with a whole umiak party, camping on the island just south of Inugsuk. He was lame in one foot, and had to hop. We thought it would be fun to visit the party, so we followed the man in our rowboat. We were disappointed to find that the people had already broken camp and were about to leave. The old man of the family was Lars Aronsen, with gray hair and a voice that was only noisy air. He spoke very slowly and with great effort, thrusting his face close to ours. He told us that his wife's mother's elder brother had lived at the house on the point of Inugsuk in 1850. There were three other men in kayaks, two of whom were married and had their wives with them in the umiak. One of these was nursing a baby. There were also some other women and children, including the half-witted woman we had seen in Naujait. The people had been to Prøven's salmon fjord and were now on their way to Tasiussaq, where the "Old Man" lives. The umiak was in a dreadful mess, with all kinds of filthy dishes and clothing lying in the bottom. There were also the omnipresent pups lying on some featherbeds beside the woman and baby.

We had given the people some candy, and they now asked us if we wanted a salmon. We thought the fish was a gift, but they asked for money. We had only twenty-five øre with us, which was more than a fair price for the fish, since it is the regular price for a bird, but the people wanted more, so we had to give the fish back. I was disappointed, because I had not tasted any salmon. It was not a true salmon, but a salmon trout, with white meat but a bright salmon-colored skin. We were angry at these natives, who seemed to think they could get anything they wanted.

We all started off then in our boats. The kayaks went on

ahead, and the umiak followed, with the women at the oars and the old man steering. They turned west toward Kingigtorssuaq. I remarked to Mathiassen how daintily the man who had stopped to see us dipped his paddle. He took short, mincing strokes and tee-tered his body. I thought from the way he acted and the way he looked at me that he was interested in girls. I told Mathiassen this, and he repeated it to Robert, who answered that the young man did want a wife. There were several young men at Naujait who wanted very much to marry, but no girl would have them, because the old man of the place was too disagreeable.

We landed at the southernmost point of Inugsuk, and told Robert that he might go ptarmigan hunting. It seems that he had obtained a few cartridges from someone. We wanted him to meet us with the boat at a certain spot in the harbor at lunchtime, but since he had no watch, we had to tell him to be there when the sun should be as far to the west of Qaerssorssuaq as it was now to the east of it. We set off along the southern shore of Inugsuk Island. Everywhere the leaves were red, the black *empetrum* ber-ries were in their prime, and the ground was hard under a thin layer of slime. The frost was beginning to make the bare patches of ground hump up and the stones come out. We followed along the high hillside above the cliffs. The umiak and its three kayaks were ahead of us, dwarfed to tiny water beetles by the distance and the expanse of the fjord. We could see the men in the kayaks shooting at birds, but it was a long time before the noise reached us.

We passed above the place where we had gone grave robbing before. Just beyond we came upon a curious structure, built of great boulders. It was about the size of a grave, but there was only the circular wall, without a cover, and on the landward side was a hole big enough for a man to crawl through. There was no sign of roof, and there were none of the smaller stones lying about which are usually heaped over a grave. There were no bones inside. Mathiassen thought this might be an empty grave, built in mem-ory of someone who had died at sea, and whose body was never found. There are many examples of such monuments in Green-land.

We turned inland from this mysterious structure, and
climbed to one of the many summits of Inugsuk. Below us lay a
chain of lakes, one of them quite large. Karl had drawn lakes on
his map but he had mixed them up. Mathiassen had been correcting this map as we walked. We could look out over the sea to the
north. The mouth of Upernivik's Icefjord was choked with ice. It
was an overcast day, but it looked as if new sea ice were forming
between the icebergs. We caught a last glimpse of the umiak
squeezing between the bergs, and surmised that they would have a
hard fight to Tasiussaq.

We decided we would visit the old umiak campsite where
Cornelius had stayed, for it was a good flat spot and might have
ruins. We had not gone far, however, before we were stopped by a
deep ravine which ran up from one of the bays toward the northeast. We followed the edge of the cliff for a certain distance until
we thought we could find a way down. We came out, however, on
a ledge halfway down the face of the rock, beyond which it was
impossible to go. On the slope opposite was a mother ptarmigan
and her chicks, eating *empetrum* berries. They did not seem frightened of us, though the mother moved them a little farther away.
We hoped Robert would have good luck with his hunting. We
turned back toward the interior of the island, and finally found a
way down into the ravine, though even here I stuck halfway down
and had to be helped. We crossed the ravine and walked up the
slope on the farther side, only to be stopped again by a cliff above
a big lake. It is extraordinary how cracked and carved up this
country is by ice and frost. There is none of the gentleness and
regularity of contour of a normally eroded land. We passed around
the lake and came down a stream to the fjord. At Cornelius' old
camp we saw the remains which he had left and the ruins of several older meat caches and tent rings, which proved that the place
was not unpopular.

Mathiassen was anxious to reach a hill on the northwestern
end of the island, so we set off again, and at such a good pace that
I had to beg Mathiassen to pity my short legs. We did not have
time to reach the place he had intended, though we did come out

on a hillside above one of the northern fjords. All along the way we had passed frozen ponds and pools, from which I had broken pieces to suck. Only the big lakes, roughened by the wind, were not frozen. We were surprised, however, to find that the fjord was covered with fresh ice. Mathiassen threw a stone down, and though it fell from quite a height, the ice was strong enough to hold it. The sea ice is not brittle like freshwater ice. It sagged a little when the stone hit it. Sea ice looks a little like snow, and is opaque and coarse, as if one could actually see the grains of salt in it. One does not slide on it as much as on lake ice.

By the time we got back to where Robert was waiting with the boat, we were twenty minutes late. He had shot only a *teist*.

This was to be our last night on Inugsuk. We had a grand feast. There was soup made from a gull and some *teist*, boiled fish, eider duck breasts fried with onions, pancakes with the last of our plum jam, and coffee. It was wonderful! By the time we were through eating and went to bed it was half past nine, and really dark, with the stars out.

We had one disappointment in the matter of food. The corned beef we had eaten the evening before we started on the trip with the *Natarnak* was so good that I had been saving the last can as a feast dish. When we opened it that last day, I found that it was spoiled. There was a hole in the can, made from the inside, as if by a nail, and concealed by the paper label. It looked like sabotage. We were somewhat disturbed, for the can was a product of a famous Danish firm, noted as outfitters for Arctic and Antarctic expeditions. This made me think of Franklin and his men, who had died of starvation, leaving behind them a great cache of canned goods, some untouched, others opened and unused. Had their tragedy been caused in some such way as this? Robert wanted to eat the meat. But Mathiassen showed him the hole, and assured him in as solemn a manner as possible that certain and horrible death was inside the can. We threw it well out into the water where he could not reach it.

The last night! What a sad, bitter thought! How much it was ending! The summer which had seemed so long and our happy life on the island, which had gone on as if it might last forever, were finished.

I woke several times in the early morning to hear the snow pattering on the roof of the tent. When we went outside, we found the ground white and wet with soft, unpleasant snow. There was a strong southwest wind, and both mountains were hidden. It looked as if we were in for a bad storm, and we wondered if the boat would be able to fetch us. We now began to look over our provisions. We had enough to last for a week with careful management, though we had only five eider ducks and one *teist*, and enough of other good things to last for only a few days. We still had plenty of salt herring (*appetit sild*), which the Greenland Trade had sent us instead of sardines, and we thought somewhat ironically that it would be hard to be reduced to these when there was nothing more filling for our stomachs. The worst was that we had burned a great deal of kerosene in the last week and did not know how much there was left. It would be pretty grim to be left on the island in this cold weather with no work to keep us busy and no fuel for the Primus. Mathiassen claims to know how to manage a blubber lamp, and since there was still a good deal of rotten blubber in our meat cache, we did not really worry. Of course, we still had our little rowboat, though it would be of no use in rough weather. I was almost hoping that we would have to stay on the island just long enough to know what it would be like under sterner conditions. I would have been quite glad to do so if there had been something interesting to do, but the digging was stopped by the frost, and we were now in danger of missing the ship. If that should happen, I knew that you and D—— in England would be terribly worried. As for Mathiassen, now that the work was over, there was nothing left for him. He was terribly anxious to be gone. He has already had all the experience he wants of camping in a tent in the Arctic fall and of starving, and he could not see any fun in being uncomfortable.

To pass the time, we went on with the index of specimens. We did not finish it for some weeks, but perhaps this is a good time to summarize the results of our summer's work.

Specimens of the Inugsuk culture from the "old midden," Tunúngassoq
(Photograph, National Museum of Denmark, courtesy of Therkel Mathiassen)

1–5. Harpoon heads. (1 is 12 cm. long.)   6. Arrowhead.   7. Wound pin.   8. Gull
hook.   9. Side prong for bird dart.   10–11. Blades for harpoon heads.   12. Blade
for arrowhead.   13. Blade for scraper (used as burin?).   14. Blade for scraper.

I have already told you about the culture of the "new midden," with its big, square stone houses; of the earlier culture belonging to the "long house" at Qamaneq, which dated from the latter half of the seventeenth or early eighteenth century; and lastly about the evidence of contact between the Norsemen and the Eskimo of our "old midden" in the thirteenth century. Mathassen dates the old midden from the beginning of the thirteenth to the end of the fifteenth century, for there was no evidence of contact with the whalers who began to come here after 1600. This old Inugsuk culture represents the last link of a chain that Mathiassen has traced across Canada and into Northwest Greenland, beginning with Naujan, northwest of Hudson Bay, in the tenth and eleventh centuries. This Inugsuk culture is not really the Canadian Thule culture, for many of the old types have dropped out and new ones have been added, nor is it quite the first culture in West Greenland, for the first immigrants from Cape York in the north must have brought the Cape York Thule culture with them, though it has not yet been found in the northern part of Upernivik District.

The harpoon heads include the Thule types with open socket, though the dominant form is a slightly younger type, known from Alaska to Greenland, with a closed socket and blade. Some of the flat heads show the beginnings of the rich West Greenland development of this type. We also found harpoon blades, foreshafts, socket pieces into which the foreshaft fits on the top of the shaft, shafts, finger rests, and ice picks for the butts of the shafts. The foreshaft is the piece that fits into the socket of the harpoon head. On the harpoons for killing seals at their breathing holes in the winter ice, the foreshaft is rigid; on the harpoons thrown from the

15. Toy ulo blade. 16. Drill point. 17. Ivory bodkin with chain link, carved from one piece. 18. Ivory bead with two pendants, carved from one piece, 19. Bead. 20. Pendant. 21. Half of wooden amulet box. 22. Wooden doll: a woman with topknot, brow band, genital apron, and boots. 23. Doll: a man. 24. Ivory doll with amulet strap. 25. Ivory bodkin with face on top. 26. Ivory bodkin. 27. Ivory comb. 28. Toy lamp. 29. Upper half of broken ivory "winged" needlecase.

kayak, the foreshaft is hinged. We also found barbed heads for bladder darts, mouthpieces for the bladder, and plugs to stop the holes. There were also lance heads of bone with stone blades. While waiting for the seal to come to his breathing hole in the ice, these old Eskimo used to sit on little wooden stools with three legs, and when they had harpooned the seal, dragged him home across the ice on a dragline with bone handle. For the spring hunting, when the seals lie half asleep on the edge of the ice floes basking in the sun, the hunter used a scratcher of wood, with toes to which were tied seal's claws. The seals thought the scratching noises made by this implement were due to another seal shuffling about, and so paid no attention to the hunter stalking them. When a seal was killed in the water from the kayak, the wounds were skewered shut with wound pins (not stopped with the modern wooden plugs), and the body was towed home. The toggles for the towing line found at Inugsuk do not belong to the Thule culture, but to the West Greenland kayak culture, just beginning to develop.

We found fragments of wooden bows, and a baleen bow. These were backed with twisted sinew lines to give them spring; the sinew was twisted with a special twister and put on with a marlinespike. There were wooden arrow shafts, with a notch at the rear end, and several different styles of bone arrowheads, some with inserted stone blades, others barbed, and others again quite plain. All had conical tangs for attachment to the wooden shaft, with the exception of one that had the modern oblique scarf. The arrow feathers had been trimmed on little boards. We found the various parts of bird darts, including the side and central prongs and the wooden shaft. These bird darts, as well as the bladder dart and the kayak harpoon, were thrown from the throwing board, though we had no piece which we could be sure belonged to a throwing board. We also got antler bola balls for killing birds, the first found in Greenland, though well known from the Thule culture and from Alaska. Other hunting weapons were bone daggers for dispatching wounded game, knives for pressing the water out of skins, gull hooks (a kind of fishhook for birds), a baleen fishhook (the first ever discovered of that material), and gorges, that is, a simple type of fishhook made of a single piece of bone, pointed at both ends and fastened to the line in the middle. We also obtained an ivory salmon decoy, the first from West Greenland, and parts of fish spears.

The sledge shoes and crossbars of sledges showed that the Inugsuk type was narrower, with straighter and wider runners, than that used in West Greenland today. It must have been like the type of sledge used by the modern Central and Polar Eskimo. Whip handles and trace buckles were also found. We did not secure many pieces of either kayaks or umiaks, though the toys showed these two types of boats. The umiaks must have been used for whaling. The kayak paddles were more slender and more pointed than the modern type, and in this respect resembled those of Alaska and the Thule culture. The kayak was just beginning to acquire that fundamental importance that it has in the modern West Greenland culture.

Although no modern West Greenlander knows how to build a snow house, and has never seen one unless the Polar Eskimo who come south in the winter with the mail sledges have made one, the Inugsuk Eskimo made snow houses, as we could tell by the snow knives, snow shovels, and snow probes that we found.

Other tools used by men were knives of various types, baleen saws (imitated from Norsemen's saws?), whetstones, adzes, bone hammers, hammer stones, mattocks with bone blades, wedges, chopping blocks of whale vertebrae, and bow drills with stone bits, bone sockets, wooden shafts, and mouthpieces of caribou astragalus. There were also hand drills, and flint flakers of walrus rib. The women's tools consisted of ulos with the simple, old-fashioned handles of the Thule culture, knives for shaving baleen (the first found in Greenland), skin scrapers with stone blades, fat scrapers of split, hollow leg bone, and one of ivory in the old Thule cup shape, bone awls, needlecases from which hung sealskin thimbles on ivory thimble holders, sewing knives, cutting boards, etc. I have already mentioned the ivory and wooden bodkins. They seem originally to have been a useful implement of some sort, and hung at the belt. Later they became purely ornamental. Many were decorated with a woman's bust and head at the top, others had only the topknot. These bodkins are found only in West and Northeast Greenland. The stone lamps were of both the Thule and the modern types. The cooking pots were rounded, not square-cornered like the modern pots. We also found an antler pothook, an antler blubber pounder, parts of fire drills and boards, lumps of pyrites (fool's gold) for striking a light, wooden bowls and meat trays, tub staves, soapstone bowls, drying racks made of an oval baleen frame filled in with baleen netting, wooden dippers, and bone spoons, the decoration of which seems to have been copied after those of the Norsemen. There were also pointed sticks of antler for serving meat, implements for digging the marrow out of bones, handles for carrying bags or quivers, even a small skin bag, and many cups and bowls made of baleen with wooden or bone bottoms. I have already mentioned the numerous platform mats or mattresses of baleen, and the baleen door.

Besides the sealskin mitten I found, we obtained two others of the same type. The dolls showed that the natives used to wear the loincloth, or *natit*, now no longer worn because the Eskimo have been made to feel that it is sinful to sit naked in the house. Both men and women wore short boots, and the hoods of the women were pointed, like those of the modern Polar Eskimo. In their boots they sometimes stuffed baleen shavings instead of dry grass, as do the Alaska natives. They had snow-beaters for knocking the snow off their clothes before coming into the house, bone combs for their hair, louse-catchers, and back-scratchers. The dolls show that the women wore their hair gathered into a knot more at the back of the head, instead of on top, as now, and they wore brow bands of ivory. We found bear-tooth amulets, and other tooth pendants, beads, and carved drop pendants of ivory.

There were drum frames and handles, for the first time made of baleen, and amulet boxes, for the first time found in Greenland, though known from the Thule culture. Other objects that ought to be mentioned though we do not know what they were used for are the wooden handles which I called sling handles, and some little rectangular pieces of bone, which Mathiassen thinks may have been men for a game. As for their games, we found several *ajagaqs*, pieces of bone with many holes, which are tossed into the air and caught on a pin, the scoring being determined according to what hole the pin has caught, and we found a sealskin ball, for the first time represented archeologically, tops, buzzes or bull-roarers, wind wheels, and a bear figure.

The children's toys were particularly interesting. There were 101 dolls—that is, there were more dolls than specimens of any other single type—and the other children's toys mirrored the culture of their parents so fully that we could have learned the essential character of this culture if only the toys had been found. Some of the toys were small implements which the children could have used, others were miniature articles for a doll's hunting or housekeeping. There were harpoons, bows and arrows, bird darts, lances, bladder darts, sledges, kayaks, umiaks, knives, snow shovels, adzes, mattocks, cooking pots and lamps, meat trays, spoons, platform mats, and the mysterious wooden handles, and all the parts that belonged to these things. A great number of the toys were made of baleen. Anybody could see that the parents loved their children and delighted to make toys for them.

In summing up, Mathiassen finds that 89 percent of the types found at Inugsuk belong to the Thule culture. The remaining types are younger and show that the development toward the modern Greenland kayak culture had already begun. The archeological material found on the now uninhabited Northeast Coast of Greenland shows close similarity to the Inugsuk culture, and Mathiassen believes that the northeast was reached by the Eskimo only after they had migrated south along the West Coast and rounded Cape Farewell. It is the tracing out of this migration which Mathiassen hopes to do in the next years.

X

Farewell

Upernivik Again

DEAR FAMILY:

We had lunch on our island that last day, still wondering how long we would have to stay, anxious to get back to Upernivik and yet sorry to go, and very restless because there was nothing to do. The Upernivik rowboat slid miraculously out of the mist, old Caspar at the tiller, and six stout men at the oars. We gave them coffee, for they were quite wet, and hurried to pack our things. This took us until nearly four o'clock. When my tent was down, I saw how terribly sooty it was on the inside. When the last of the alcohol was used up, we had primed the Primus with kerosene, and that made a dreadful smoke. (1930: True kerosene, of course, cannot be burned without a wick. The fuel we used in our Primuses behaved much like gasoline and was probably a product midway between our American kerosene and gasoline.) The top of Mathiassen's tent was dirty also where the little snow buntings had once

255

perched. They had not found it easy to balance in the wind on top of the tent, and had slid off several times.

The men all helped us, or tried to help us, with the packing, and ran about picking up quite useless junk which we had thrown away. They seemed to set great store by scraps of paper and even such trifles as broken or bent Primus needles—why, I can't imagine, since not one of them could have owned a Primus. We could not take the heavy boxes of specimens with us in the rowboat, so these were left in a pile with the waterproof bed sheets over them. The Upernivik schooner was to pick them up on her trip back from the north. The smaller boxes, my trunk, and our suitcases came with us. At the last minute, when we were all aboard and ready to go, Robert appeared dragging the foul seal meat which we had not been able to eat for days, and put it in the boat. Evidently he was so pleased with his seal he could not bear to leave any of it behind. Robert washed his hands, we cast a last, sorrowful look at our old home, and the boat pushed off into the dirty weather.

We watched our island as long as it was in sight behind the icebergs. The midden showed black and inviting to the end.

Caspar had some letters for me, much to my surprise. They had reached Copenhagen too late to catch the *Gertrud Rask*, but had come on the third trip of the *Hans Egede* to Ūmánaq, and from there had wandered by devious ways up the coast.

It was a long, cold trip. Mathiassen and I had a blanket to wind about our legs, but the cold seemed to come up through the very bottom of the boat. The men rowed standing up and facing forward, except for occasional short intervals when they sat down facing the stern. They rested hardly at all. By the time we came to the stretch of open water between the last island and Upernivik Island, the snow was falling thick, and for a while we could not see the land at all. Mathiassen had given Robert his old digging coat. In spite of the cold and the snow, Robert did not put on this new raincoat until we were just about to land, saving it, no doubt, for that important occasion. He had washed his white knitted cap with the tassel before coming to town, and he looked most impressive.

Upernivik Island was much longer than I had remembered, and it was eight o'clock before we reached the harbor. Of course, there was no one at the little dock to receive us and help us land our stuff, and it seemed to take hours before someone came in answer to Mathiassen's telephone message to the governor's house. We put our boxes in the storehouse and walked to the "White House." How curious it was to be back in civilization again! We felt dirty and weather-beaten, and our sealskins were much too warm for the heated rooms. Mrs. Otto had a supper prepared for us, and the white people gathered round while we devoured the food. Mathiassen exclaimed constantly over how good everything tasted, but I was disappointed, because the civilized food was somehow not as delicious as I had expected it ought to be. I was really sad that the work was over, and could have wished that the summer was beginning again. Mathiassen was quite happy; because, I think, he knew that he could come back again and again, while I was so uncertain about my future. Everyone asked questions about our work, and when we started to tell them what we had done on the island, I was astounded to hear how strange our answers sounded. What had been our real life five hours before was already a myth, a dream left behind in the mist and snow. How little one can keep of such an experience! Now it was only words, cheapened and made vulgar by the telling to others who could not really share. One cannot express what once was real and living. That is incommunicable, and to try to force such an experience into words is to kill it. It becomes set and crystallized; one remembers only the words, not the feeling they hide. I realized now with a pang that in the days to come I would be homesick for the little desert island, for the sweet smell of rotten blubber from the fresh-thawed midden, the warm sun on my stiff sealskins, the cold wind in my face, the happy voices of the Eskimos, the rich savor of seal meat and eider ducks, and at night the knocking of ice against ice beyond my tent door. Will these ever be mine again?

We were in Upernivik for ten days, while we gradually got the dirt washed off, though our hands were not really clean until the calluses had peeled. The mitigations of my boredom were the work on our specimen index with Mathiassen and the feeding of two pups.

The pups were the best fun. Their history was long and complicated. Originally one of the finest dogs in Governor Otto's team, Felice, had pups. All but one died, and this one was killed, because it hardly seemed worthwhile to raise only one. Felice, however, stole two pups, but by this time she had no more milk. Another dog, perhaps the original mother, stole them again, and eventually all the dogs in the pack joined in eating the unfortunate creatures. Felice, however, not to be cheated, stole two more pups, and now was managing to feed them a little, though there was not enough milk and they seemed to be dying.

I asked to see them, and the maid brought them in while we were having after-dinner coffee. For an experiment, I gave them a little condensed milk, and it was a pleasure to see how greedily they drank. Mrs. Otto gave me permission to feed them. It was difficult at first, for they wanted to suck and could not understand the technique of lapping. They stuck their paws into the saucer, spilled the milk all over themselves and the floor, and then yelped because they could not get anything to eat and were cold. I fed them three times a day, and this necessitated scrubbing the kitchen floor every time. The mother was chained in the yard, and had a barrel full of straw to live in. She did not seem to mind my taking the pups from her, though she subjected the poor little things to a most energetic licking when they were returned. Even during the short time of our stay, the pups improved. They learned to walk, and would come tumbling out of their barrel when they heard me call. The smaller one was still inclined to howl for his food when it was only an inch from the end of his nose, though one day he bit his brother when the other pushed him from the dish, and once the bigger pup actually managed a little squeaking bark. I loved the pups dearly, and it was hard to refuse Mrs. Otto's offer to give them to me.

The day that stands out most clearly in our minds was that when Mathiassen and I climbed Qaerssorssuaq. We had talked of it for some time, but everything depended upon the arrival of the colony's new motorboat. It had started in August from Úmánaq, with a crew of Eskimos under the very white Greenlander, Peter Dalager, and everyone was worried because it had not arrived. Imagine our delight, however, when it was sighted just before sunset on the eighteenth. It was Dr. Krüger's old *Hawlit*, the boat that had given such a lot of trouble with the screw. Peter had spent the time in visiting every single village on the way. We were present when Governor Otto received him, and gave him a calling down. I will say this for Peter—he is the only man who does not seem small in the presence of the governor.

Our climb was scheduled for the twentieth. It was arranged that we were to touch at a small island, Nord Ø, southwest of Upernivik, to put ashore some men who were to build a beacon, and that we were also to visit some house ruins on another island, Bruun Ø, which was also nearby. We had to get up at five o'clock. Mrs. Otto with her usual thoughtfulness had prepared a wonderful pile of sandwiches to take with us, and had left our breakfast on the table. There were also two bottles of home brew, "Greenland beer." The *Hawlit* was up to her usual tricks, and did not get started until seven. I had brought a pair of dry *kamiks* with me, and put the beer bottles in them to carry them to the dock. On the way someone dropped a boot, and not only was the bottle broken, but my *kamik* was soaked. It still smells of beer.

At Nord Ø, where we put the men ashore to build the cairn, there were two house ruins, which seemed quite old. The blacksmith was in charge of the gang and had foresight enough to bring a tent, Primus, and cooking outfit. As they finished their work by one o'clock and we did not pick them up until eight, they had need of warmth and food.

Bruun Ø is really two islands, lying quite by themselves in the open sea, and separated from each other by a very narrow channel. The ruins were actually on the half that was not Bruun Ø. There were six houses in all, ranging in age from the old Thule ruin, half washed away by the sea, to the large square stone house with high walls. There were a number of graves on the hillside in back. This would have been an excellent place to excavate were it not for the position of the island. Lying so close to the open sea, it would be drenched with rain and fog all summer, and few people would care to come so far to visit. The ground was frozen hard as iron, even the turf crackled as we walked, and it was impossible even to poke along the edge of the midden.

It was almost noon when we reached Qaerssorssuaq. We ran into a broad, unprotected bay, south of the famous auk cliffs and out of sight of Upernivik. The shore was lined with enormous piles of glacial debris which hid the land from our sight. It took some time to find a place where we could get ashore from the boat, for there was quite a little surf running. Peter Dalager agreed to anchor the boat a short distance from shore and to wait there for us.

There was plenty of snow, even at the water's edge, and we slipped clumsily over icy rocks and frozen hummocks. It seemed as if more than half one's energy had to be spent in keeping one's equilibrium on the rough ground. We could walk but slowly. We were in a wide valley, leading up to the northeast, and flanked on the right by a long spur reaching down from the summit, up which Dr. Falkenberg had told us he had climbed. At first we followed the north bank of the stream, but when the stream narrowed and offered a good frozen passage, we crossed over. Here we had a choice of routes: We could scramble up the steep side of the valley to the top of the spur, from which we knew we could follow the doctor's route to the summit, or we could go up to the head of the valley, certainly an easier route for the first part of the way, but one which might offer hidden difficulties when we came to the shoulder of the mountain. I was all for taking the sure route and risking nothing, so we made for the ridge. It was painful climbing. The snow was so soft that we sank through, and it offered no cushion for our stumbling feet. It only hid the rocks, and these were cracked into sharp edges that pressed through the thin soles of our *kamiks*. We had not had any dry grass in our boots for many days. I had neglected to bring a digging stick to use as a cane, so to keep my balance I had to walk doubled over so that I could touch the rocks above me. Although we were soon very warm, I had to wear mittens to protect my hands, so they were too hot.

It was about one thousand feet in elevation at the top of the ridge. From below we had seen the edge of it outlined with bare rocks, and had hoped that the top might be free from snow. Our hopes were disappointed, but nevertheless the going was easier than on the lower hillside. The slope was gentle, and there were wide patches of bare gravel where one could pick one's way. Between these the snow lay drifted. We zigzagged up from one bare island to the next. We were glad that there had been no thaw since the cold weather came, so that we did not find the rocks coated with ice.

We climbed for hours. The slope grew steeper, the bare spaces fewer and smaller, the drifts wider and deeper. I floundered along in Mathiassen's wake. We rested often, lying at full length in the snow, our faces bathed with sweat, our feet aching from the sharp stones. The barometer gave us great encouragement. The last stretch up onto the shoulder of the mountain was for me the most tiring part of the day. In spite of my exertions, Mathiassen kept getting yards ahead of me. I would step off hidden rocks into drifts that were up to my knees, up to my hips even. Just when I was almost despairing, the slope fell away before me, and I emerged half running onto the level shoulder. There was a great boulder on which we rested.

We were three thousand feet high. Just behind us as we sat was the last summit, hardly more than a pile of loose rocks. Below us lay snow-covered slopes falling away to the fjord. Lakes shone black in the hollows of the valleys. To the south, behind the tumbled, chaotic islands of gneiss, stretched the level, dark headland of Svartenhuk, the black layers of basalt striped with snow. Between us and it lay the islands on which were the outposts of Prøven and Søndre (Southern) Upernivik, and the island, Dark Head, against which Mathiassen's ship, the *Bele*, had run in a fog at the very beginning of the Fifth Thule Expedition. The sun was hidden by purple clouds. From the southwest a storm was riding up out of Baffin Bay. Sea and sky merged in orange and purple. The few great icebergs out in the open water were infinitely small and remote. We could have sat for hours just looking if the top were not challenging us.

The last six hundred feet were the hardest, but they were the most fun. Almost at once we were lost in waist-high drifts, out of which we had to scramble onto overhanging boulders. At the last, not only did I have to brace myself and try to guide Mathiassen's feet into safe holds, but even to let him climb onto my shoulders and finally onto my hands stretched out against the shelving rock above my head. Then he would reach down his digging stick and haul me onto the rock beside him. Sometimes one or the other of us lost his hold and we both fell, laughing, into the drifts below.

We came suddenly to the top. I, at least, was surprised at the quickness of our climb. As a matter of fact, it had taken us four hours to climb the 3,560 feet registered on the barometer. The view was superb. Behind the tangle of lesser mountains and islands stretched the Inland Ice. How little the land seemed, hemmed in between that frozen ocean and the open sea! To the north we could see the whole complex of islands, beginning with Pamiua and Upernivik at our feet, past Târtoq and Inugsuk, which Mathiassen claimed to recognize, up to where Tugtoqortôq lifts its monstrous hippopotamus head from the water—a distance of some hundred miles. The point of Svartenhuk that shut off the view to the south could scarcely have been less than seventy-five miles away.

The warmth of our climb quickly ebbed from us. No sooner had we laid down the glasses and got out our cameras than our fingers became stiff with cold. The mercury sank to 20 degrees Fahrenheit, but it felt much colder because of the wind. Of all the pictures I had intended to take, I could manage only three, and I was shivering so hard that I was sure I had spoiled them. Mathiassen, being fatter and more hardy, lasted longer than I did. We had sandwiches, and I was hungry, but there was so little pleasure in eating in that cold that we packed up as quickly as possible and, after one last look at the most beautiful and extended panorama either of us had ever seen, plunged boldly into the first snowbank.

We missed our trail on the way down and did not strike it until we were almost down to the shoulder. I was impressed with the steepness of the ridge as we came down it, and was not

ashamed of being so tired and discouraged on the way up. Mathiassen laughed and told me he had not thought I would be able to
make the top. We were both hot and thirsty again, and I began to
eat snow. This is the poorest way of getting water. All snow can do
is chill the face and wet the tongue. It seems to excite rather than
to satisfy thirst. Ice is better. Mathiassen told me that on his hurried flight from Southampton Island, when they dared not miss an
hour because of the scarcity of their food and the danger that the
ice between them and the mainland would break up, they had not
risked an ounce of extra weight. They had no lamp, and so had to
live for several days on frozen meat, unable even to melt snow for
water.

We followed our tracks down the ridge to the stream. The
slope of the valley seemed steeper than before, and the rocks
sharper. The sun had set, and we were so cold and lame that we
could only limp. I had to laugh at Mathiassen hobbling ahead of
me. I had been looking forward to a refreshing drink at the stream,
but the water was so cold that one mouthful was all I could swal-
low. Yet no sooner had I walked on a few steps than my thirst was
as insistent as ever. This has been my usual experience.

It was a great comfort to see the motorboat waiting for us. We
had some difficulty in making the men on board hear our yells.
Peter Dalager is a "very great man." He had had a Primus running
in the cabin all day, so it was cozy and warm.

It was well after dark and quite cold when we picked up the
beacon builders. It must have been nine o'clock when we returned
to the colony, and Governor Otto had had lanterns set out on the
dock to guide us. We felt that this trip was the official end of our
expedition, and we were both happy that it had ended in such a
fine way. We were proud, too, that we had been able to climb the
mountain so late in the year. In fact, we skaaled ourselves quite
properly.

The day after our climb the Upernivik schooner, Sælen
("Seal"), came back from Kraulshavn, bringing the things we had
left on Inugsuk. Her new skipper from Copenhagen, Captain
Saugman, is such a nice fellow that we are glad we are to go south

with him to meet the *Gertrud Rask*. We did not leave Upernivik until September 25, however, for the radio brought the news that the ship had been delayed by storms off Iceland and was not expected in Disko Bay until October 4.

We spent our last day in Upernivik making goodbye visits. It was hard to leave. Everyone had been so good to us, from the governor and his family, the doctor and his wife, down even to Mrs. Otto's native servants. One of them gave me an embroidered scissors case made of sealskin. I gave Ruth Otto my last two packages of cigarettes. They were only cheap Virginia cigarettes that I had bought in Copenhagen, but they tasted good here after the rich diet of Abdullas and Benson & Hedges. Because there is no tax on tobacco or wines, the government officials in Greenland can and do afford the best, but these strong cigarettes soon tire the tongue, and one is glad to return to cheap brands. Governor Otto gave me a pipe.

We went on board the night before we were to sail, for we had to get away early in the morning. Our accommodations were very limited. Forward was the forecastle with six bunks, but we took on easily a dozen natives, men, women, and children, besides Peter Dalager and the crew of six Greenlanders. How they slept is the wonder. They traveled free, but had to bring their own food. The galley was amidships, and was so tiny that I could hardly stand upright in it. Aft on the quarterdeck was the companionway to the main cabin. The skipper slept in a little alcove off it. On the other side was a locker let into the side of the ship, which served as Mathiassen's bunk. Beside the companionway was a microscopic room which was used as a rope and sail storeroom. One of the lockers had been cleared out for me to sleep in. It was very amusing. The "stateroom" itself was so small that I almost had to go out when I wanted to turn around. The bunk was quite comfortable, and when inside it was absolutely black, and I could hear the water slapping against the side of the ship. The wheel was aft, right over my head, and the compass was lighted from below by a lamp hung in my "stateroom."

After we were established on board, Mathiassen remembered

something that he had left behind, so he and the captain went ashore, while I stayed on deck watching the brilliant phosphorescence that flashed about their oars.

Southward Bound

On board the *Seal*
September 25–October 3

When I woke next morning it was to find the captain standing by my bunk with some bread and butter and a cup of coffee. The schooner was chugging merrily along.

We came to Prøven, Robert's home town, at six that night. The outpost manager came aboard, and we offered him hot rum. He invited us to his house, and we followed joyfully, thinking we were to get supper. Alas, the family had already eaten, and we were entertained on coffee, liqueurs, and whiskey and soda until ten o'clock, and our heads spun.

The next day, September 26, was the King's Birthday, and the outpost manager persuaded us to stay for the dinner his wife was preparing in celebration. In the morning we visited old Jonas, whose acquaintance I had made in Upernivik when we first arrived. He has quite a fine house, fitted up with several things taken from the wreck of the *Bele*, including a parcel rack that hung above the door. There were five alarm clocks of various persuasions, and the walls were covered with autographed photographs that included several of Rasmussen and other famous explorers. I was interested to see one of Professor Hobbs, for whose dynamite we had been detained so long at Helsingør. Mathiassen got out the Visitors' Box to show Jonas. I always feel sorry for the women and children when Mathiassen is showing his treasures, for he talks exclusively to the head of the house, and they never get a chance to see things. There was one little girl, suffering from what I thought was toothache, and I lifted her onto my lap so that she might see, too. It was some time before it occurred to me that she might have mumps, and then I was all in a sweat until I could get rid of her. She did have mumps, I was told, and the poor child, like the others in the village, had been operated on by the ignorant half-breed nurse. I don't know what the woman did, but in some way she had slit the throats of all the children! There must have been a dozen with their necks bandaged. Apparently the cure had been effective, for they all recovered. I had never had mumps, and was now terrified that I would catch it. All during the voyage back to Denmark I was anxiously feeling my throat for the dread symptoms, but fortune was kind.

The dinner was very fine, and consisted of caribou meat fried in onions, caribou tongue, raw white whale skin, and many cold Danish sandwich dishes. The caribou meat was so dressed up that I could not catch the vension flavor. It was my first taste of *matak* (white whale skin), but this was mixed with lobster salad, so I could not tell what it really was. I would have preferred these native dishes *au naturel* in a tent, where their simple goodness could have been appreciated. Here I could only imagine how good caribou meat would taste after a month of seal meat.

We stayed until afternoon coffee, washed down, Danish fashion, with chocolate served in the same cups. Now it was quite dark, but we had to reach Søndre Upernivik that night. To run after dark meant extra pay for the crew, but since we had spent the daytime in enjoying ourselves, we pitched in to contribute the extra amount, for we did not think the government should have to pay for our amusement.

Søndre Upernivik is the last village north of Svartenhuk. Here the character of the country was already changed. The rounded gneiss of the north had given way to the level terraces of black basalt. The outpost is in a particularly desolate spot, on a low, flat strip of land under a grim hill.

The outpost manager at Søndre Upernivik is a brother of the outpost manager at Tugssaq. We went to see him, of course, and had a long walk over a rough path, crossed by ditches, into which I kept stumbling. The northern lights gleamed palely. We were still too far north to see them at their best, Mathiassen told me. The North Star shone bright above our heads. The house looks like a European house, but the domestic economy is that of a Greenlander's. The manager's father had been a Dane, but he had died without giving any real education to his sons, the lack of which they felt as a great handicap. The man told us, for example, that his great ambition had never been realized, he had never been "*hjem til Danmark*" ("home to Denmark"). This simple phrase coming from such a man, in such a place, struck me as one of the most pathetic things I had ever heard. The man had tried to do the best he could for his children, he told us, but it was almost impossible to teach them Danish when their mother and all their companions spoke only Greenlandic. He was one of the few half-breeds I have met whose birth has made him a misfit.

We sat for hours, it seemed to me, in that hot, stuffy room, and I was tortured with sleep. I could hardly keep my eyes open when we finally stepped outside into the cold. It was inky black except for the feeble northern lights, the stars, and the phosphorescent water. It took the combined efforts of the captain and Mathiassen to lead me down to the dock and get me into the boat. When we were aboard, the captain hauled up a bucket of water so that we might inspect the phosphorescence at close hand. After a little stirring, the water would no longer sparkle, and when poured out on the deck, its magic was gone.

We sailed early next morning, and as usual I was wakened by the captain bringing my breakfast of coffee and bread and butter. He had the coffee made in the engine room, where there was plenty of heat to boil the water. I had to do less cooking in the galley than I had feared. It was very small and inconvenient, and so filled during the day with Eskimos boiling fish that we usually managed with bread and butter and cold meat or sausage for lunch. The first day I had cooked a large potful of prunes, so that Mathiassen often insisted on prunes and oatmeal for lunch, much to my disgust. My dislike of oatmeal has always amused him. At night we usually had fish, which I fried. When Robert left us at Prøven, Mathiassen gave him a few *kroner*. His wages had been paid in full, and Robert had spent every cent, but Mathiassen did not like to leave him behind completely destitute. In return, Robert had brought us a magnificient salmon as a farewell gift. The captain had also brought some eider ducks and some baby ptarmigan. Every time I looked at the latter, my mouth watered. We had the breasts of the eider ducks stewed in margarine and water, with bits of pork threaded through them. This last was hard to do, for I attempted it on deck late in the afternoon, when it was dark, and so cold that the birds' blood seemed to freeze on my fingers.

We made Dark Head about the middle of the morning. It is a low basalt island lying between Flad Ø, which is all that its name suggests, and Skal Ø, a precipitous island to the south. On the eastern part of Dark Head are two hills, joined by a saddle on which the monument commemorating the wreck of the *Bele* is built. We came to Dark Head for several reasons: one to repair the monument, another to let the captain look for a possible shelter in a southwest storm, and last, but certainly not the least interesting, to have a look at the wreck of the *Bele*, lying on the extreme southwest point of the island. We anchored in a shallow bight halfway between the wreck and the monument. There was quite a little surf running, and since the beach consisted of enormous boulders against which the boat pounded violently, it was difficult to get ashore. The captain got quite wet holding the boat for us.

The land is very flat and very barren. The winter ice along the beach has pushed up a wall of rocks behind which is a swamp. We first visited the spot where the crew and passangers of the *Bele* had built their camp. It had never been more than a shelter made of boxes of provisions, barrels, crates, even hams and sacks of potatoes piled up to form walls, and roofed over with a sail. I looked for traces of this camp, but found nothing—doubtless the Eskimos had carried off anything that had been left behind—and even Mathiassen could not remember the exact site. We came upon two house ruins, however, both built of stone. Mathiassen thought them to be quite modern, and suggested that they had been built by the natives who came to plunder the wreck. Near one of the houses we found a broken kayak. The skin was too dry and stiff to be good for anything, even for mending boots, so we did not take it.

The last part of our walk was over a frozen lagoon, dammed

back by the high wall of boulders at the point on which the *Bele* was. The wreck lay along the bar. Only the stern of the ship was left. Amidships the skeleton dwindled away into a chaos of twisted girders. The bottom of the ship and all the forward part had disappeared. The propeller shaft and screw lay some yards out in the pounding surf. The bowels of the ship were strewn along the beach for several hundred yards to the north. If I had not seen all this with my own eyes, I would not have thought the sea strong enough to have destroyed an iron vessel so completely. We scrambled through a hole in the side and climbed up onto the stern deck. Every scrap of wood, except that which was screwed to the steel crossbeams, had been sawed off and carried away by the Greenlanders. They had not been able to remove the lower deck. Here we could see where the dining table and chairs had been bolted to the floor, and where the walls of the cabins had been. It was hard to imagine that once this had been a warm and sheltered interior.

When we had tired of looking at the wreck, we walked slowly back to the spot where we had landed, and the captain signaled the men to come ashore and fetch the cement which was needed to repair the monument. On the way up the hills we passed some Cape York or Thule house ruins. It was such a hot walk that I had to take off my sealskin pants, which I had been wearing over my knickers. The monument is a beacon about ten feet high, built of granite brought from Sweden, because the *Bele* had been a Swedish ship, chartered by the Greenland Trade. On the top of the pile is a stone cut into the shape of a crown, and on the western side, which faces the wreck, is a stone tablet with the Danish inscription: "On this spot King Christian and Queen Alexandra of Denmark rescued the crew and passengers of the ship *Bele*." It seemed ridiculous to erect a monument in such a spot where none, except perhaps a party like ourselves, would ever see it, and foolish too to choose a spot that neither the king and queen nor the party of the *Bele*, except Mathiassen, had ever visited. The captain had to use salt water to mix the cement, since the men had forgotten to bring the fresh water he had asked for.

When we were ready to go aboard again, there was a strong

wind blowing up from the southwest, with every promise of a storm, so the captain was anxious to get out of the bay, which offered anything but shelter. The anchor had to be hauled up by hand. It was very hard work, for the wind was blowing stronger every minute, and the anchor had fouled. When it came up at last, we were distressed to see that one of the flukes was broken off. Fortunately, we carried an extra anchor—a necessary precaution.

That afternoon we rounded Skal Ø, and when we went to bed the schooner was beating into the wind off the point of Svartenhuk. It was very cold. As I lay in my bunk, I could hear the man at the wheel dancing and stamping on the deck over my head to keep his feet from freezing. For dinner we had put up the racks on the table, and all the time the ship was pitching more and more heavily. Captain Saugman had turned in right after eating, but was up again at eleven. At two o'clock I woke to find the ship rolling and tossing so that everything in the cabin—chairs, table, and all—was hurtling from one end of the room to the other. The captain, looking very cold, came down, and I got out of bed to join him in a cigarette. He told me that he had turned the ship back. The wind was so strong that we had been fighting for eight hours to pass a certain point of land. We put in to Maligiak Fjord, one of the few bays on Svartenhuk. But even behind the land it took us an hour to work our way up the bay to a safe anchorage. The bay led to the southwest, and down the valley at the head the wind roared as in a tunnel.

There being nothing better to do, we lay abed until twelve-thirty the next day. The wind was still high, and we could not even put ashore in the small boat, much less leave our shelter. On the northwest shore of the bay, about a mile above us, are two huts, built as shelters for the mail sledges that cross Svartenhuk in the winter.

We tried to pass the time with deck tennis, but it was not successful. We could not catch the ring with mittens, and it was too cold to leave them off. We called up one of the men, who played the accordion while the captain and I danced. We took a long nap in the afternoon, and went early to bed, after drinking the last of the rum in honor of my mother's birthday. That day I think we spent sixteen out of the twenty-four hours in bed.

The next day the wind had dropped a little, which was a great relief. That afternoon we were able to chug south, and the next day, September 30, we reached Iglorssuit at five-thirty in the morning. This is a tiny outpost on the eastern shore of Ubekendt Ø.

The entire population of the village raced down to the beach to welcome us. I was very much excited to recognize a Polar Eskimo girl among the crowd of women. Her long ivory-colored sealskin boots and microscopic foxskin pants were conspicuous among the ordinary red boots and sealskins of the West Greenlanders. Mathiassen went up to speak to her, but she was so shy that she clung to the arm of her companion and would hardly look at us. Mathiassen mentioned all the names of the Polar Eskimo who had been with him on the Fifth Thule Expedition, and though this seemed to please and reassure her, she would not say anything. Mathiassen says that all Polar Eskimo women are very retiring.

The outpost manager invited us up to his house, and we expected coffee, of course. Imagine our horror when beer—horrible home-brewed "Greenland" beer—was produced, and four large glasses filled. It was the most poisonous stuff I have ever tasted, short of castor oil. I dawdled with my glass, hoping I would not have to finish it, but Mathiassen told me that it would be most discourteous if I did not. There was still a little left in my glass when the manager's wife came in and filled up the men's a second time. They had stepped into another room, and I could hardly keep from bursting with laughter when I saw their expressions as they discovered the beer. They did their duty manfully, however, and it was with great relief that we all set down our empty glasses. Peter Dalager came in then on some errand, and to do him honor the woman produced another glass and two more bottles, and before anyone could prevent her, filled up our glasses again! I felt sick, even the men were dizzy, when the ordeal was over. Drinking that awful beer at six o'clock in the morning on an empty stomach was the worst experience we had in the Arctic.

At Iglorssuit we acquired a very seedy-looking individual who introduced himself to us as B——, the brother of an Upernivik man. He was a typical beggar. Mathiassen gave him a few pennies because he had nothing. After that he was always running up to us whenever we appeared on deck, always telling us in his whining voice how unfortunate he was, and that he and Karl were "one." He offered to send dogskins to us in Denmark if we would only pay him in advance. He had probably never owned a pup in his life, and was certainly not the sort of fellow one would ever trust. He was a disgusting example of the corruption that our white man's civilization spreads everywhere, and nothing could have been more striking than the difference between this servile fellow and the hunters of the north, who entertained us as great men entertain distinguished guests and sent us away with princely gifts of seals.

All morning after leaving Iglorssuit we ran south under towering walls that rose straight from the bottomless fjord, lined by slanting dikes of basalt and broken by ravines so precipitous that no one could possibly climb them. I slept in the afternoon, and when I came on deck, the sun was gone, we had already rounded the northern point of Nûgssuaq, and Ûmánaq was out of sight. I should have liked one last glimpse of the most beautiful fjord in Greenland.

We arrived at Qutdligssat, the coal mine in Disko Island, and found little change since June except that the snow lay deep to the water's edge. We went on shore about nine o'clock, and Mr. Gissing, the Swedish mining engineer in charge, invited us all to breakfast.

During the next few days the captain was busy getting his cargo of coal aboard, and Mathiassen and I had nothing to do but take long walks on the beach. There were many eider ducks about Qutdiligssat, gathering in flocks for their flight south, but the natives did not hunt them much. They seem to have been busy at the mine.

Although Mr. Gissing had entertained us for every meal, our last night, as it happened, we ate on board the *Seal*. We had a fine dinner with fried fish, soup from the baby ptarmigans that had been making my mouth water for so long, and pancakes. That evening the inspector's motorboat, *Leif*, the same one that had taken us to Inugsuk, arrived from Godhavn to fetch us.

October 3 is my birthday. When I came into the cabin in my pajamas for our last breakfast, I found that the captain and Mathiassen had constructed a beautiful and fearful birthday cake of pancakes, with prune and condensed-milk icing, on which burned twenty-three Christmas candles. The prunes had been suggested by a remark of mine the previous day about a way of making jam from prunes, and they had tried in vain to whip the condensed milk. I was tremendously pleased, though it strained my capacity to eat my share of the cake.

At ten o'clock we went on board the *Leif*, after saying good-bye to everyone. It was with much sadness that we left the captain, for he was one of the nicest men I have ever known, and we were sorry that the days of our voyaging together were at an end.

(Mathiassen writes me, February 1933: "Sad things have happened in Greenland last fall. The schooner *Sælen* [on which we traveled] disappeared on its way from Upernivik to Holsteinsborg with Captain Saugman, Governor and Mrs. Otto and their daughter, Ruth, and everyone on board. Nobody knows what happened, but there was a bad storm. The 'Old Man of Tasiussaq' has died. Dr. Falkenberg dwells now here in Søborg [a suburb of Copenhagen]; he has two boys, and we have seen him several times.")

The Last Greenland Towns

Godhavn and Jakobshavn
October 3–14

It was bitterly cold on the motorboat. There was a strong wind, and, being poorly designed, the boat rocked and pitched. We did not reach Godhavn until one o'clock the next afternoon. Here the assistant's wife gave us a magnificent lunch. Her little boy was a perfect cherub of a baby. The good food, the warmth, the happy company suddenly loosened my tongue, and to both Mathiassen's and my own surprise, I began to talk Danish for the first time.

Dr. Porsild had invited us to stay with him at the Arctic Station until our ship should come, so after lunch we went over to his house. Our hand baggage was hauled up from the dock by a dog sled, the first I had seen in actual operation. They let me ride on the load part of the way.

Dr. Porsild was very kind to us. He brought out all the pictures he had made of specimens excavated at Sermermiut, a site near Jakobshavn. It was fine to be able to talk about our work with a scientist who could understand it. At his house we also met the members of the famous Wegener expedition. Besides Dr. Alfred Wegener, the leader, there were three younger men, Dr. Sorge, tanned and bearded, Dr. Giorgi, somewhat less hirsute, and Dr. Löwe. There was also with them another young German, an assistant to Fräulein Schmücher who had been studying the effects of glaciation in Jakobshavn District.

We had heard much about Dr. Wegener's work. He and his three comrades had come to Ūmánaq District early in the spring, and had spent the summer on or near the Inland Ice. They had mapped several hitherto unsurveyed fjords, and had measured the rate of the advance of several glaciers, before they had accomplished their main objective of finding a place where they could climb onto the great ice cap itself. The most wonderful part of their work was measuring the depth of the ice. This they had done at several places—at the edge, and at least forty kilometers inland, if I remember correctly.

Dr. Sorge speaks English very well, and explained how they had done this. They had made use of a seismograph to record the length of time it took for a disturbance in the ice, produced by an explosion of dynamite, to be reflected from the bottom. This was a method which they had previously perfected on Swiss glaciers. Forty kilometers inland from the edge of the ice, where the nunatak peaks rise to heights of 2,000 or 2,500 meters, the surface of the Inland Ice is 1,500 meters above sea level. Of this, only 300 meters (975 feet) is land; the rest, 1,200 meters (3,900 feet), is ice!

Even in Upernivik we had heard the extraordinary news that Dr. Sorge and Dr. Giorgi had climbed Ūmánaq. So many had attempted the ascent and had failed that Ūmánaq was believed impregnable. Imagine the astonishment of the colony when they looked up one day and saw two figures standing on the top, and "winking" at them, as Sorge put it!

The days in Godhavn passed pleasantly. We were royally entertained by Dr. Porsild, by the assistant governor, by the people at the magnetic observatory, and by the radio operator.

The *Gertrud Rask* came on October 7. We sailed for Jakobshavn the next morning, and arrived late in the afternoon. Everything was buried under deep snow, and there was fresh ice in the harbor. The dogs were running out onto the cakes, sniffing eagerly at the water, perhaps hoping for fish. Many people were already wearing their winter clothes. The dogs seemed very happy. They love winter, for then they have work to do and are fed regularly. We saw many of them curled up in the snow, the tips of their bushy tails over their noses. At the places where they had lain, they left little ice-lined pits. Yet they did not seem to be cold.

We sailed on October 14.

The Voyage to Denmark

On board the *Gertrud Rask*
October 14–November 2

DEAREST FAMILY:

Tonight we will pass Cape Farewell, and then nothing of my Greenland experience will be left to me but memories. I knew that I should have a good time when I sailed, but how could I realize the hold which this experience—the free life, the happy, fascinating natives, the absorbing work, and the loyal comradeship—has obtained over me. I feel as if I could never be content with ordinary living again, unless it were to be broken by a return to the Arctic. It makes me very sad to know that I have found my ideal vocation in such an inaccessible place. It was hard to leave just as the winter was coming on, when everyone—natives, white men, and dogs—seemed so happy in the anticipation of sledge traveling. They tell me the winter is the best time, and this, mind you, is from people at Upernivik where it is really dark. I had a taste of riding on a sledge at Godhavn, so I can imagine how glorious it would really be. . . .

Now it is no longer freezing, there are no northern lights at night, no phosphorescence in the water, no North Star just over the mast—only rain and wind. It seems muggy and hot. Me for the North! . . .

The ship is late. She was a whole month coming from Denmark on account of bad storms. We are running into them now, but the wind is favoring us, so we are flying home with all the big sails set and the engine pounding. We roll so much that we cannot sleep at night, and it is very tiring even to sit in a chair. . . .

How good it will be to come home! Dearest family, I dare not begin to think too freely of how splendid it will be to be with you again, for there is still so long a time to wait. I am dreadfully homesick now that we have left Greenland, and Bryn Mawr seems like the best place on earth. The only cloud on the horizon is the thought that I may have to live in England and won't get to the Arctic again. I know too well what I want. I feel as if a crisis in my relations with D—— were approaching. How to persuade him to come to America? I am afraid and troubled. I wish you were here to help me. Perhaps I don't deserve the happiness I want.

Love,
FREDDY

On the ship there were now, besides Mathiassen and myself, Dr. Wegener and his three men, a mining engineer, five geodeters, including our old friend Sørensen, Fräulein Schmücher, and her assistant. This was a distinguished company, and I looked forward to the voyage. It was anything but pleasant. The ship had to fight against violent winds, and rolled so savagely that we could find rest neither night nor day. Many nights we lay awake till dawn, or thought ourselves lucky if we could catch an hour's troubled sleep. The food on board was poor, for all the fresh stuff had been eaten up on the long voyage out. My cigarettes were all gone by now, and the beer soon gave out, much to the men's distress, but I was too exhausted to miss either. We seemed to live only on the vitality that we had stored up during the summer.

Exhaustion like this plays curious tricks. I noticed that, friendly as we had been at the beginning of the voyage, we now had little to say to each other. Each expedition kept much to itself.

One day the wind was so strong against us that the motor was stopped and we lay rolling in the waves for half a day. That was the hardest time of all.

All voyages end. On the last day of October the weather cleared, the sea was calm, the sun shone. We ran out on deck, everyone was happy, we all began to talk, the ship was transformed. The next day was Dr. Wegener's fiftieth birthday, and we resolved to celebrate it in a fitting way. Everyone admired him. The spirit in his expedition could not have been finer or offered a stronger contrast to that of Krüger's. We asked Sørensen for news of Krüger and Bjare, since he had been near them most of the summer, but he could not bring himself to speak of them. They had sailed on the Canadian police boat for Canada, and that was the last he had heard of them.

(1930: It was, indeed, the last that any of us were destined to hear. On the *Gertrud Rask* I had a strongly prophetic dream, which brought together both the beginning and the end of the summer. I dreamed that we were on board the ship, and the hold stood open, ready for the supplies that we were to take on for Dr. Krüger in Ellesmereland. But just as we had had to wait for Dr. Hobbs' boxes, so we had to wait now, and delay was fatal. When at last the cases of provisions arrived, we knew we were too late to meet Krüger at the rendezvous, and that he and Bjare were doomed to starvation. Perhaps that was how they actually died. We may never know; we are only certain now that they are dead. I know that Sørensen had no hope for them, even at the start, and that was why he could say nothing.

Dr. Wegener is dead, also. I wish that I might write a tribute worthy of him. The next year, 1930, he returned with a larger expedition for the whole winter. Drs. Sorge and Löwe spent the winter alone on the Inland Ice making meteorological observations. Bad weather delayed the dispatching to them of supplies until late in the spring. When at last a relief expedition set out under Wegener and Giorgi, storms set in again, and most of the Greenlanders who were with them turned back from superstitious fear and because of lack of proper clothing. Wegener, Giorgi, and one Eskimo pushed on alone. They found Sorge and Löwe alive, though the latter's toes were frozen. They had, of course, to be amputated. The grisly operation, without anesthetics, had to performed with only a pair of wire shears and a penknife. There was not enough food for all of the men at the camp, so Wegener and the Greenlander set out alone for the base camp. Dr. Wegener died of exposure on the return journey. His body was eventually recovered beside the skis which the Greenlander had set up in the snow to mark the spot.

Just as his comrades would have died for him, Dr. Wegener gave his life to save theirs. It was a privilege to have known him even for a few weeks. I shall not soon forget that thin, vigorous figure, the kindly face and sensitive mouth, nor that dignity and greatness of soul that inspired the respect and admiration of all. The loss to science only his colleagues can evaluate.)

[1975: It seems incredible that at this time no one mentioned the theory of continental drift which Dr. Wegener had proposed. Though originally received with skepticism, it is now accepted as proven fact.]

The last day aboard was very happy. We had a big party to celebrate both Dr. Wegener's birthday and our homecoming. Because of the fog we could not land that night, but had to anchor a little distance offshore. Everyone was gay; even Mathiassen, for all his restlessness, was content—he had received a radiogram from his wife.

We had prepared all sorts of funny presents and jokes. Dr. Wegener was given a map of the Inland Ice, according to the results of his expedition, in natural colors, etc. It came with all the praises of the critics, just as books have on the blurb dust jacket. The map, however, was only a completely blank piece of white paper! Then he got a figure, made of cotton wool and matchsticks, of *"Lille Smule"* (Danish for "just a little drop"), one of the dogs of his expedition who would never do anything they wanted him to do. He came with a funny poem parodying a child's prayer. Then Mathiassen and I gave him a dog sled and team cut out of paper (I did that), with an Eskimo driver, bringing him a real "Inland Ice dinner." Mathiassen wrote the menu. It was very funny, and the Eskimo words impressed the company. He also got a walrus carved from a potato (with Eskimo ivory needles for tusks, given by Fräulein Schmücher), which brought him the screw from his motorboat which had been lost in the ice in Disko Bay, together with a poem parodying one of Goethe's. There were so many things that the poor man was overwhelmed, and we all laughed at our own jokes. That night we had a lot of whiskey, and Gabel-Jørgensen [commanding geodetic officer] and I had great flirtations. Also Mathiassen confided in me that he wished Rasmussen had been the kind of leader Wegener is. Wegener is a real scientist, besides being a good manager, leader of men, comrade, and expert on Arctic exploring techniques. It seems that Rasmussen is not really a scientist, and it must have been disappointing not to have him appreciate what the scientists were really doing. I was rather interested to hear that. I almost feel that I had gone on the Fifth Thule Expedition. I know exactly how Mathiassen felt all the time. . . .

Copenhagen. The long voyage is over. Friends, relatives, reporters are swarming all over the ship. What joy to be welcomed back! How good everything looks! Houses, streets, trees, automobiles are familiar and beautiful. Yet everything is delightfully strange, too. There is a few minutes' wait at the customs, then the taxis roll up, and we say goodbye to our fellow voyagers. Dr. Wegener's three companions are still wearing their Greenland *kamiks* and *anoraks*—they have lost or worn out their ordinary clothes—and stride off happily, swinging their duffel bags. Mathiassen puts me into my taxi. Now at last, after so many months, I am alone. I feel crushed by the complexity of the city, and almost terrified at facing it again. But it is saddest to say goodbye to the comrade of so many happy experiences, the teacher to whom I owe so much.

Epilogue

Copenhagen
November 4, 1929

DEAREST FAMILY:

I sent you a cable yesterday. . . .

Thank you so much for the money. I wanted it just to be on the safe side. . . . But now I hope to be able to return with something left of it. My whole summer, counting the round trip from London to Copenhagen, will come to some $500 or $600, which is not so bad, considering that it includes a voyage across the Atlantic. . . .

I go to England on the seventh, spend a few days in London, then two weeks with D——, including a visit to Wales. I am sailing on the *Majestic* from Southampton on the twenty-seventh and will get to New York six days later. . . .

I am terribly homesick. I can hardly wait to get home. I don't anticipate seeing D—— as much as I do seeing you. Is that wrong? It would be horrible if that indicates any change in my feelings toward him. But I don't think so. But this dreadful matter about living in England tortures me every night. Ever since I have been away, I have rehearsed the possible conversations we may have on the subject. If I have to live in England, it may embitter my life, I feel. I wonder if I can ever be happy there—whether the thought of the happy work I might be doing in America and the person I might have been would not stand between me and my husband. But if I force him to come to America, then he may feel the same way toward me. I suppose what will happen will be that I will leave him in the same horrible uncertainty as now, that I will have to marry him, still not knowing what that means. . . . [If we live in England], then my only chance for professional work might be to be Dr. Mathiassen's assistant another time. But I want to do something on my own. . . .

One thing that has happened to me is that I have grown much more independent. I have had to take care of myself so much that it has made me very self-centered, I'm afraid, and it will be hard for me to accommodate myself to another's wishes, if they are contrary to mine. D—— is very independent, too, so we will probably have some bad times before we settle down. For that reason I think it was a great mistake that we did not marry that first June, in spite of the economic situation, for there are things more important than money. . . .

I am anxious to be married in America. When I first wrote you, I did not think there was any hope of D——'s being able to come to the United States. He writes that he has talked with his boss, and that a vaction can be arranged. I want to be married in Bryn Mawr if that is possible. . . .

I was very distressed to hear about Mother's and Father's illness. I was so afraid that things would not go well while I was away. That is one reason why I don't want to be far away from you when I am married. How good it will be to see you again. I do hope you will not look older. . . .

Goodness, now I am slipping back into the old ruts of worrying again! I wish one could live forever on the mountaintops of Greenland. One had nothing to worry about there. It was marvelous. The only things that troubled me were worries that I had not been able to leave behind. . . .

Best of love to you all,

FREDDY

[1975]

D—— was generous and forgiving about the spoiling of his summer vacation with me, which was now shifted to the damp English autumn. We stayed with his mother, whom I called "Mum," and I also visited him at his boardinghouse in Wales. That dreary countryside, with its piles of mine tailings and the barren stone hills, where the pit ponies searched for grass, and the grim towns, offered little comfort. And, like other miners' women, I also waited in the late afternoon for my beloved to come up from the shaft. When I saw him, gaunt and black to the eyes with coal dust, I could have wept. No man should be made to look like that. He bore it without complaint.

"Mum" sailed with me on the *Majestic* and visited us in Bryn Mawr for a month or more. After Christmas I resumed my studies at Columbia, where I won a fellowship for the following year, to finish my dissertation.

But all the time I was plagued with doubts as to whether I was being fair to myself and to that honorable man who waited patiently for me and who expected the kind of wife I knew I could never be. So in the spring I sadly sent him back his ring. "Mum" said I had done the right thing, and to the end of her life continued an affectionate correspondence. D——, as if to compensate him for all that he had suffered, finally was married to just the right woman, a wife who gave him happiness and children. In the summer of 1930, Dr. Birket-Smith wanted me to go to Alaska with him. At the last moment he was taken ill, so I went alone with my brother as helper, our Danish-American expedition postponed until 1933. I have led many other trips to the North, but as yet none has taken me again above the Arctic Circle.

My Thanks to:

Danes and Greenlanders for their kindness;

Therkel Mathiassen and Helge Larsen (chairman of the editorial board of *Meddelelser om Grønland*) for permission to use pictures and text;

The American Philosophical Society for a grant from the Phillips Fund; and

Karl Dimler, photographer for Bryn Mawr College, for salvaging my photographs;

Susan Kaplan for drawing the maps;

Pamela Burr for introducing me to the publisher and helping me to prune my text;

George Brockway and his skillful staff for making this into a handsome book.